Checking on Banks

Checking on Banks

AUTONOMY AND ACCOUNTABILITY
IN THREE FEDERAL AGENCIES

Anne M. Khademian

BROOKINGS INSTITUTION PRESS
Washington, D.C.

About Brookings

The Brookings Institution is a private nonprofit organization devoted to research, education, and publication on important issues of domestic and foreign policy. Its principal purpose is to bring knowledge to bear on current and emerging policy problems. The Institution was founded on December 8, 1927, to merge the activities of the Institute for Government Research, founded in 1916, the Institute of Economics, founded in 1922, and the Robert Brookings Graduate School of Economics, founded in 1924.

The Institution maintains a position of neutrality on issues of public policy. Interpretations or conclusions in Brookings publications should be understood to be solely those of the authors.

Copyright © 1996
THE BROOKINGS INSTITUTION
1775 Massachusetts Avenue, N.W., Washington, D.C. 20036

Library of Congress Cataloging-in-Publication data:

Khademian, Anne M., 1961–

Checking on banks : autonomy and accountability in three federal agencies / Anne M. Khademian.

 p. cm.

Includes bibliographical references and index.

ISBN 0-8157-4922-8 (cl.: alk. paper). — ISBN 0-8157-4923-6 (pbk. : alk. paper)

1. Banks and banking—United States—State supervision. 2. Bank failures—United States. 3. Administrative agencies—United States—Reorganization. 4. United States. Office of the Comptroller of the Currency—Evaluation. 5. Board of Governors of the Federal Reserve System (U.S.)—Evaluation. 6. Federal Deposit Insurance Corporation—Evaluation. I. Title.
HG1778.U5K46 1996
322.1′0973—dc20

9 8 7 6 5 4 3 2 1

The paper used in this publication meets the minimum requirements of the American National Standard for Information Sciences—Permanence of Paper for Printed Library Materials, ANSI Z39.48-1984

Set in Garamond Book

Composition by AlphaTechnologies/mps, Inc.
Mechanicsville, MD

Printed by R.R. Donnelley and Sons Co.
Harrisonburg, Virginia

For my parents,
Richard and Martha Péwé

Acknowledgments

In the summer of 1992 I began the first of many weeks shuttling between the Federal Deposit Insurance Corporation, the Office of the Comptroller of the Currency, and the Federal Reserve in Washington, D.C., to interview staff members with expertise in banking supervision. My thanks to them and their colleagues in various districts across the country for the long hours, valuable insights, and patience in sharing their knowledge with a political scientist.

Many thanks to Donald Kettl, Dennis Dresang, and Melvin Dubnick for their careful reading of the manuscript and for the perceptive comments that were crucial for sharpening and improving the argument. Conversations with Don Kettl reinforced my enthusiasm and energy. Also, thanks to an anonymous reviewer at Brookings, three external reviewers who provided excellent comments for revising the manuscript, and an anonymous expert in banking who checked the text for factual accuracy. Paul Quirk and Hal Rainey read portions of the manuscript in the form of conference papers and provided valuable commentary, and my colleagues at the University of Wisconsin La Follette Institute of Public Affairs and the Department of Political Science patiently listened to me talk about the project for three years, offering comments and insights along the way. My appreciation to the students who took heavy doses of banking supervision, CAMEL ratings, and discussions of the bank resolution process in courses on regulatory policy, the policy process, and organizational theory. Their questions and discussion of the material helped me to think through many parts of the manuscript.

Special thanks to Nancy Davidson, acquisitions editor for the Brookings Institution Press, who provided enthusiastic guidance and support for more than three years. Many thanks to James Schneider who edited the manuscript, Jonathan WeaverDyck who verified its factual content, and Deborah Patten who compiled the index.

Four students at the La Follette Institute provided assistance: Sandy Deyoe, Timothy King, Eric Pearson, and Jonathan WeaverDyck.

The La Follette Institute of Public Affairs provided support for time off to conduct research in the early stages of the project and travel support to conduct interviews. A grant from the Gerald R. Ford Presidential Library made it possible to examine developments in banking supervision and discussions of consolidating the banking agencies between the late 1960s and 1970s. The papers of Arthur F. Burns, former chairman of the Federal Reserve Board of Governors, were particularly useful and comprehensive. Finally, the University of Wisconsin Graduate School provided a summer's support.

To my husband Zarir who has patiently withstood my numerous trips to Washington and each rewrite of this text; who has tolerated my index cards, photocopies, and stacks of annual reports around the computer; and who (even after being on call for forty hours, or in the middle of studying for the medical licensing exam) has always listened and has enthusiastically supported my projects, my love and my thanks. And to our daughter, Gordiya Parsi, my love and my thanks for the sheer joy and happiness you give me each and every day.

The views in this book are my own, and should not be ascribed to the persons or organizations mentioned above, or to the trustees, officers, or other staff members of the Brookings Institution.

Anne M. Khademian

Contents

1

Why Banking
Supervision?

The Clinton administration has offered an impressive plan to "rationalize and simplify" the "needlessly disjointed and convoluted" structure of banking supervision: consolidate the responsibilities currently exercised by three federal agencies—the Office of the Comptroller of the Currency (OCC), the Federal Reserve Board, and the Federal Deposit Insurance Corporation (FDIC)—into a single agency to be called the Federal Banking Commission.[1] In one simple action, it is argued, consolidation would improve the administrative efficiency of banking supervision, increase its effectiveness, and improve the accountability of bank supervisors.

The administration's plan is part of a larger effort to downsize, streamline, and reorganize government agencies to improve effectiveness and accountability. Clearly, something must be done to improve the performance of government generally and cut costs. As the savings and loan

---

1. *Consolidating the Federal Bank Regulatory Agencies*, proposal requested by the Senate Committee on Banking, Housing, and Urban Affairs (November 23, 1993), p. 3. The proposal also includes consolidation of the activities of the Office of Thrift Supervision. The OTS is a bureau in the Treasury Department responsible for supervising savings and loans that have a national charter.

The administration's proposal is one in a long series of efforts to reform the supervisory system. See "The Report of the President's Commission on Financial Structure and Regulation," December 1971, pp. 87–95, folder "Hunt Commission," box 3, John G. Carlson Files, 1972–77, Gerald R. Ford Library; memo from Jim Connelly and Harry Meyers to Deputy Secretary Stephen S. Gardner, "Proposed Financial Institutions Act of 1976," February 6, 1976, folder "Stephen Gardner," box 132, L. William Seidman files, Gerald R. Ford Library; Task Group on Regulation of Financial Services ("Bush Task Group"), *Blueprint for Reform: The Report of the Task Group on Regulation of Financial Services* (Government Publications Office, July 1984); and the Bush administration proposals for regulatory consolidation as contained in S. 413, 101 Cong. 1 sess. (1989). See also Robert S. Pasley, "Consolidation of the Federal Financial Regulatory Agencies," graduate thesis, Stonier Graduate School of Banking, University of Delaware, June 1989.

1

crisis of the 1980s showed, when government agencies lack explicit policy guidelines and accountability is blurred, performance suffers and costs mount. Thousands of thrifts under the supervision of the Federal Home Loan Bank Board failed at a cost to American taxpayers of more than $300 billion. But just what *is* the solution for improving performance and reducing costs? That depends on whom you ask and where you look.

Ask an elected official in Washington and he or she will argue that government agencies need to be more accountable. Agencies are hidden in the hierarchy of massive executive departments or set adrift as remote government corporations or commissions. Program duplication and the overlap of jurisdictions among programs blur responsibility for implementing government policies. The daily functions of many agencies are obscured by the legalese used to shape regulations and take administrative actions. As the official might see it, consolidation of obscure and disparate agencies into single visible entities and codification of bureaucratic procedures will improve accountability and performance and control costs.

But ask federal bureaucrats how to improve performance and reduce costs, and they will probably emphasize the necessity for greater autonomy on the part of public managers and line personnel. It is the continual efforts to reshuffle and reorganize agencies and the suffocating rules and procedures imposed by elected officials seeking to hold bureaucrats accountable for every action that compromise good performance and raises the cost of government programs.

Thus the trade-off between accountability and freedom of action bedevils efforts to reform American bureaucracy. How can Americans ensure that bureaucrats are held accountable for their actions without stifling the flexibility and creativity of the public managers who must tackle difficult mandates with minimal resources? Does better bureaucratic performance result from granting agencies more autonomy or structuring the oversight of agency activities more rigorously? Is there a formula or organizational scheme that will improve accountability as well as performance? Or is the answer more complex than the American public and its elected officials care to believe?

Consider the little-known task—or art as its practitioners are wont to say—of banking supervision. Public management of this 130-year-old function is conducted by three federal agencies, each responsible for scrutinizing the safety and soundness of institutions under its jurisdic-

TABLE 1-1. *Overview of the OCC, Federal Reserve, and FDIC*

Characteristic	OCC	Federal Reserve	FDIC
Supervisory jurisdiction	Supervises national banks	Supervises state-chartered banks that belong to the Federal Reserve system, and bank holding companies	Supervises state-chartered banks that do not belong to Federal Reserve system
Agency type	Bureau in the Treasury Department	Independent regulatory agency	Government-chartered corporation
Regional and field organization for supervision	Six districts that oversee duty stations	Twelve Reserve banks	Eight regional offices that oversee field offices
Mandates other than supervision	Administration of the national banking industry	Regulation of the money supply	Management of the Bank Insurance Fund

tion (table 1-1).[2] The Office of the Comptroller of the Currency is the primary supervisor of all banks chartered by the federal government. The nation's central bank, the Federal Reserve Board, is charged with supervising banks with state charters that belong to the Federal Reserve system and overseeing bank holding companies that bring a variety of individual banks under one corporate umbrella. The Federal Deposit Insurance Corporation supervises all state-chartered banks that do not belong to the Federal Reserve System, in addition to managing the bank insurance fund.

These three agencies all have the same general mandate—to supervise the banking industry—yet they manage it in very different ways with different results, an observation made evident at the height of the worst banking crisis since the Great Depression. But why do they operate so differently? The answer lies with the distinctive organizational structure of each agency and the relationship each has with political overseers. For example, the Federal Reserve's unique structure and officials' dependence on its expertise as the nation's central bank allows it to distance

2. State governments supervised banks earlier than the federal government. In 1829 New York and several other states began supervising state-chartered banks that contributed to a state insurance fund designed to protect depositors and note holders in the event of bank failure. See Ross M. Robertson, *The Comptroller and Bank Supervision: A Historical Appraisal* (Office of the Comptroller of the Currency, 1968), pp. 25–26.

itself somewhat from political demands. This autonomy translates into a management style that has produced fewer and less costly failures for the banks under its supervision than for those under the supervision of the other two agencies, as well as very stable supervisory practices. During the 1980s banking crisis Fed-supervised banks failed at the lowest rate, and at the lowest cost to the insurance fund, under the agency's long-standing practice of conducting full examinations for every bank under its jurisdiction every year.

It does not follow, however, that the FDIC and the OCC (or all government agencies, for that matter) need greater autonomy if they are to perform better. A low rate of bank failures is just one definition of successful supervision; others could include promoting the healthy growth of individual banks and the industry, encouraging innovative banking, and assisting the overall competitiveness of the industry. A well-rounded system of supervision will not only prevent banks from failing, but will accommodate the risk-taking necessary for growth and competitiveness. Here is where the OCC comes into its own. In contrast to the traditional practices of the Fed, the OCC's supervisory style is defined by innovation, which is important for keeping the system of supervision apace with the changing banking industry. The OCC's style, in turn, is directly related to the agency's greater exposure to heavier and more conflicting external political demands than those faced by either the Fed or the FDIC. As the most consistent innovator of the three agencies, its successes and failures have informed the Fed's and the FDIC's efforts. The agency's weak autonomy and innovative supervision are the products of both its formal structure and historical and political factors that allow members of Congress and the executive branch to be intrusive in calling for agency accountability.

The way agencies are structured and held accountable thus determines how they do their jobs. The question then becomes, what can these three agencies teach us about bureaucratic reform? More specifically, is consolidation an appropriate solution for improving the supervisory process and grappling with the problem of inefficient bureaucratic performance more generally? If three agencies manage the same task with different results, why not pick the one that does the best job and consolidate authority in that agency? But before agencies are combined to do a certain job, there must be agreement on what the best way is. Questions of administrative design and the exercise of accountability are fundamentally political questions that cannot be answered in the abstract.[3]

Just as the OCC, the Federal Reserve, and the FDIC each have a structure and a relationship with political overseers that is defined by unique political and historical factors, an agency created by consolidation would have its own design and its own political circumstances surrounding its establishment. There is no guarantee that supervision would be conducted in the manner deemed most appropriate or best before consolidation. And because each of the agencies contributes something valuable to the overall soundness of the banking system, it is not clear that Americans would want to do away with any or all of those components through consolidation.

As Congress moves to allow banks to compete with one another across state boundaries and to compete with insurance companies and investment banks, the banking system needs sound supervision to protect the interests of depositors and borrowers, investors, and taxpayers, who ultimately bear the risks when the system does not work. Therefore policymakers need to understand how banks are supervised and preempt hasty efforts to consolidate agencies or impose a uniform management style that might make a deregulated banking system more vulnerable in the long run. The challenge of this book is to illuminate the art of banking supervision; explain the connection between structure, political oversight, and the way supervision is managed; and demonstrate why the current system is not only a healthy arrangement for the banking industry, but represents a cautionary illustration for overzealous reformers.

The Puzzle

In 1987 the number of bank failures escalated from 5 a year, a figure that had held steady since the Great Depression, to more than 200.[4] Between 1943 and 1981 the FDIC (which also manages the federal bank insurance fund) collected more income from the insurance premiums charged to banks than it needed to pay off depositors in failed institutions. In 1983, however, insurance losses began to exceed assessment

---

3. For an excellent study of the connection between administrative design and politics, see Jack H. Knott and Gary J. Miller, *Reforming Bureaucracy: The Politics of Institutional Choice* (Prentice Hall, 1987).

4. Federal Deposit Insurance Corporation, *1991 Annual Report* (1991), p. 132.

revenue as 43 banks failed.[5] By the end of the decade, more than 1,000 had failed, and in 1991 the FDIC projected for the first time a negative net worth of $7 billion for the fund.[6]

The timing was poor. Congress was already facing painful votes to allocate hundreds of billions of dollars for paying off insured depositors in the crumbling savings and loan industry. The specter of a similar meltdown in commercial banking prompted a congressional inquiry. Government examination and supervision of banks was studied by congressional staff and academics, audited and evaluated by the General Accounting Office, and explored in the financial and mainstream press.[7] The scrutiny was aimed at finding out what was wrong with the regulatory framework governing banks' behavior—from limitations on banking powers to the federal guarantee of deposit insurance—and was focused on the way the examination and supervision of individual banks' activities was exercised by the OCC, the Federal Reserve, and the FDIC. What constituted a bank examination for each agency? How often were banks examined? When were informal efforts used to alter banking practices, and when were civil monetary penalties and other formal sanctions used? What was considered a safe amount of capital for a bank by examiners in each agency?

A congressional staff report was prepared for the House Banking, Finance and Urban Affairs Committee to identify the primary causes of the bank insurance fund's insolvency.[8] The report detailed significant differences between the examination styles of the three agencies and

5. FDIC, *1991 Annual Report*, p. 1.

6. Panos Konstas, "The Bank Insurance Fund: Trends, Initiatives, and the Road Ahead," *FDIC Banking Review*, vol. 5 (Fall-Winter 1992), pp. 15–23.

7. The congressional study was James R. Barth, R. Dan Brumbaugh Jr., and Robert E. Litan, *The Banking Industry in Turmoil: A Report on the Condition of the U.S. Banking Industry and the Bank Insurance Fund*, report of the Subcommittee on Financial Institutions Supervision, Regulation and Insurance, House Committee on Banking, Finance and Urban Affairs (December 1990). The report was updated in Barth, Brumbaugh, and Litan, *The Future of American Banking* (Armonk, N.Y.: M. E. Sharpe, 1992).

For the General Accounting Office assessment, see *Bank Supervision: Prompt and Forceful Regulatory Actions Needed*, GAO/GGD-91-69 (April 1991); and *Bank Supervision: OCC's Supervision of the Bank of New England Was Not Timely or Forceful*, GAO/GGD-91-128 (September 1991).

Press reports included Jim Mctague, "Feeling Good about Feeling Bad, *American Banker* (October 13, 1986), p. 10; Joel Glenn Brenner and Carlos Sanchez, "D.C. Knew Firm Had No Bank Charter," *Washington Post*, December 7, 1990, p. A1; John M. Berry, "Regulators to Ease Up on Banks," *Washington Post*, December 15, 1990, p. A1; Fred R. Bleakley, "Tough Guys," *Wall Street Journal*, April 27, 1993, p. A1.; and David S. Bizer, "Examiners' Credit Crunch," *Wall Street Journal*, March 1, 1993, p. A14.

8. *Analysis of Bank Deposit Insurance Fund Losses*, staff report to the House Committee on Banking, Finance and Urban Affairs, 102 Cong. 1 sess. (September 1991).

stark differences between the failure rates of banks under each agency's jurisdiction. Two basic stylistic differences among the agencies were the frequency of examinations conducted on location and the breadth of each examination. Whereas 97 percent of banks supervised by the Fed were examined on location every year, 64 percent of the FDIC's banks received such examinations and only 36 percent or less of national banks supervised by the OCC.[9] The Federal Reserve's on-site exams typically constituted a thorough review of each bank's practices, compliance with banking law, and management system. The agency's examinations of the more than 6,000 bank holding companies under its supervision were equally thorough. The scope of the FDIC's exams was similar, with a bit more reliance on off-site data analysis. The OCC, however, focused its supervisory and examination resources on those national banks and banking activities deemed most risky, while relying on off-site monitoring systems to examine less risky banks.

The staff report identified the number of failed banks under the jurisdiction of the agencies and the cost of those failures for the bank insurance fund. Between 1986 and 1991 the fund lost $12.4 billion to protect depositors of failed banks or to inject capital into troubled ones.[10] National banks under the supervision of the OCC accounted for 73 percent of the losses, half of which ($4.9 billion) were attributed to the failure of small banks, those with assets of $1 billion or less. FDIC-supervised banks accounted for 35 percent of all losses during the same period, while Fed-supervised banks actually contributed more to the bank insurance fund through insurance premiums than was required to resolve those few state member banks that failed.[11] The report's findings are summarized in figures 1-1 and 1-2.

The OCC's targeted approach to supervision in the 1980s was unique among the three agencies and controversial. It was built on the concept of a hierarchy of risk. At the top of the hierarchy the agency placed systemic risk, or risk related to banking activities posing an industrywide threat, and it focused examination resources and staff on these practices. A greater number of examiners than usual could be sent to deal with banking problems in one region, or they might be assigned to large multinational banks whose troubled status or failure would have sys-

9. *Analysis of Bank Deposit Insurance Fund Losses*, p. 21

10. *Analysis of Bank Deposit Insurance Fund Losses*, p. 2. The fund spent $24.9 billion during this period to resolve failed institutions or to assist troubled banks, but it brought in only $12.5 billion in deposit insurance premiums.

11. *Analysis of Bank Deposit Insurance Fund Losses*, pp. 2-3.

FIGURE 1-1. *Average Share of On-Site Bank Examinations and Bank Insurance Fund Losses, by Bank Supervising Agency, 1986–91*

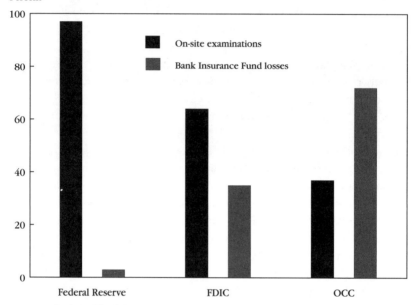

SOURCE: *Analysis of Bank Deposit Insurance Fund Losses*, staff report to the House Committee on Banking, Finance and Urban Affairs, 102 Cong. 1 sess. (September 1991).

temic consequences. Similarly, the most risky activities in an individual bank and its systems for managing the risk could be targeted by a special examination. In practice this meant that banks in the most troubled condition and healthy banks whose potentially weakened condition would threaten the health of the whole system received concentrated attention. Those deemed safe and sound and posing the least risk (typically smaller banks that had been determined to be safe in past years) would receive less, if any, on-site attention but would be monitored through the data that banks routinely submit to their primary supervisor.

The House report dealt a blow to what critics in Congress called the OCC's drive-by style of examination by connecting the agency with the rate of national bank failures and the cost of resolving those failures. An interval of eighteen months or longer between on-site visits by an examiner was cited as the reason for the OCC's lower rate of success in preventing failures—those of small banks in particular.[12] The Fed's pol-

12. *Analysis of Bank Deposit Insurance Fund Losses*, p. 4.

FIGURE 1-2. *Share of Bank Insurance Fund Losses of Small Banks, by Bank Supervising Agency, 1986–91*

Percent

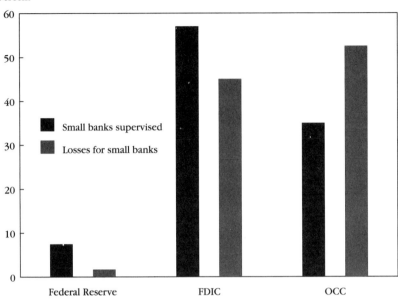

SOURCE: See figure 1-1.

icy of examining every state member bank and bank holding company once a year and conducting a full exam was considered the best approach.

The report's findings suggested an obvious question: Why did these three agencies, with similar expertise and similar mandates for ensuring a sound banking system, pursue different examination techniques that apparently had important implications for the viability of the banks under their jurisdiction? At a time when bank failures were escalating, why didn't the Federal Reserve or the FDIC also adopt a targeted approach?

The question prompted a closer look at banking examination and supervision and its management by each agency that revealed an apparent contradiction. The managers responsible for supervision in each agency shared a common interpretation of the challenges posed by their task and aspired to a common ideal of how the task would be most effectively carried out. Simply put, they considered every bank unique in its combination of risks. They saw no formula to guarantee safe operation because the quality of management differs from bank to bank, as does the quality of loan portfolios, earnings capacity, liquidity, and capital. The bank examiner must therefore have the training necessary to exercise independent judgment case by case to determine whether any given combination of banking risk is safe. This is why bank supervision is an art, not a science.

Yet despite this shared interpretation, the agencies' approaches are distinct. An examination of the management systems of each from 1979 to 1994, the years preceding and immediately following the banking crisis, shows three very different attitudes toward central direction of field operations that has implications for the way examiners conduct exams and are held accountable by their field, district, and Washington-based supervisors. During these years there were consistent differences in the way each agency organized headquarters policymaking and operational functions, the way each delegated authority to the regional and field office management and personnel, and the way each trained and hired personnel, all of which matter for the way examination and supervision are conducted.

The question is why, and what are the ramifications for bureaucratic reform?

Building Character through Autonomy

Walk into the lobby of the Federal Deposit Insurance Corporation offices in Washington and you are met by a large, temporary display of artwork by amatures from the area, a comfortable grouping of boxy chairs and plants, the bustle of bicycle messengers carrying packages to the front security desk, and the clang of the elevators accommodating a constant stream of people. Upstairs, the pace is fast yet informal. Sleeves are rolled up, ties are loosened, comfortable shoes are the norm. The wide-open offices facilitate constant exchanges between managers and staff.

Walk out of the FDIC, located two blocks from the White House, take the metro to southwest Washington, and walk from a highway underpass and the background of the rail yards into the new building and the bank-vault atmosphere of the Office of the Comptroller of the Currency. Beyond the security desk in the large, empty, marbled entryway and behind a clear secured door a receptionist signs visitors in. They wait in the dark paneled reception area for someone to come down from the upper floors to take them to their appointment. Elevators announce their arrival with a low pong and a softly lit frosted circular lamp. Upstairs the hallways are long and empty, lined by gray and dark blue panels and pictures of past comptrollers of the currency. Without a guide a first-time visitor could easily become lost in the maze. The atmosphere is formal, the work takes place behind closed doors, and the visitor never quite shakes the feeling of being an intruder.

Another metro ride to northwest Washington and a short walk brings one to the Federal Reserve buildings. Prominently placed between Constitution Avenue, the State Department, and the White House, the administrative building of the Fed sports a garden and tennis court, perks agencies in southwest located near the railroad tracks do not enjoy. The lobby is dominated by a large security desk and metal-detector gates. The security guard is relaxed, confident, and professional. He gives careful attention to visitors, but his primary concern is maintaining control over access to the Fed offices. Upstairs the work is collegial, the emphasis on specialization and expertise, and the confidence of the security guard is everywhere. Administrators are open and frank. A quick lunch in the agency's dining room on the top floor reveals a trivial but typical feature of the Fed—there are no garbage cans, only a small window in the wall that takes one's tray and trash away.

Every government agency has a character (or culture as it is more commonly called), and necessary to understanding this character is the extent to which an agency is independent of elected officials, constituencies, and other organizations that might share the same responsibilities.[13] Character evolves out of an agency's efforts to address external expectations for its performance while it grapples with the internal challenges of managing its responsibilities. As certain technical routines, formal structures, and efforts to engineer control are repeated; as politicians' expectations, at times conflicting, for performance clash with internal resources and operations; and as the agency adapts internally to reduce friction, motivate personnel, and blend work, a character evolves that is manifest "through the elaboration of commitments—ways of acting and responding that can be changed, if at all, only at the risk of severe internal crisis."[14] Those agencies that can exercise some

13. The term is Philip Selznick's from *Leadership in Administration: A Sociological Interpretation* (Harper and Row, 1957), esp. pp. 38–56. Selznick applies the concept to organizations in general, not just government agencies.

14. Selznick, *Leadership in Administration*, p. 40. Like Selznick, I view character, or culture, as an integrating feature, stitching different work components and different expecta-

operational autonomy without setting off fire alarms in the halls of Congress or the office of the secretary in an executive department, those that take actions regardless of the preferences of their primary constituencies, and those that can act without having to coordinate their efforts with another agency will have characters that more prominently represent the internal priorities of managing their task.

The characters of the Fed, FDIC, and OCC explain the translation of their mandates to examine and supervise banks and the styles of their top managers. The character of each agency is represented by commitments articulated and defended formally in its publications and presentations and informally by its personnel. These commitments guide the agencies through the expectations of elected officials, the demands of constituent banks, and the priorities of other financial regulatory agencies, and provide a sense of identification and purpose for agency personnel. The commitments also define what is special about the work of the agencies when they come to be evaluated. Most important, the commitments provide a context within which top management makes decisions to coordinate, direct, and develop an organizational approach to the examination and supervision of banks.

This is where one must look to explain the different management styles of the OCC, Fed, and FDIC. The priorities of political overseers in Congress and the executive branch, the leadership efforts of politically appointed executives, or the demands of constituent groups tell only part of the story.[15] The styles must instead be understood in the context of the organization that translates the priorities into policy.[16] External

---

tions together to facilitate the work of an organization. However, there are other ways to view character. See Joanne Martin, *Cultures in Organizations: Three Perspectives* (Oxford University Press, 1992).

15. Each is a popular explanation for bureaucratic behavior in political science literature. The emphasis on elected officials, in particular, has created a cottage industry of efforts to explain bureaucratic behavior by focusing on the ability of Congress, the president, the courts, or a combination of them to control that behavior. Each approach, however, reduces the bureaucracy to a single actor to be controlled instead of grappling with the complexity of the bureaucracy as an organization. For an excellent summary of this literature, see Thomas Hammond and Jack Knott, "Who Controls the Bureaucracy? Presidential Power, Congressional Dominance, and Bureaucratic Autonomy in a Model of Multi-Institutional Policymaking," paper prepared for the 1993 annual meeting of the American Political Science Association.

16. Others have made a similar argument. See Hal G. Rainey, "Public Organization Theory: The Rising Challenge," *Public Administration Review* (March-April 1983), pp. 176–82; Terry M. Moe, "An Assessment of the Positive Theory of 'Congressional Dominance,'" *Legislative Studies Quarterly*, vol. 12 (November 1987), pp. 475–520; and Marc A. Eisner, "Bureaucratic Professionalization and the Limits of the Political Control Thesis: The Case of the Federal Trade Commission," *Governance*, vol. 6 (April 1993), pp. 127–53.

efforts to shape an agency's behavior will be filtered through the character of the agency. Character serves as a nexus between a mandate from the political arena and management of the mandate. In this nexus the task is deciphered and its execution is given meaning; here, hiring, training, and promotional decisions will have consequences for the way policy is executed. Efforts to hold personnel across the country accountable to headquarters must be weighed against the need to encourage autonomous judgment. And the resources of the agency bump up against political expectations for effective performance.

This is not to argue that the character of each agency defines its style of managing independent of the efforts of the top management to bring the art of supervision to fruition. Managements in the agencies share a vision of their supervisory task, and they view management challenges in a common manner. They must make their strategic decisions to achieve their supervisory ideal, however, in distinctive contexts. The character of each agency constitutes a set of constraints that extends beyond the organizational structure, the formal mandate, the expertise of examiners, and the allocation of resources and personnel.

To understand an agency's organizational character, one must examine the autonomy it has from elected officials, constituent banks, and other financial regulators to conduct its mandated responsibilities. The Fed is the most autonomous of the three on all counts, followed by the FDIC and then the OCC. Although each is subject to political scrutiny in an effort to hold it accountable, each is subject to a different kind of scrutiny and is different in its response to that scrutiny. These varied levels of autonomy are products of political and historical factors that combine to provide (or restrict) the flexibility of each agency to conduct banking supervision.

Autonomy is contingent upon four factors.[17] First, some agencies are granted a degree of formal independence from the political process

---

17. Use of the term *autonomy* and the factors that lead to organizational autonomy (such as clear goals and a clear bottom line) draws directly on the work of Herbert Simon and Victor Thompson. In an article acknowledging the forty-first year since the publication of their text, *Public Administration*, they argue for a more careful examination of organizational "self-containment" (autonomy) and the unitary nature of an organization's goals. An organization that is a "master of its own fate and can proceed with its decisions without extensive consultation and negotiation with other units" is self-contained. An organization that is unitary has "a clearly defined, and relatively single-directional goal whose attainment can be measured." See Herbert A. Simon and Victor A. Thompson, "Public Administration Revisited," *Society*, vol. 28 (July-August 1991), p. 42. In *Public Administration* the authors elaborated the connection they saw between these two concepts: "Very often we find that units with a high degree of self-containment possess another characteristic—these units often have an organization goal that is thought of by many people as a worthwhile activity in its own right.

through their organizational structure. For example, the OCC, Fed, and FDIC are self-funding, exempting them from the annual congressional appropriations process. But the OCC is a bureau in the Treasury Department and unlike the others is subject to more oversight of its operations by Treasury officials and representatives of the executive branch. It must also abide by more federal rules and procedures than the Fed or FDIC, which are entities independent of any executive branch department.

Second, autonomy is contingent upon the clarity of formal mandates and the extent of the consensus among constituencies, elected officials, and the American public. The more precisely stated an agency's mandate and the broader the support for it, the more likely the agency will have some flexibility in managing its task. In the case of the Federal Reserve and FDIC, the formal mandate is broader than bank examination and supervision, but the clarity of and support for this broader mandate provide both agencies with some flexibility in how they conduct banking supervision.

Third, autonomy depends on how much elected officials and other agencies respect an agency's expertise. If an agency must compete with others to provide that expertise, it must demonstrate competence far superior to theirs to achieve the autonomy enjoyed by agencies without competitors.

Fourth, autonomy will be enhanced by a clear indicator that elected officials agree can be used to assess the performance of an agency without probing procedures and decisionmaking activities. A clear indicator can also motivate an agency's employees by providing a barometer of their performance.

An agency with a great deal of formal independence will not necessarily have operational autonomy. If there is little support for its mandate, little respect for its expertise (or competitors with the same type of expertise), and no indicator that can readily be used to assess its performance, the agency will be very cautiously attuned to the concerns of political overseers, constituents, and possibly other agencies. Its character will reflect its lack of autonomy, and it will provide employees with guidelines for balancing such a variety of concerns.

An agency with a single, clear, widely accepted indicator of its performance is likely to have extensive autonomy. Political overseers will not

---

. . . Organizations possessing such a socially meaningful goal we will call *unitary organizations.*" See Herbert A. Simon, Donald W. Smithburg, and Victor A. Thompson, *Public Administration* (Knopf, 1950), p. 268.

be drawn off into contentious debates about how well it is doing its job; if the indicator is acceptable, the agency will be considered accountable and will most likely have flexibility in how it fulfills its responsibilities. An organization need not, however, have a clear performance indicator as a necessary condition for being allowed considerable autonomy. General respect for its expertise and competence in performing a task could leave the interpretation of what constitutes its success in the hands of the agency itself. In the case of the OCC, Fed, and FDIC, it is precisely because the agencies share expertise in bank examination and supervision that competitive claims occur from time to time. With claims to competence can come greater autonomy and hence an organizational character that emphasizes managing the task at hand rather than meeting a plethora of external demands.

Banking Supervision and Bureaucratic Reform

Critics of the current system of bank supervision contend that all three agencies are long on autonomy and short on accountability. Those who support the Clinton administration's proposal to consolidate them say that the reform would improve the ability of elected officials to oversee the overseers. One agency (the Fed), they argue, is responsible for monetary policy, one (the FDIC) for bank insurance, one (the Securities and Exchange Commission) for regulating the securities markets, and so on.[18] Why not apply the same principle of functional specialization, and thus improved accountability, to banking supervision?

With greater accountability, they contend, will come administrative efficiency and a reduced regulatory burden for the banking industry. Consolidating training programs, district and regional offices, and legal staffs and creating a single cadre of examiners would have to be less costly than maintaining three of each. And a single supervising agency would make life much less complicated for bank holding companies that own a variety of state and nationally chartered banks, each of which can now have a different primary supervisor.

Immediately following the 1980s banking crisis, critics expressed concerns about the accountability of the examiners and supervisors who operate within such a disjointed and convoluted system. Were examiners allowing banks to operate with capital levels that were too low?

18. L. William Seidman, "A New Way to Govern Banks," *Wall Street Journal*, February 3, 1994, p. A14.

Were they investigating banking activities thoroughly, or merely looking at samples of a bank's activities? Had examiners and their supervisors allowed a climate of careless, or simply stupid, banking practices to take hold with the full faith and credit of the U.S. government backing the risk taking? Were enforcement actions actually being applied by supervisors to make banks correct risky conditions, or was "forbearance" (delaying the enforcement of supervisory mandates that might unnecessarily worsen a bank's condition) the rule?[19]

In response to these concerns the work of examiners and supervisors was exposed to a flurry of studies that produced a collective yes to each of the questions. Congress addressed what was the FDIC's accountability problem in the Federal Deposit Insurance Corporation Improvement Act of 1991. The primary purpose of the legislation was to provide the bank insurance fund with a $30 billion line of credit in 1991, but it also took an important step toward limiting the discretion exercised by bank examiners and supervisors to assess the condition of banks and bring enforcement actions against problem banks. The art of the task, in other words, was to be replaced with standardized procedures.

The message of the legislation was clear: fewer banks would fail if supervisors were mandated to take more prompt enforcement actions against banks, more thoroughly examine and document a standardized set of banking activities, and limit risk taking by banks that depleted capital below specified levels of safety. Examiner and supervisory discretion was to be limited by simple, across-the-board rules identifying the aspects of operation most critical to a bank's overall health and thus most critical in determining whether it would require disbursements from the bank insurance fund in the future.

The current system of supervision is not so tidy. National banks are chartered and supervised by the OCC, while the Fed and the FDIC split authority for state-chartered banks. The FDIC is also responsible for managing the bank insurance fund and resolving failed institutions, while the Fed is the nation's central bank. The supervisory system was not planned in any comprehensive manner. It arose out of piecework efforts to spread the protection of the national government over the nation's supply of money. As one report recommending consolidation commented in 1937, the structure is the "result of historical accident

19. Bank supervisors exercise forbearance when they determine that enforcing particular supervisory mandates might unnecessarily worsen a bank's condition rather than improve it. Enforcing a severe monetary penalty against an ailing bank, for example, or setting aside large loan loss reserves might push it toward insolvency.

rather than of any consistent plan."[20] If a simple and rational (that is, a readily comprehensible and centrally directed) structure is required for accountability, the current arrangement falls short.

Nor is it a simple matter to pin down the work of bank examiners and their supervisors. Much supervision, arguably the most effective, is exercised informally, with examiners and bank staff working together to return a troubled bank to soundness. If the bank's decline is turned around, there are no headlines applauding effective supervision, but only, as one examiner said, "an audible sigh of relief" among bank staff and examiners alike. Examiners assess such intangibles as the quality of bank management (relying not only on the performance of the bank but also on the responsiveness of bank management to past supervision) and the performance record of the manager. The examiner's instincts about managerial competence are also important. Competent managers might be given greater opportunities than managers who are considered incompetent to pull a bank out of trouble. If a bank fails after a supervisor has placed confidence in the skills of a good manager, the supervisor can be judged guilty of forbearance, and prompt corrective formal enforcement actions instituted.

Yet in the rush to make these agencies more accountable, policymakers have not paused to investigate what it is that each of them might do particularly well—individually and in conjunction—in supervising banks. Nor have they considered the challenges supervision poses for public managers, the organizational responses to these challenges, and the historical and political factors that affect the efforts of each agency. Consolidating and codifying bureaucratic procedures does not guarantee better performance.[21] Indeed, there might not be a simple formula that can simultaneously improve the accountability and performance of government agencies across the board. Instead, improved performance might have to be a creature of case-by-case review and come at the expense of accountability defined by neat organizational charts and bureaucrats who supervise by the book. Policymakers must ask, "What will the banking industry, the banking public, and the taxpayers who ultimately guarantee banking deposits gain from consolidation, and what will they lose?"

20. *Investigation of Executive Agencies of the Government*, Preliminary report of the Select Committee to Investigate the Executive Agencies of the Government, S. Rept. 75-1275 (GPO, 1937), p. 213.

21. Donald F. Kettl, *Reinventing Government? Appraising the National Performance Review* (Brookings, 1994), esp. pp. 58–59.

Bureaucracies vary greatly in the ways they perform. Some resist leadership and direction; others are more responsive, perhaps to their detriment and eventual demise.[22] Some agencies confront the challenges of changing mandates, new constituencies, and increased conflict; others are debilitated by such complexity.[23] Some agencies manage the procurement of goods and services adeptly, while others continually incur cost overruns.[24] And some agencies, given the same mandates and the same political overseers, will simply manage their responsibilities differently and accomplish their goals from different directions—the focus of this book. These variations in performance, responsiveness to leadership, and management and implementation style would be lost in the abstract efforts to consolidate and codify to improve accountability.

If policymakers accept at face value the argument that consolidation and codification will improve accountability, they forgo a public dialogue about the challenges of managing public programs and the ways these challenges might be met. This is especially critical when legislators charge agencies with achieving goals that are vague and difficult to realize because of the conflict surrounding a program or because elected officials know they want to do *something*, they are just not sure what or how to do it. In either instance, bureaucracies play a fundamental role in translating vague goals articulated with conviction and flourish into tangible policies. Bank regulators in the Fed, FDIC, and OCC, for example, have responsibility for supervising banks' risk taking. They must

22. For resistance see Donald P. Warwick, *A Theory of Public Bureaucracy: Politics, Personality, and Organization in the State Department* (Harvard University Press, 1975). For responsiveness see Wallace Earl Walker, *Changing Organizational Culture: Strategy, Structure and Professionalism in the U.S. General Accounting Office* (University of Tennessee Press, 1986). For the role of a leader see Thomas K. McCraw's discussion of Alfred E. Kahn and the Civil Aeronautics Board in *Prophets of Regulation: Charles Francis Adams, Louis D. Brandeis, James M. Landis, Alfred E. Kahn* (Harvard University Press, 1984).

23. For discussion of agencies that have adapted see Martha Derthick, *Agency under Stress: The Social Security Administration in American Government* (Brookings, 1990); Glenn W. Rainey and Hal G. Rainey, "Breaching the Hierarchical Imperative: The Modularization of the Social Security Claims Process," in Donald J. Calista, ed., *Bureaucratic and Governmental Reform* (Greenwich, Conn.: JAI Press, 1986), pp. 171-95; Terence J. Tipple and J. Douglas Wellman, "Herbert Kaufman's *Forest Ranger* Thirty Years Later: From Simplicity and Homogeneity to Complexity and Diversity," *Public Administration Review*, vol. 51 (September-October 1991), pp. 421-28; Daniel A. Mazmanian and Jeanne Nienaber, *Can Organizations Change? Environmental Protection, Citizen Participation, and the Army Corps of Engineers* (Brookings, 1979). For a discussion of failure to adapt see Terry M. Moe, "The Politics of Bureaucratic Structure," in John E. Chubb and Paul E. Peterson, eds., *Can the Government Govern?* (Brookings, 1989), pp. 267-329.

24. Donald F. Kettl, *Sharing Power: Public Governance and Private Markets* (Brookings, 1993), pp. 267-329.

sufficiently limit risk to prevent bank failures and drains on the insurance fund, yet allow for enough risk to ensure the commercial banking industry thrives as a competitor in providing financial intermediation. Without a concise congressional definition of a "safe and sound" banking system, clear guidelines for the "maintenance of the public's confidence," or accurate indicators for the "systemic health" of the banking industry, it is up to these agencies to identify the parameters, and it is up to the bank examiners to translate policy into real behavior by the banks.

Just what that responsibility looks like and how each agency tries to implement its responsibilities are worthy of careful inquiry. This is, after all, the regulatory arrangement designed to protect depositors and ultimately taxpayers from costly bank failures and to provide some certainty in markets for financial intermediation. It is the system behind the familiar sticker on the bank window, "Member, FDIC," that gives people the confidence to place paychecks, savings, and retirement plans with an institution and to finance homes, cars, and their children's education. Americans are quick to criticize bureaucracies for policy failures and target them for reform. But reform efforts should be better informed by an understanding of the management challenges posed by the task and the potential variation between agencies in their competence to perform particular mandated responsibilities.

Study Design

Throughout 1992 and 1993, I conducted open-ended interviews with past and present examiners, supervisors (in the field and regional offices and in the headquarters in Washington), and officials in the Fed, OCC, and FDIC to learn about banking supervision and the resulting management challenges, and to find an explanation for the distinctive management styles in each agency. Statements from these interviews are included throughout this book to illustrate the connection between the autonomy of an agency and its management style. The examiners and supervisors in the three agencies share a common understanding of banking supervision and describe similar challenges in managing a process considered more art than science. Of course, like any professional group whose power and prestige rests upon its command of a particular expertise, the argument that examination is an art that cannot be codified and packaged is perhaps predictable. Yet it is precisely this predictability and the strength of common professional concerns that makes the varied management styles a puzzle to be explained.

The study begins with this puzzle. The commonly held ideal of bank examination and supervision and the management challenges they pose are the focus of chapter 2. Chapter 3 presents the distinctive management styles of the three agencies. In each, managers must have some central direction of examiners spread across the country, yet they must allow examiners some discretion. The way each agency tackles this challenge has implications for other management concerns such as hiring, training, and maintaining an examination force able to assess the condition of banks varied in size, composition of risks, condition, and location. Both chapters 2 and 3 focus on the three years preceding and succeeding the banking crisis of the 1980s. An explanation for the management styles, however, is more historical, encompassing the formative years of each agency to the present.

Chapter 4 discusses the concept of agency autonomy and its connection to the development of each agency's organizational character. Each is exposed to political scrutiny in an effort to hold it accountable, yet they differ in the kind of scrutiny they receive and their responsiveness to it. An explanation for this variation focuses on the structure of each agency and the political and historical factors experienced by each. Chapter 5 examines the organizational characters of the Fed, FDIC, and OCC, represented by sets of commitments, and the connection between characters and management styles.

Chapter 6 examines the organizational characters in action as each agency grapples with common mandates for supervising the responsibilities of banks toward their customers and communities. These "compliance" mandates and the expectations for performance from the political arena initially clashed sharply with each agency's organizational character. In particular, the mandates clashed with the professional motivations of the examiners and the broader mandates for which each agency has traditionally been held accountable. The agencies had to adapt their commitments to the way work is done in some instances, and managements had to make significant adjustments to incorporate the new expectations into their respective responsibilities. Just how they did this has depended on their autonomy or their need to be responsive to a variety of demands.

In the constant search for better accounting of the activities of bureaucracies, the American political system typically searches for simplicity. As Woodrow Wilson argued, power, visibly exercised, can be readily held accountable. Yet there are important administrative advantages found in the complex systems that together supervise the commercial banking industry. This is the topic of chapter 7. The Fed, FDIC, and OCC have jousted (at times vigorously) over jurisdiction, and efforts to coordinate their supervisory styles often result in minor compromises. But they also learn from each other techniques for managing the supervision of risk taking by banks and check each other when a seemingly sound decision is not necessarily safe for the bank insurance fund or is contrary to the stability of the system.

Officials at all levels of government talk a great deal about reinventing the administration of government—delegating authority more broadly to agencies and to those out in the field, giving agencies the elbowroom to pursue their mandate with accountability maintained by assessing performance and injecting competition into the delivery of goods and services. The good news is such an arrangement can work well. For more than half a century the three agencies have individually and in tandem provided a test case of the principles of "reinventing government." The bad news is that when a banking crisis or some other crisis arises, the political response is typically to demand greater accountability through stronger hierarchy, greater consolidation, more procedural constraints, and less autonomy.

The Federal Deposit Insurance Corporation Improvement Act, or the "so-called improvement act" as many bankers and regulators are fond of saying, took a step toward standardization and codification of the supervisory process with a conviction reminiscent of Frederick Taylor's that there was one best way to scientifically manage a task. But the wisdom of another management scholar, Martin Landau, offers a more appropriate approach to thinking about the management of supervision.[25] Landau contends that a little duplication and overlap can be a smart way to design an administrative system, especially when it is not clear what the "one best way" to approach a task ought to be. The argument is borne out when the historical record of banks under the jurisdiction of each agency is examined in the final chapter. Indeed, the innovation and learning that has taken place through administrative overlap, especially

---

25. Martin Landau, "Redundancy, Rationality, and the Problem of Duplication and Overlap," in Francis E. Rourke, ed., *Bureaucratic Power in National Policy Making*, 4th ed. (Little, Brown, 1986), pp. 470–83; and Landau with Russell Stout Jr., "To Manage Is Not to Control: The Folly of Type II Errors," *Public Administration Review*, vol. 39 (March-April 1979), pp. 148–56.

in the past twenty years, is fundamental to a safe and sound system of supervision.

Coming out of the crisis of the 1980s, the three agencies are not anxiously returning to past techniques and standard operating procedures. Instead, examiners and administrators are trying to make examination more preemptive—to isolate and quickly resolve systemic problems, to make training more sophisticated, and to harness technology more effectively for better supervision. As long as we value banking examination and supervision as a public policy, the operation of these three management systems, in the aggregate, works well.

Now, to the puzzle. Just what *is* banking supervision, and how is it managed?

2

The Art of Bank Examination and the Management Challenge

Visit the headquarters of the Office of the Comptroller of the Currency, the Federal Reserve, and the Federal Deposit Insurance Corporation and the differences between the agencies are manifest in architectural design and furnishings, patterns of interaction among staff, and the language that characterizes their mission in the broader scheme of financial intermediation. Yet speak with top management in each agency about bank examination and supervision or visit the regional and field offices of the agencies and the distinctiveness blurs. In the daily management and implementation of examination and supervision common perceptions of the task predominate. Bank examiners are the line professionals in supervising banking risk and maintaining depositor and investor confidence.[1] They use their expertise to assess the risks in a banking operation and recommend necessary changes.[2]

The position of bank examiner is a career position in each agency, with opportunities for advancement. Many field office supervisors, regional or district directors, and headquarters division management in each agency began as field examiners.

Examiners are hired with four-year college degrees in business, finance, or, increasingly, accounting, but they receive examination train-

1. For a history of state and federal supervisory efforts, see Federal Deposit Insurance Corporation, *Federal Deposit Insurance Corporation: The First Fifty Years: A History of the FDIC, 1933-83* (1984), pp. 111-12; and Ross M. Robertson, *The Comptroller and Bank Supervision: A Historical Appraisal* (Office of the Comptroller of the Currency, 1968), pp. 23-27, 71-76.

2. Bank examination is a field of expertise defined and maintained by the three government agencies in response to a government need—what Frederick Mosher calls a "public service profession." Frederick C. Mosher, *Democracy and the Public Service*, 2d ed. (Oxford University Press, 1982).

ing on the job and through agency classroom instruction. Although the agencies do have a few common training classes, each has its own training division that designs and develops curriculum, independent-study courses, and on-the-job training programs. Each agency determines its own length and makeup of course work, examination standards, and other requirements for becoming a commissioned examiner.

Yet regardless of the agency, the sequence of schools, or their college background, examiners in the field and in management positions embrace two common principles that define the "art" of bank examination and supervision. First, every bank is considered unique in the combination of risks it represents. One supervisory prescription for soundness does not fit all banks. Second, effective supervision rests on the competent and independent judgment of the examiner, who must be able to assess these unique circumstances.

Drawing upon these two principles, managers at the Fed, FDIC, and OCC face a common challenge. The ideal examination process, as defined by the profession, maximizes the independent judgment of the examiner. But there must be some form of central direction to train, coordinate, and hold accountable the several thousand examiners employed by each agency and spread across the country. Accomplishing direction without suffocating independent judgment is a central challenge. Further, and most critically, the ideal depends heavily on the quality and experience of an examiner for preventing supervisory problems that might require formal, contested enforcement actions. Examiners need, in other words, sufficient training and experience to develop expertise to deal with both the banking industry's common products and problems and its more sophisticated ones.

The Task

Bank examination begins in field offices, sometimes called duty stations, across the country. An FDIC field office in the midwest is typical: a few desks, rather dated computer terminals, and a receptionist. The supervisor works out of a room off the main office filled with agency manuals, guidances, and examination reports on the floor, the desk, and in filing cabinets. A few casually dressed examiners work at the terminals doing preexamination work. Large schedules with the names of examiners and banks to be examined hang on the walls.

Here supervisors deploy teams of examiners, typically led by a senior examiner, to evaluate four areas of a bank's operations: the soundness of commercial activities, the effectiveness of consumer protection and community reinvestment activities (also known as *compliance*), the integrity of trust department functions, and the effectiveness of internal controls for operating the institution's electronic data processing activities.

Most examiners and resources are concentrated on commercial activities—the traditional examination function and the one considered the most prestigious among examiners. The focus of commercial examination is the CAMEL rating, and the product is the examination report. Each letter in the CAMEL index represents an indicator of commercial performance: Capital adequacy, Asset quality, Management competency, Earnings, and Liquidity. For the community bank in Olivet, Michigan, as well as the largest multinational bank in New York City, the examination often generates anxiety. Examiners assess the distinctive components of the CAMEL index, rating each on a scale of 1 to 5, and assign an overall rating to each bank. Banks scoring 4 or 5 are placed on the FDIC's "troubled" list and receive more specialized and frequent supervision from examiners and analysts of the primary supervising agency. A ranking of 1 is reserved for the safest banks. The examiners then prepare an eleven-page report that details the condition of the bank and recommends various actions to bring the bank in line with safer and sounder practices.[3]

Review of the report and a plan for enforcing the recommendations brings agency supervisors at the field and sometimes regional levels into the process, particularly for banks rated 3 or higher. A field office supervisor explained the process and the burden of proof placed on the examiner's shoulders when a bank or the examiner's own supervisor questions the assessment and recommendations:

> If a bank is rated a 4 or 5, I specifically do want to see the report. I will look at what the examiner is recommending and why, and help him think through what actions to recommend, not to force him to take specific actions. . . . The examiner must sign the report, I don't; so he ought to send in what he feels is the right recommendation. . . . Then,

3. The common eleven-page examination report is a recent development, the product of an interagency initiative to standardize supervision procedures between the three agencies. However, it has not gone far in altering the variations in practices between the agencies. This situation is discussed at greater length in chapters 2 and 6.

if the regional office believes a certain action should or should not be taken, they might question it. . . . But if [the examiner] thinks the assessment is correct, he ought to send it in. He's the one who will be on the stand in an administrative action [if the bank challenges the report].

The bank's board of directors is given a copy of the report, and any recommendations (particularly for troubled banks) will be discussed in a meeting between the field supervisor and examiners and the board. If the bank does not follow the recommendations, the agency can take action to bring about the recommended changes. Enforcement can be a combination of arm twisting and tough talk with the bank board or formal actions such as fines or cease-and-desist orders.

For the examiners and their supervisors this process, from assessment to enforcement, is far from straightforward. "It's more art than science," explained a field office director. "In terms of an exam, you probably don't realize as much until you are in problem banks . . . and you see that something didn't feel right, didn't look right, so you dug deeper until you found something." Although examiners are armed with an agency manual, supervisory letters, job aids, and, in the case of the OCC, e-mail bulletin boards connected with Washington headquarters, examiners and their supervisors comment that it is often only the blatant violations of banking law—reckless lending, poorly structured internal control systems, and outrageous management—that present examiners with easy evidence for a troubled or soon-to-be troubled operation. For the great majority of well-managed institutions, there are few hard-and-fast rules that fit all situations to indicate when a bank is clearly on the right or wrong path for the long term.

Examiners contend that it is the art of assessing the unique combination of risks in each institution and rating its overall condition—from capital to management to earnings—that makes examination and supervision distinct from regulation. Supervision requires judgment in the application of agency policies; regulation requires the application of a standard or rule across the board to determine whether a bank is in compliance. And, examiners add, it is the review and evaluation of the risk in a bank's portfolio of loans and its operating systems that distinguishes examination from an audit of financial statements or an accounting of financial activities.

In 1993 the General Accounting Office recommended that the three agencies standardize what bank examiners focus on in an exam, how they make their assessments, and how they record their activities.[4] In their responses to the GAO, the agencies disagreed.[5] In reference to the studies, a senior examiner from the Fed argued, "We don't require every section [of an exam] to have a checklist. . . . I keep trying to explain to the GAO the difference between auditors and examiners. . . . The GAO wants every little section to have a checklist, but you don't need guidance in a lot of areas." A seventeen-year veteran of the FDIC in the Southwest recalled originally taking a $9,200-a-year examiner position because of the "financial end" of the job. "Notwithstanding people's perceptions of what we do," he stated, "we are *not* auditors. We audit when necessary, but we are not auditors!" Rather, he said, a commercial exam "is a credit analysis, and that's basically finance. . . . It's subjective. It's a true business art."

Yet, what the profession defines as the exercise of artful expertise, others define as the "culture of ad hoc discretion."[6] In 1991 Congress passed the Federal Deposit Insurance Corporation Improvement Act (FDICIA) requiring each of the three agencies to develop *regulations* for the safe conduct of particular banking activities (previously defined by agency policy) to be applied across the board to all institutions. Further, the law mandates that one component of the CAMEL rating, capital, should serve as the standard indicator of a bank's condition and the main concern of supervisory actions. Capital, many examiners contend, is now being regulated rather than supervised.

Capital is the excess of a bank's assets over liabilities. Once represented by silver, gold, and other possible assets paid in by a bank's investors and physically present in the bank, capital is now represented by securities and other instruments of a bank's long-term finance. To determine a bank's total capital and assess its adequacy in relation to the bank's assets, examiners typically add to this equity capital the reserves set aside for possible loan losses. The FDICIA allows banks considered

---

4. General Accounting Office, *Bank Examination Quality: FDIC Examinations Do Not Fully Assess Bank Safety and Soundness*, GAO/AFMD-93-12 (February 1993); *Bank Examination Quality: FRB Examinations and Inspections Do Not Fully Assess Bank Safety and Soundness*, GAO/AFMD-93-13 (February 1993); *Bank Examination Quality: OCC Examinations Do Not Fully Assess Bank Safety and Soundness*, GAO/AFMD-93-14 (February 1993); *Bank and Thrift Regulation:Improvements Needed in Examination Quality and Regulatory Structure*, GAO/AFMD-93-15 (February 1993).

5. See, for example, GAO, *Bank Examination Quality: FRB Examinations and Inspections*, p. 54.

6. Richard Scott Carnell, "The Culture of Ad Hoc Discretion," in George Kaufman and Robert E. Litan, eds., *Assessing Bank Reform: FDICIA One Year Later* (Brookings, 1993), pp. 113–21.

"well capitalized" by examiners to function without specific supervisory restrictions. Supervisors of banks that fall into one of the four lower categories of capital adequacy can gradually restrict the banks' ability to pay dividends to shareholders or expand through branching and acquisition. The banks can also be required to replace bank officers, divest themselves of risky subsidiaries, or terminate high-risk activities.

A traditional role for capital has been to provide a cushion against potential losses. Should liabilities grow, the well-managed bank can draw upon accounting equity and loan-loss reserves to meet obligations to depositors and shareholders. Under the FDICIA, the primary function of a bank's capital is to provide a resource for protecting the bank deposit insurance fund. Before a bank draws down all its capital in its final days of solvency, the FDICIA requires "critically undercapitalized" institutions, or those with capital equal to 2 percent of assets, to be placed in receivership within ninety days. Resolution costs (paying off insured depositors or facilitating the transfer of deposits to a healthy bank) can then be drawn from the bank's remaining capital rather than have the FDIC insurance fund bear the full burden.

With the FDICIA Congress has taken a step toward defining a standard formula for bank examination and supervision based on capital adequacy, redefining the primary purpose of bank capital as it is considered in bank examinations and fundamentally redefining the task of the bank examiner and supervisor. The profession defines the art of examination as the ability to assess a bank's condition by looking at a combination of factors. The FDICIA defines capital as the crucial indicator of any bank's condition; it emphasizes the examiner's responsibility in identifying problem institutions by using a regulatory standard and closing them before their capital runs dry.

Nevertheless, although Congress has tried to redefine the task and its implementation, in practice the mission has not changed nor has the fundamental training that examiners receive. Despite making capital king, the law still requires the examiner to conduct full on-site exams of each bank, paying attention to all the indicators in the CAMEL index. Indeed, in a 1991 report on enforcement activity, the GAO argued that "bank capital typically was a lagging, rather than a leading, indicator of bank problems" and that examiners needed to improve their early assessments of management and assets, for example.[7] To the extent that a

---

7. General Accounting Office, *Bank Supervision: Prompt and Forceful Regulatory Actions Needed*, GGD-91-69 (April 1991), p. 3.

bank is well capitalized, and most are, the corrective actions mandated by the FDICIA do not come into play.[8] It is still the role of the examiner on-site and the judgments he or she makes that will be crucial to the way a potentially unsafe situation is handled.

The analysis and judgment of the examination team determines when a bank is performing well because of its sharp management or because of a short-term stroke of luck with real estate investments. This same analysis and judgment determines when a bank's policies for lending decisions or preventing discrimination in lending are in compliance with the law but are perhaps not effective. Analysis and judgment also determine when a loan should be "classified" because of the risk that a borrower will not make payments or when it should be considered good. As a result, this analysis and judgment will characterize the quality of a bank's assets (diminished by classified loans) and thus the adequacy of its capital (the difference between assets and liabilities). Most critically, it is the quality of examiner assessments that serves as the premise for supervision exercised by the Federal Reserve, FDIC, and OCC. As noted by the field office supervisor quoted earlier, the examiner signs the final report indicating the bank's condition, and the examiner is the one who will take the stand to testify if the bank challenges the report in an administrative action. Consequently, an assessment must be able to withstand scrutiny by agency supervisors, the bank and its attorneys, and possibly the courts. Describing the advice he offered to examiners, one regional administrator cut to the point: "Knowing where the risks are, you [the examiner] have to be willing to accept risks yourself."

Balancing Unique Combinations of Risk

Banking is a business of risk that depends on depositor and investor confidence. The examination profession must facilitate that confidence by restricting risks that threaten safety, while allowing for sufficient risk taking to ensure a viable operation. A variety of risks might threaten safety. If borrowers default on their loan payments, the bank faces a credit risk. If the bank makes too many loans in one geographic area or relies too heavily on a particular product (to encourage deposits, extend credit, or manage its customers' credit), it faces a concentration risk. The value of its fixed-income assets and the price it must pay for deposits depend on interest rate risk. If assets are not readily used to

---

8. James R. Barth, R. Dan Brumbaugh Jr., and Robert E. Litan, *The Future of American Banking* (Armonk, N.Y.: M. E. Sharpe, 1992), pp. 23-24.

meet current liabilities, the bank faces liquidity risk. And finally, a poorly run or inefficient institution faces operations risk.[9] High risk related to any of these, or a combination, could push a bank to failure.

Depending on the size of a bank, the community it serves, its affiliates, and the extent of its business dealings, failure could disrupt financial intermediation in a community and across financial markets. At the same time, banks must be allowed to take sufficient business risks to remain competitive. Banks are no longer unique. Pension funds, mutual funds, insurance companies, mortgage companies, and a diverse profusion of financial service companies now compete for deposit funds and to extend and manage credit, service loans, and buy and sell loans packaged as securities. More than ever, if a bank does not compete aggressively in these ways, it also invites failure.

The effort to balance concerns for safety with those for maintaining soundness or competitiveness is most clearly manifest in the policies agency management makes to guide field examiners. "We have always emphasized balance," said a Fed policymaker. "We want to ensure the safety and soundness of loans, but we want credit to be available to borrowers for the economy to grow. . . . Everyone is striving for balance; of course, one person's balance is not the same as another's." Consensus might be achieved among supervisors in one agency, or even among the three supervising agencies for a particular policy designed for banks that are well capitalized with quality assets, well managed with stable earnings, and liquid. But policies must provide a standard against which the poorly managed and perhaps reckless institutions can be held accountable without stifling the competitive behavior of well-run institutions. A member of the OCC's top management group described the effort:

> With policy . . . you are trying to walk a fine line. You do not want to regulate in a way that affects the entire industry to control the practices of a few banks that you are concerned about. . . . If you have a hundred banks, and three are engaging in certain activities, you don't want to limit the other ninety-seven. . . . It's a trade-off of regulating the level of risk in the entire banking system without stifling the management ability to deal with other issues, and to do it in a way without regulating to the lowest common denominator.

9. John P. O'Keefe, "Risk-Based Capital Standards for Commercial Banks: Improved Capital Adequacy Standards?" *FDIC Banking Review*, vol. 6 (Spring-Summer 1993), pp. 1-15.

The trade-offs are just as prevalent at the very end of the supervisory process, when supervisors can take formal and informal enforcement actions. They might recommend increases in a bank's capital or a recapitalization, better systems for managing lending, more competent officers, a halt to dividend payments that might cut into a low capital reserve, or stopping lending practices that concentrate risk. They can enforce the plan informally through meeting with bank officers and the board of directors, requiring a resolution or letter of commitment from the board stating the corrective actions to be taken, or drafting a memorandum of understanding specifying the corrective action plan. Supervisors can also take formal action. They can invoke a written order specifying required actions, assess a civil monetary penalty, order the suspension or removal of an officer or director from banking operations, issue a cease-and-desist order, or, in the case of the FDIC, eliminate deposit insurance.

What makes these actions formal is their enforceability in an administrative proceeding or in court by the legal staff of an agency. Yet a formal action to bring about corrective action entails risks of its own. Indeed, once a bank is in a troubled condition, the enforcement process pits potential risks to shareholders and investors against the risk to the FDIC's insurance fund (and potentially taxpayers) should the bank fail. Enforcement actions intended to change a bank's operations can have unintended consequences for its capital cushion. A particularly onerous civil monetary penalty might deplete limited capital or draw away money needed by the bank to meet its obligations. Enforcing the suspension of dividend payments might prompt a sharp drop in the market price of a bank's shares; if the share value is depressed, the bank's ability to raise equity capital will be reduced. Suspending or removing a bank's managers or its board of directors could send depositors and investors scurrying to institutions they perceive to be better managed. Indeed, as the frontline officials in the supervision of risk, bank examiners' simple presence, if prolonged, can signal real estate markets, potential customers, and bank investors of trouble. "When you have an industry built on confidence," observed one top manager, "and you introduce uncertainty, you are asking for it."

The ultimate penalty, shutting a bank's doors, revoking its charter, and putting it into FDIC receivership, decides the game of risk to the disadvantage of the shareholder and, if some equity capital remains, to the advantage of the bank insurance fund. If an institution is closed before its net worth reaches zero (a power given to the supervising agencies under the FDICIA), the FDIC can share the resolution costs with a bank's creditors. But closing the doors before capital is depleted also has its risks. "We might protect the FDIC insurance fund, but what about Joe shareholder? The minute we take away the bank," said one official responsible for supervisory policy, "the value goes to zip. . . . Once you take away the bank, the loans are no longer worth squat."

This balancing act between sufficient and excessive risk and between enforcement that prevents failure and enforcement that prompts it is complicated by what agency managers identify as the basic challenge of banking supervision: every bank is unique. Each component of the CAMEL rating is considered important because banks have different strengths and weaknesses. Low levels of capital in one bank, for example, might not pose as significant a risk as they would in another if the bank's management has a good track record. A bank that has low earnings might be in sounder condition than a high earner drawing income from high-risk real estate loans or financial instruments that are very sensitive to interest rate fluctuations. And one bank's diversified earnings from activities other than lending might diminish the risk associated with its loan portfolio, while a similar portfolio in another bank with earnings primarily from its lending activities could increase risks. Referring to the FDICIA's emphasis on a sufficient cushion of capital as the basic indicator of a bank's condition, an official charged with policymaking argued that "hard capital sounds so real. . . . But capital is not an indication of condition; it's not just a question of how much capital. . . . Some banks may have a little capital but be healthy. Others might have a lot of capital but be in a risky condition. . . . A bank might have 2 percent capital, but it might have bottomed out and be on its way back."[10]

Bank examiners and their supervisors will argue that the unique combination of risks in any bank requires examiner flexibility and the use of examination policies rather than the application of across-the-board regulations.

My first lecture on the art of examination and the supervision of risk came during an interview with one of banking's veteran philosophers (as he was described to me by others), whose regulatory experience, research, and commentary are widely valued within the industry. The

---

10. The counterargument, discussed later, is that the decision to wait for a bank to "come back" allows banks headed for inevitable failure to deplete their capital in a last-ditch effort to meet obligations.

FDICIA, he observed, was an attempt to remove examiner discretion by regulating rather than supervising capital. "Bank capital is something you can't regulate because the differences between assets [and] liabilities—capital—the appropriate level depends so significantly on management. . . . You can get capital figures, but no one knows what [a bank] needs." The condition of any given bank, he argued, depends on a combination of factors, and it is up to the examiner to determine whether the particular combination is a sound balance of risks. He illustrated the point by relating his experience as a young examiner and the way in which the *supervision* of capital was used by a senior examiner to bolster other aspects of a bank's operations.

The supervision of small banks used to entail some rough justice. . . . I can remember telling a small bank to "get $75,000 in new capital by Monday, or you're closed!" and he did. . . . When I was training in Mississippi, I was with a great, experienced examiner. . . . We went into one bank one day, and it was fine. . . . Then we went into another bank that was identical to the first . . . even the same cows in the field. . . . [But] the examiner classified everything under the sun [classified loans are those considered risky in terms of the ability of the borrower to repay] and told the banker that he had no capital. . . . I asked him, "Why did you do that? It was in the same condition as the first bank." . . . He said that the difference was that in the second bank the CEO was a high school teacher whose father was a banker, and he was taking over the bank at age twenty-eight, and [the examiner] wanted to scare the hell out of him [to prompt him to become a better manager]. *Now* he has no capital . . . and the way you got at him was through capital.

As in the past, such rough tactics are still overseen by an agency's field office supervisors or those at the district level or, when necessary, those in Washington. In the 1990s, however, politicians and reporters are also involved, often bringing instances of apparently arbitrary actions to the front pages of the business press. With relative anonymity, the examiner from Mississippi could tell a young CEO what he needed to do to improve the soundness of the bank and his own management skills; the examiner that is hard on a bank CEO today might earn the *Wall Street Journal* headline, "Regulator from Hell."[11] Regardless of the level of scrutiny under which examiners operate or the specificity with

11. Fred R. Bleakley, "Tough Guys," *Wall Street Journal*, April 27, 1993, p. A1.

which their task is defined, their job and that of their supervisors remains the same. They must assess risk, then balance and trade off one set of risks against others.

Once an assessment is made, however, the art of supervision is to get a bank to make changes in its practices before manageable problems become ones that place it on the troubled list or push it into failure. If examiners have the discretion to assess the risks and judge when enforcement actions need to be brought, a measure of their expertise is a healthy industry with few (or at least low-cost) failures.

The "Walk around the Block"

Too often, a former OCC official commented, "the bank examiner is the one who shows up on the battlefield after the battle is over and shoots the wounded." The examiner, in other words, often has the job of confirming the failing or failed condition of a bank. What is needed, he continued, is an "orientation toward trying to keep the battle from happening in the first place." If examiners cannot identify and successfully prevent problems, they will be relegated to overseeing troubled banks slip into failure. Yet convincing the directors of a bank to make changes in their operations before problems become manifest and acute is not easily accomplished, particularly when the bank has high earnings or a high ratio of capital to assets. It is the equivalent, as one former examiner said, of "walking around the block": the supervisor and bank officials walk in circles without the bank's taking corrective action. How to preclude problems is crucial to the effectiveness of bank examination and supervision.

This same examiner, now a manager in Washington, illustrated the walk around the block by describing the efforts of his agency in the early 1980s to get Continental Illinois National Bank to alter its management practices just when the bank was at its earning peak and its position was viewed very favorably in the corporate world:

> The year the cracks [in the foundation] were showing [the management] was named banker of the year. . . . They were at the height of public perception . . . and then some bureaucrat making $30,000 a year is going to tell them they need a management change? When it is proper to push for change, how do you influence it? . . . You fight with the bank for usually two years. . . . I call it the walk around the block . . . and ain't no CEO or president will say "right"; they will say

"bullshit!" . . . So in that two years, you lose the corrective period. . . . The problem is endemic in the concept of supervision.

In 1984 Continental Illinois required the largest, most elaborate disbursement of FDIC insurance funds ever made up to that time to prevent collapse.

Two fundamental difficulties prompt the walk around the block. First, enforcement actions are intended to bring about corrective action so that a bank headed for trouble will turn itself around. Yet simply bringing an informal or formal enforcement action against a bank will not guarantee timely corrective actions or that the bank will be able to take any at all. Corrective actions must be taken by bank officers and directors, and the earlier the better. For examiners and their supervisors, the question is how best to elicit early cooperation or ensure compliance. Without question, examiners and supervisors in the Fed, FDIC, and OCC prefer an informal, cooperative approach. In response to a GAO report that recommended "prompt corrective actions" instead of informal efforts, the Fed argued:

> The prompt corrective action proposal, as it has been presented to date, has focused on prescribing actions and measures that supervisors should require institutions to take (or be constrained from taking) and has *been silent on the means to be used by supervisors to see that these orders are complied with.* GAO has concluded from its study that in the past supervisors have not been as effective as they might have been in getting institutions to take appropriate corrective measures, because they relied too greatly on informal rather than formal enforcement actions.[12]

Examiners and supervisors will argue that bringing about early corrective action is achieved through persuasion and jawboning. As one agency supervisor said, "You just have to keep in mind that you don't get things done by administrative action. . . . We are sales people, and some things are a tough sale." Convincing bank management to make changes to reduce risk is a tough sale, even when the bank is in trouble. "Banks," observed a senior examiner, "will always fight the concept that they are troubled institutions." It is a particularly tough sale when the institution is making a healthy profit or has a high level of capital, and it

12. GAO, *Bank Supervision*, p. 62 (emphasis added).

is tougher yet to have a supervisory action stand up in an administrative process where hard evidence that a problem exists is required.

As each of the three agencies pointed out in their response to the GAO, informal enforcement actions are not only less costly to pursue than formal administrative or judicial actions, but they can foster a cooperative relationship that facilitates supervisory access to the bank for fact finding and can create a greater likelihood that the bank will work with the supervisors to meet the recommendations of the supervisory plan rather than contest a formal enforcement action in court.[13] The measure of a successful enforcement process, the OCC argued, "is not the number of actions taken or even the type of actions taken. . . . Rather, it is the accomplishment of the supervisory goals in light of the facts and circumstances in each case."[14] The walk around the block, in other words, is not necessarily to be expected just because informal efforts are used. Bank examiners will argue that for every walk around the block, there are many more successful corrective actions brought about through informal enforcement actions or simply persuasion on the part of the supervisors.

For Congress, however, which was facing the largest number of bank failures since the Great Depression and the possibility of a taxpayer bailout as large as the one required by the savings and loan industry, informal enforcement actions seemed only to prolong the inevitable failure and to deplete capital cushions. The FDICIA attempted to correct for the walk around the block (or the stroll to bankruptcy, as it was portrayed in congressional hearings) by mandating self-executing restrictions on a bank's actions when capital reaches particular critical levels. For example, whether or not the bank's primary supervisor requires it, an undercapitalized institution cannot make capital distributions (payments to shareholders or management fees), it must have a capital restoration plan in place, and if it allows assets to grow, capital must grow accordingly. Yet these provisions are only self-executing if the

---

13. An interesting literature on cooperative regulation supports the agencies' argument. See, for example, John T. Scholz, "Reliability, Responsiveness, and Regulatory Policy," *Public Administration Review* (March-April 1984), pp. 145–53; and Scholz with Jim Twombly and Barbara Hendrick, "Street-Level Political Controls over Federal Bureaucracy," *American Political Science Review*, vol. 85 (September 1991), pp. 829–50. Scholz argues that a cooperative strategy (employing the game theory strategy of tit for tat) does facilitate regulatory compliance and prevents the dysfunctional consequences of regulation by strict application of the rules. See also Ian Ayers and John Braithwaite, *Responsive Regulation: Transcending the Deregulatory Debate* (Oxford University Press, 1992), for a similar argument grounded in sociology rather than the formal theory employed by Scholz.

14. GAO, *Bank Supervision*, p. 70.

bank is able to raise new capital. In its written response to the GAO report on enforcement, the FDIC argued, "It is one thing to require additional capital but it is quite another for management to raise or otherwise restore capital within some reasonable time frame."[15] The agencies can halt or restrain the payment of dividends, acceptance of high-risk brokered deposits, interest paid on deposits, and other activities more promptly under the FDICIA, and they have the authority to remove bank officers or board members with limited due process constraints. Again, however, "It is one thing to constrain or seek the removal of a marginal or incompetent officer, by whatever means, but it is quite another to find a more suitable replacement."[16] Most critically, with its emphasis on trip wires for primarily undercapitalized institutions, the FDICIA does not give the examiner additional means to bring about changes in a thriving Continental Illinois Bank's operations before it is too late. The law does little to prevent the walk around the block.

Assessing the "M" in CAMEL

The second difficulty that prompts delays in action is the bank examiners' assessment of management. Nowhere is the art of examination more evident than in judging management capability. As in the story told by the young Mississippi examiner, examiners have always made informal assessments of management, but formal rating as part of CAMEL has been often predicated on the overall condition of the organization. Examiners can assess the financial condition of a bank based on its capital, assets, earnings, and liquidity. But management is difficult to assess independently. Thus if capital is adequate, assets and earnings solid, and liquidity sufficient, management is often assumed to be sound as well. Many supervisors, in fact, simply refer to the CAEL index because management is so difficult to measure independently. "Traditionally," a field office director stated, "it was always argued that the CAEL drives the M." If a bank's CAEL components were 2, 1, 2, and 2, the M would be plugged in as a 2 also. Yet, as field office directors and as most managers in agency headquarters acknowledge, the condition of the bank does not necessarily show overall safety and soundness if management is not competent to deal with a major economic downturn, the collapse of a real estate market, or the consequences of volatile interest

---

15. GAO, *Bank Supervision*, p. 53.
16. GAO, *Bank Supervision*, p. 53.

rates for rate-sensitive products. The problem with *not* relying on CAEL, however, is that the indicators for sound management are not clear.

"In a pure world," said a member of management at the FDIC, "the condition of the bank is a good starting point. . . . But you must look beyond, not just whether conditions are good or bad, but what led to the bad." The best way for an examiner to anticipate the troubled condition of a bank, he continued, is to have a means to assess the competency of management independently—a proposal more complicated than it might seem. "If a manager recognized early on in the process that certain assets were going to hell in a handbasket and tightened up the screws, that's good. . . . But if the bank failed anyway, was management bad?" The task is made more difficult when earnings, in particular, are high. According to the same senior manager, "We can tell them, 'we are concerned that you are making loans with little equity. . . . We don't care if your earnings are going up; this is not smart management.' . . . But it's hard to hit someone over the head who is successful."

Nevertheless, supervisors have made strong efforts to ensure that examiners are striving to assess management independently. One OCC district supervisor said, "We constantly tell examiners, when you analyze management, don't stop with the symptoms, get to the cause. . . . What role did management's decisions play? Were there procedures in place? Did it make sense to make that decision? . . . Don't be satisfied with good results. . . . There is a lag between bad management decisions and poor results."

Field examiners try to assess management competency by using the exam itself as well as considering the responsiveness of management to past supervisory efforts. "I can tell you what our policies and procedures say, but I will tell you that you cannot look at management in a vacuum," said one senior examiner. "You have to look at the history, the performance, and the prospects to make a determination as to management capability." This same examiner resisted the notion that some single indicator could be especially useful. "It might be tempting to look at the policies and procedures . . . to determine whether the institution is OK, but some managers are so good they have no need for policies and procedures. . . . We are stressing the substance of management rather than procedures." As part of the review of assets, for example, the examiner conducts an ongoing discussion with a bank's management. The structure of assets and the ability of managers to discuss the objectives behind that structure reveal, according to some examiners, management quality.

Defining quality management, separating it from performance, and rating it is something examinations have yet to achieve, but the interest in doing so is high. A manager involved in the OCC's Research and Resource Management Division noted that

> just as the OCC looks for qualities of management to run the OCC, as any organization looks for quality of top management, we could pull together those factors and use them to supervise a bank, to be better at assessing the quality of management. It's not totally impossible. We evaluate personnel based upon certain standards, and I think management should be evaluated too. . . . I think it can be put together.

The problem, as he and others noted, is a management rating, measured independently of performance, that is distinctively different from the CAEL rating will require an examiner to stick his or her neck out. An FDIC regional supervisor noted that if an examiner rated a bank manager a 3 without the bank's having severe loan problems, the examiner's report would be rejected by the district office. Instead, the examiner will typically take a conservative approach and will rate management on a par with performance. "You have to be able to explain poor management and high performance," stated the OCC official, and today "any subjectivity (on the part of the examiner) flies in the face of the current [FDICIA] directions."

Yet if examiners want to prevent battles with supervisors and bank managers over the soundness of bank operations rather than simply exercise their responsibilities to put failing banks out of their misery, they must become more competent to assess management quality independently of banking performance indicators.[17] Referring to the concentration of banking failures in the Northeast in the late 1980s, an OCC supervisor noted, "There were cracks in the foundation before the economic bust. . . . We're trying to look at the little cracks before the mess, to start being more preemptive."

The Good Examiner

The examiner who is able to balance risk, use measured enforcement that prevents walks around the block, and assess management compe-

17. Office of the Comptroller of the Currency, *Bank Failure: An Evaluation of the Factors Contributing to the Failure of National Banks* (1988); and Federal Reserve Bank of Chicago, *Management Assessment: Report by the Taskforce of the Federal Reserve Bank of Chicago* (1993).

tency has a parallel in the regulatory literature. In their study *Going by the Book*, Eugene Bardach and Robert Kagan contrast the "newly evolved, tougher breed of inspector" with the "good inspector." The former "too often seems to take unreasonably costly bites from good apples along with justifiable bites from bad apples, thus provoking resistance and ending needed cooperation."[18] In contrast, the good inspector would make an effort to preserve cooperation between regulators and regulated to reduce resistance and improve the likelihood of achieving regulatory goals. This inspector would represent a "more sophisticated type of enforcement official" armed with "modern enforcement tools" but capable of using them "flexibly and selectively." To secure responsible social behavior from the regulated interests, the good inspector would offer responsiveness, a fair and serious hearing of the regulated firm's difficulties in reaching compliance; forbearance, a willingness to back off on strict enforcement when the activity is of secondary importance or when enforced compliance would be unreasonable; and would offer information as to how the regulated might come into compliance in a cost-effective manner and an explanation regarding the objective of the regulation.[19]

In the world of bank examination, then, the good examiner would be willing to let slide violations that did not affect a bank's safety in return for more effective management efforts to improve internal control systems, make better loans, or improve management oversight. The good examiner would work with the banks, taking into consideration the uniqueness of each risk portfolio and the particular costs of compliance with banking law, to find workable compromises. Yet the good examiner would be willing to turn to formal enforcement if good will did not produce good faith efforts toward sounder practices.

The ideal of the good examiner represents a careful balance between the maintenance of cooperation that produces desired behavior and the independence of the examiner to make enforcement a viable threat. This is particularly important as the banking industry confronts mergers, experimentation with new financial instruments such as derivatives, and other changes. One director of supervision noted the importance of training examiners to keep up with these developments; especially at a time of economic difficulty for the industry, examiners must have a

---

18. Eugene Bardach and Robert A. Kagan, *Going by the Book: The Problem of Regulatory Unreasonableness* (Temple University Press, 1982), p. 123.
19. Bardach and Kagan, *Going by the Book*, p. 131.

thorough grasp of the banking business as well as solid communication with the banks to understand the consequences for individual banks. However, he continued, "we're not cheerleaders for the banks. . . . In interviews with officers it's clear we have [at times] more of an adversarial relationship."

Achieving and maintaining the balance between cooperation and independence requires that both bank and examiner see the benefit. As a deputy comptroller in the OCC noted, there will always be those banks that "oppose any regulation," those that "feel it stifles creativity," and those bad apples that make "poor decisions . . . banks with no good systems of policy . . . lenders that don't use the proper standards." When an agency's cooperative, informal effort is met with disregard, cooperation is typically replaced by formal enforcement. "The worst thing is to say you will do something and not do it," the comptroller continued. "Then we will go to an enforcement action, maybe assess monetary penalties . . . maybe a cease-and-desist order."

The ideal of the good examiner is clearly challenged by the philosophy of the FDICIA. What examiners consider a failure of the cooperative process—the need to enforce supervision with formal actions—is the remedy prescribed by reformers.[20] And the logic underlying the law is that prompt enforcement actions, based on explicit standards of safe and sound banking, are the remedy for cooperative efforts that too often grant a bank forbearance. Although the backers of the legislation can surely see the logic of cooperation both for the effectiveness of tailored enforcement solutions and for the flexibility granted to the supervised banks, evidence for the effectiveness of the approach is ambiguous, particularly at the height of a banking crisis. For members of Congress seeking to prevent a bailout of the banking industry, solid indicators by which to assess supervisory effectiveness and on-the-job behavior is the goal. This is a direct challenge to the professional autonomy of bank examiners and is met with discomfort and disregard. Based on his own experiences in New York during the 1960s, a former examiner, now a manager in Washington, argued for the effectiveness of an informal approach:

> If there was a problem, the chief examiner would talk to management. "Charlie, the guy you have in the loan office is not doing you any good.

---

20. *Federal Deposit Insurance Corporation Improvement Act of 1991*, sec. 131. See also GAO, *Bank Supervision*.

You are going to have to talk to him or replace him." And when we came back the next time, that would be done. . . . Then we started this crap that Congress pushed . . . that examiners shouldn't make judgments . . . and now the examination process is a laundry list. . . . It forced banks to get lawyers in there . . . and consequently everything is much more formal. . . . I liked it better the old way.

The Management Challenge

The task of banking examination and supervision, and the good examiner ideal, present top managers in the Fed, FDIC, and OCC with common challenges.

Hiring Competent Examiners

Until the one best way to operate a bank is codified, examiners will have to depend on expertise in assessing the condition of a banking operation. Consequently, the initial challenge for agency managers is to hire competent people and train them to understand the banking business; as an OCC director stated, "Getting a good staff and developing them takes a long time." Examiners work from field offices often miles from their regional or district office and further yet from Washington—just the way many examiners prefer it. Yet if they are to provide field, district, and Washington supervisors with competent information and recommendations, they must have quality training and sound judgment.

When they are hired, most examiners are recent college graduates who arrive on the job with a degree in business, finance, or perhaps accounting. All three agencies compete for this pool of potential employees, and managers in each agency are well aware of the competitive advantages and disadvantages of their agencies. Some emphasize pay and benefit differentials, others the variations in requirements for becoming a commissioned examiner able to specialize and earn a higher income.[21]

In recent years all three have gone outside the pool of new graduates to hire people with some experience in the private sector. A Federal Reserve bank supervisor described these efforts as a way to strengthen

21. Before 1989 there were significant differences in the salaries and benefit packages offered by the three agencies. Passage of the Financial Institution Reform, Recovery, and Enforcement Act of 1989 provided some flexibility for the OCC, allowing it to be more competitive in its hiring. The differences were directly related to the extent of autonomy enjoyed by each agency. For a discussion of the differences, see chapter 3.

specific types of expertise: "We also hire experienced bankers. . . . We don't bring in examiners right out of school. . . . We try to find people with a specialty area and then we emphasize that. . . . Traditionally the Fed has hired entry-level college grads . . . but as products have developed, and the needs have become more specialized, we've gone for more experienced people." The agencies are thus also in direct competition with the private sector, particularly banks and accounting firms, which can pay higher starting salaries. Attracting good people requires not only good benefit packages and opportunities for advancement but also the ability to offer an interesting professional career within which the new examiner can develop expertise and exercise independent judgment.

Training Competent Examiners

Once agencies have hired new examiners, the next challenge is to prepare them to exercise informed independent judgment and keep pace with changing banking technologies and products. Led by the OCC, all three agencies altered their examination procedures in the early 1980s from a predominantly bottom-up, bean-counting orientation to a more top-down examination focused on bank management that uses sampling techniques to assess the condition of the bank. A former OCC official recalled his experience as a teller when the bean counters came to examine his bank:

> One day the bank examiners showed up, and they ran in and ordered us to stop doing what we were doing, and they sealed the cash drawers, and first they balanced the teller windows, and then they counted the cash in the vault, and then they looked at loans in the loan portfolio that were over a certain amount. . . . It was very mechanical, but it didn't help much in terms of how the bank operated on a daily basis.

A senior manager in Washington described the approach today as "a more structured sampling of loans to verify if a bank's internal loan system is sound." Rather than require the examiners to "put their fingers on each dollar, count cash, every dollar in the vault," as one former examiner recalled, an effort has been made to evaluate the systems of checks and balances in place—from lending to trust operations, asset acquisitions, stockholder dividend practices, and reimbursement practices—and to sample aspects of the bank's operations.

The transition reflects changes in the way banks do business, particularly since the liberalization of banking practices allowed by the Deregulation and Monetary Control Act of 1980 and in response to the dramatic increase in competition from nonbanks in the provision of financial intermediation.[22] The complexity of today's financial instruments and services demands a form of examination quite different from counting the cash in the bank vault and determining the secure status of safety deposit box systems. Restricted in their ability to sell insurance or securities, banks have nevertheless been innovative in developing new products for customers and new means to manage and diversify their own portfolios. Twelve out of the nation's top twenty players in the rapidly growing market for derivatives, for example, are banks, operating as dealers between customers seeking to hedge against contrasting forms of risk or as purchasers from other dealers to hedge their own risk exposures.[23] Examiners assessing these operations must understand the derivative as a product, the nature of the market, and be able to judge the soundness of the warehousing system banks are required to have in place to maintain a balance in their exposure to opposing types of risk.

The growing frequency of bank mergers and acquisitions poses another challenge because they consolidate resources, concentrating risk with potentially harmful consequences. Examiners must understand the implications of product diversity and risk concentration for individual banks and the entire banking system. In addition, because regional economic downturns require agencies to dispatch examiners from one region to the next, other examiners must be able to pick up the slack.

Deciding how the challenge can best be met with limited resources is a primary concern for managers charged with designing and implementing training. Examiners must be taught the basics of examination, including the basic operation of a bank. At the same time, they must be kept abreast of changes in the industry and new legislation or regulations governing the activities of banks. And they must be taught in close coordination with the policy development that takes place in each agency. Agency trainers must identify the skills that have to be learned for examiners to develop competence in a particular area of examination. The areas requiring training are many, from the fundamentals of a

22. Thomas F. Cargill and Gillian G. Garcia, *Financial Deregulation and Monetary Control: Historical Perspective and Impact of the 1980 Act* (Stanford, Calif.: Hoover Institution Press, 1982).
23. General Accounting Office, *Financial Derivatives: Actions Needed to Protect the Financial System*, GAO/GGD-94-133 (May 1994).

banking operation and the basic assessment and classification of loans to the ability to give a presentation to a board of directors and testify in a deposition, hearing, or trial regarding a supervisory action against a bank. Trainers must then develop appropriate courses using combinations of on-the-job training, instruction in Washington and in the district offices, independent study, job aids, and joint schools offered by the Federal Financial Institutions Examination Council, a coordinating body for the three agencies.

Finally, training directors must develop ways to test the proficiency of trainees before they become commissioned examiners who exercise considerable autonomy and are responsible for training other examiners. In addition to completing other requirements, new examiners are required by each agency to pass a final examination. If training fails to keep pace with the changes in the industry, or simply fails adequately to prepare examiners, the foundation of the supervisory process is at risk. "It's like Newton sitting under the apple tree and the discovery of gravity," as one director of supervision in the OCC commented. "Without a knowledge of physics, [the falling apple] would have just hurt. . . . It's the same idea with examiners. If you don't have knowledge of banking, you don't know if something is a problem or not. . . . You can't exercise judgment unless you understand banking." Preparing examiners for the exercise of judgment is fundamental. "We are always talking about judgment," said one director of training programs. "We have these college graduates who would love to have a cookbook—a pinch of this, a dash of that. If that was the case, there would be no need for examiners."

More than simply producing well-prepared examiners, however, training also has to coordinate with supervisory policy. Before an examiner can be trained to assess a bank's management of derivatives, for example, there must be a supervisory policy in place and a standard for the way the assessment should be conducted. "But sometimes," as one training official noted, "there will be a new policy, and no clear understanding of what the performance should be. It's scary, but training can establish policy." The coordination of policy and training is most difficult with respect to cutting-edge issues in the banking industry. As another training director described the situation,

There are some very technical changes in the banking industry today. One hot button is derivatives. It is difficult to provide training when even the experts can't define it. Some say it is a swap, others say it is a strip coupon. . . . We can't train until there is a policy. Once the policy is written, the impulse is to get it out there. But it is difficult. We sometimes have to weave policy through a number of classes.

The training challenge for management is nothing short of running a graduate program in professional bank examination. Managers responsible for training must provide the courses in a sequential and timely manner with instructors who have to balance their teaching load with their regular examination responsibilities. In each agency, senior examiners serve as part-time instructors, usually for several years. Identifying examiners willing to teach regularly, able to convey the necessary information and skills, and available to teach, as one director of training pointed out, is akin to being a college dean.

I think of my job as being like that of the dean of a school, and I'll tell you why. It's not quite the same but close. What's a dean's function? To bring in good people to teach, to have the right number of students in courses, to ensure that students get the courses they want and that they are happy with the instructors, and to ensure that the instructors are happy, which usually means making sure that they don't have to teach too much. . . . The dean's job is to keep all the balls in the air. It is not an exercise of the exertion of my will on someone else. . . .You can order people to teach, but it doesn't mean they will do a good job. For our instructors, it's not a full-time job. The vital activity of training is not their primary activity. . . . So the logistical details are difficult. We are beholden to the good will and cooperation of the instructors. Each has his or her own way of teaching, and we must work with that, and work to keep everyone in the same general path. It is not a characteristic problem, just a challenge. . . . In a college a faculty member may decide that he needs to go off and contemplate their navel on a mountain top or on a lake. The analogy is the same here. Good instructors may do that, or their boss [at the regional level] may decide they are more useful somewhere else.

Commitment to the Profession

Once the examiners are trained, the agencies must provide incentives for them to make a long-term commitment to the agencies and the profession of banking examination. Longevity of service sharpens the expertise that examiners can then share. This is critical, in large part because of the way young examiners are trained. Both on the job and in the classroom, the agencies depend on the expertise (sometimes in very specific areas) of the senior examiners. Some turnover is good to bring in fresh perspectives, but controlling turnover reduces hiring and training expenses. Examiners' commitment to an agency and close identification with their profession might also reduce the likelihood of their straying from agency policy or becoming too dependent on bank management for determining a bank's condition.

Crucial to longevity, supervisors agree, is an agency's ability to motivate personnel and reward good performance. But although supervisors in all three agencies said they were allowed the flexibility to pay employees a higher salary than other government agencies or to establish regional pay differences (a more recent development for the OCC than for the others), they also consistently commented on the difficulty, endemic in government service, of sorting out the excellent performers from the mediocre and concentrating higher wages or bonuses on the best. "The FDIC is better than most agencies," noted one senior supervisor, "but the hiring and firing of personnel is difficult. . . . You can't reward people for high performance and you can't punish people for poor performance." Another said, "The biggest constraint is motivating employees to do the job. In the government service, even if you perform only satisfactorily, you get an increase. . . . Someone who is outstanding might receive an extra $800, but he or she will look and see that Johnny got just as much for doing nothing."

A former OCC official recognized that some loss of examiners was acceptable, but he still worked to improve the compensation package to reduce turnover:

There was a crying need to remove the disparities in compensation among the agencies and with private industry. . . . Many of the staff were leaving to work for banks. . . . In one sense that is good. It's healthy to have turnover so that there can be some mobility and opportunities for advancement, and you have people with good supervisory skills in the banks and theoretically influencing their behavior. . . . But the turnover rate had gotten to an intolerable state.

The OCC's turnover rate was not necessarily any more intolerable than the Fed's during the early 1980s (it ranged from 12 to 15 percent a year), and dropped below that of both the Fed and the FDIC from 1984 to 1992 (figure 2-1). Relative to this lower 7 to 8 percent (closer to the

FIGURE 2-1. *Annual Turnover of Bank Examiners, by Bank Supervising Agency, 1980-92*

Percent

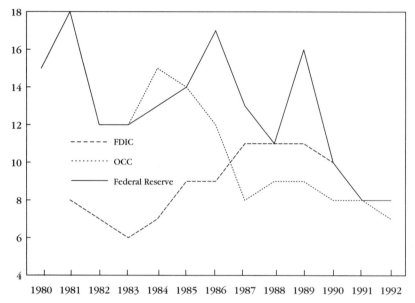

SOURCE: Data on the number of new hires each year, the total number of examiners each year, and turnover are from agencies responsible for personnel management. Where there were gaps in the data (not all the agencies kept turnover statistics in the early 1980s, for example), information regarding the number of examiners and new hires was collected from the agencies' annual reports, and the turnover rate was calculated. OCC data for 1980-83 were not available.

agency's historical average), however, the 15 percent high in 1984 was perhaps "intolerable."

Not every supervisor connected motivation exclusively with monetary rewards. Some emphasized the importance of promoting and protecting the professional culture of banking examination. One director in the FDIC identified his most significant challenge: "How do I as a manager, a leader, pass on to new people what they need to do their job? . . . Bank examiners are going against bank presidents. . . . You need an attitude to do that, and a corporate culture that must be passed on. . . . It's learned along the way." It was the ability to inculcate in employees an agency's esprit de corps, a sense of mission, that he identified as the key to long-term motivation for the job.[24]

24. In the FDIC the esprit de corps shared among examiners is closely related to the agency's mission to protect the deposit insurance fund. For a discussion of the role this mission plays in examiner behavior, see chapter 3.

Another manager, a regional director of supervision, emphasized the need to maintain the enthusiasm that young examiners brought to the field and protect the professional culture from the political and news media pressures focused on examiners at the height of the banking crisis. "The biggest concern I have is the number of people who are getting whipsawed. I try to counter a lot of that. We have some *very good* people. They come from outstanding schools. . . . They are bright, bright people . . . and they fit right into what we need. I don't want to destroy that enthusiasm with everything they see. . . . They're the ones out on the firing line." An FDIC field supervisor made the same observation: "We have some exceptional people now, but they feel the tug. You don't want them to become disillusioned by all the talk and criticisms of government bureaucrats. . . . It's easy for the first four to five years because the benefits are pretty good, but then it becomes difficult." Noting the barrage of criticism examiners in all three agencies were receiving at the time, the regional director observed that the key to maintaining esprit de corps was to emphasize the agency's and the profession's culture of independence. "There is a professional condition that is necessary for examiners. . . . I tell them that if you take a strong position, and it is well supported, we will support you."

Central Direction with Discretion

Management in the Federal Reserve, FDIC, and OCC must offer some deference to the priorities of the profession for exercising independent judgment yet provide sufficient oversight and direction to enforce policy consistency among examiners spread across the country. Central direction is also important for the supervised banks. If examiners are given broad discretion, there has always been concern that it will lead to inconsistent treatment among banks and generate uncertainty as to the practices an examiner will or will not find acceptable on a return visit—a negative report, after all, has costly consequences for a bank.

As in any organization dominated by a strong professional group, there is a tension between autonomous expertise and hierarchy or central control. In 1963 Victor Thompson wrote of the "imbalance between ability and authority" as the "most symptomatic characteristic of modern bureaucracy."[25] In the Fed, FDIC, and OCC, the imbalance is somewhat muted by the predominance of former examiners in top

25. Victor A. Thompson, *Modern Organization* (Knopf, 1964), p. 6.

management. Nevertheless, the tension is present. A Washington-based OCC supervisor emphasized the "strong anti-Washington bias" in his agency and the strength of the district offices as an impediment to his ability to compete for more personnel or resources.

> Washington is seen as a waste of bureaucracy . . . and it's so hard to demonstrate that two more people would allow us to do so much more when there is such opposition from the field. . . . There is no chance to increase the number of personnel because it doesn't play well in Peoria. . . . There is a lot of power housed in the districts of this agency . . . the people out there examining the banks, and for any number of reasons the Washington agency staff is not likely to grow at the expense of the districts.

Where this OCC manager stressed the tension in terms of organizational strength, a regional supervisor for the Federal Reserve emphasized the distrust field personnel had for political appointees to the board of governors and the influence that they had over the examination and supervisory staff in Washington. "I recently had a heated discussion with a board staff member on the relative role of the board of governors. Out there [in Washington] they are God's representative on earth. [Washington staff] never question the board and wait for them to provide insight. I tell them the governors are political appointees, and they are relying on you to provide bureaucratic expertise."

Despite the strong sense of autonomy expressed by examiners and supervisors in all three agencies, they do recognize the necessity for central direction. A senior examiner and part-time instructor in the FDIC contrasted Reserve Banks' significant autonomy from the Fed's board of governors and the autonomy of the FDIC's regional offices from the agency's Washington headquarters.

> As a goal, standardization is good. There are eight regions [in the FDIC], and within the field offices there is so much difference, so much diversity of reports, philosophy. . . . The Federal Reserve banks are too autonomous. Each is a separate entity with responsibility for what they do there. I wouldn't want to go to that, but from a field standpoint, it is a pain in the butt to have paperwork rammed down your throat [in an effort to standardize across regions], rather than be allowed to use your judgment.

The challenge to management to provide central direction and policy consistency without overwhelming the field offices with paperwork or excessive restrictions is similar to that posed by Herbert Kaufman in his 1960 study, *The Forest Ranger*. Kaufman was interested in the way forest rangers, "the lowest-ranking line executives and operators in the national forest administration," translated policy statements into action.[26] This was particularly challenging because rangers were spread across the country, often in the most remote areas, and subject to the preferences and pressures of local communities and economic interests that might be in conflict with agency policy. Kaufman found that the Forest Service institutionalized particular techniques to control these "centrifugal forces that might be expected to fragment" the agency. Bank examination also requires a geographically dispersed workforce in close proximity to the banks they supervise. Indeed, the professional ideal of the good inspector requires examiners to have good communication and rapport with the banks they examine.

Today exerting central direction is much more manageable than it was in the late nineteenth century, when the OCC was the first of the three agencies to take up the task. As is still the case, funding for the OCC's activities came from assessments charged to the national banks each time they were examined. Without any centralized means for collecting the fees, the agency relied on the examiners to make collections. The fees were then used by the examiners to pay for any staff they hired as well as their own travel and living expenses.[27] The organizational tension was clear. To do the job, examiners required sound knowledge of the banking business and some rapport with the banks they examined (especially if they wanted to get paid), yet at the same time they needed a sufficient premise for independent judgment and assessment of the banks' operations.

Examiners no longer collect the supervisory fees and central direction is greatly facilitated by technological advances, but the tension posed by encouraging cooperative on-site relations in order to conduct thorough exams and to prevent walks around the block is still crucial for the management in Washington. The tension is particularly strong when the agencies are training new examiners on the job. When asked to describe the working relationship between bank officials and their primary super-

26. Herbert Kaufman, *The Forest Ranger: A Study in Administrative Behavior* (Boston: Resources for the Future, 1960), p. 4.
27. Ross M. Robertson, *The Comptroller and Bank Supervision: A Historical Appraisal* (Office of the Comptroller of the Currency, 1968), pp. 76–79.

visors, the senior vice president of a large midwest national bank replied, "A lot depends on the experience of the [examination] staff. Where bankers are concerned is when someone conducting the exam is fresh out of school. They might not have even had a checking account before . . . [and] they are asking questions that some bankers think are dumb. In a sense, we are training them." An official in another bank expressed the same frustration: "Last time [the examiners] were in here they warned us ahead of time that we were going to be a training ground for a bunch of greenhorns. So last year [the exam] took a month. . . . I'm tempted to send them a bill for the training." When the agencies rely on on-the-job training, the line between the independent examiners and the banking professionals is thin indeed. But making sure that the line stays drawn is the challenge of management.

Bankers profess an effort to cooperate with the examiners—from training greenhorns to providing the office space, personnel, and information necessary to complete an exam. "I've always found that if we attempt at the front end to make the exam as comfortable and as open as possible, that's the best approach," commented a bank vice president. "I would still think there is stress even if you come at it from the open door. . . . But it should be congenial. . . . An adversarial approach is not appropriate, no matter what the situation." Referring to the tone of a typical examination, a senior FDIC examiner stated, "When there is a problem, it is not an enjoyable process for anyone, but it is not necessarily as antagonistic as it seems." Continuing, he indicated his sensitivity to the stress of bank directors and their employees when a bank was in trouble:

> Part of the reason I like to travel is to see the bankers. . . . After a bank has survived a difficult time, you can hear an audible sigh of relief. . . . When a bank is in trouble, it affects a lot of people—the bankers, their employees, and then the examiners have more work and more stress too. . . . It can be personally hard. . . . The personal side is still there. . . . [and] the relations are not as antagonistic as outsiders might think.

Yet before examiners hear that audible sigh of relief, they must have the clout to make banks bring about difficult but necessary changes. That requires the backing of agency policy and strong support from supervisors, as well as the confidence on the part of the examiner that comes through training and experience—both of which depend on central management and direction. Just how the Federal Reserve, FDIC, and OCC manage this challenge is the topic of chapter 3.

3

Three Ways to Manage the Supervision of Banks

Despite a common interpretation of their mandated task, a common view of the management challenge posed by it, and their embrace of a common ideal (the good examiner), the OCC, Federal Reserve, and FDIC manage examination and supervision very differently. Essential to these differences is each agency's approach to centralized direction of field personnel. On-site bank examination and supervision require agency employees to be stationed across the country, close to both large urban banks and community banks in rural areas. The management challenge is to ensure that examination and supervision are conducted in line with agency policy without compromising examiners' exercise of independent judgment or disrupting the necessary lines of communication between the banks and the examiners.

Each agency management operates from some concept of central direction. It is manifest in the way they organize their headquarters policymaking and operations and delegate authority to supervisors and examiners. Each system of central direction also determines the context within which the hiring, training, and career promotion of personnel take place.

The focus in this chapter is on the agency management systems in place from just before the 1980s banking crisis to the mid-1990s. The agencies made changes in their systems during this time, but the basic premise of each remained constant, despite operating under leaders appointed by three presidential administrations, enduring the most distressed period in American banking since the Great Depression, and coping with the most successful banking era in terms of annual profits.

Centrally Directed Innovation in the OCC

At the core of the management style at the Office of the Comptroller of Currency is a simple concept: innovation and lots of it. During the 1980s and 1990s the OCC's style was characterized by consistent, centrally directed innovation in examination and supervisory policy, change in the structuring of functional responsibilities in headquarters and in the level of operational autonomy allowed in the field, and the use of technology to improve skills, resources, and central direction. The agency has had a strong legacy of autonomy in the field (see chapter 4). As a result, agency headquarters drew mostly on the routine development of new supervisory techniques and guidelines for examiners to ensure adequate control of field operations.

During the late 1970s, OCC examination policy emphasized the problems of industrywide risk such as real estate lending; its supervisory policy focused on identifying and limiting such risk. These emphases cut against the ones that were embraced by financial analysts, who wanted examiners to emphasize detecting potential failures of individual banks and closing them promptly to preserve remaining capital and minimize losses to the federal deposit insurance fund.[1] In 1979 the OCC began a special program of continuous, on-site supervision of the nation's largest multinational banks and of the entire banking system. It broke away from the practice of thorough examination of individual banks from the bottom up.[2] In subsequent years its management has experimented with targeting only the most troubled banks for thorough examination. It has also instituted changes in examination reports to make them more usable to banks and has experimented with providing examiners more specialized training in safety and soundness, compliance, trust, or electronic data processing as well as developing generalists competent in all four areas.

In the most obvious sense, policy initiatives from headquarters provide direction in the field for the way an examination is to be conducted, the resulting report prepared, and supervision exercised. But a routine flow of initiatives also forces field offices to turn to Washington for clarification, interpretion of on-the-job situations in the context of

1. Paul M. Horvitz, "A Reconsideration of the Role of Bank Examination," *Journal of Money, Credit, and Banking*, vol. 12 (November 1980), pp. 654–59; and Patrice Gordon and Thomas Lutton, *The Changing Business of Banking: A Study of Failed Banks from 1987 to 1992* (Congressional Budget Office, 1994), p. 30.

2. Office of the Comptroller of the Currency, *1979 Annual Report* (Department of the Treasury, 1980).

new policies, and the training of examiners to carry them out. And the initiatives encourage professional growth among examiners. Some provide career personnel with avenues for advancement in the agency and greater autonomy in the field.

The Hub of Policy Innovation and Delegation

Below the comptroller the OCC's management is organized into two main divisions: Bank Supervision and Policy and Bank Supervision and Operations. Each is headed by a senior deputy comptroller and two deputy comptrollers who oversee their division's more specialized functions. Within Operations one deputy directs supervisory operations for multinational banks (all national banks owned directly by one of seven major bank holding companies), and another directs them for special banks (the national banks in the most critical trouble as well as others that require monitoring).[3] In conjunction with the senior deputy, these two oversee all field work in the agency's six national districts and numerous duty stations.

A much larger management group in the Policy Division develops and communicates policy through directives; examiner manuals and handbooks, circulars, and electronic bulletin boards; interpretation; and guidance. The group consists of a senior deputy comptroller, a chief national bank examiner responsible for developing safety policies for national banks, and two deputy comptrollers charged with policy for international banking and consumer and community rights concerns. The offices of the deputy comptrollers and the chief national bank examiner are staffed by directors responsible for more specialized concerns in each area.

The chief national bank examiner is the driving force for examination policy (but not international or compliance policy). This office monitors OCC policies, reviews information coming from the field and questions from examiners, evaluates economic trends affecting the industry, and oversees changes in banking products and practices. The chief examiner then initiates policy changes to address concerns. A policy group consisting of the OCC's chief counsel, the senior advisor to the comptroller, and the five senior deputy comptrollers from each functional division (operations and policy, plus the support divisions of administration,

---

3. The seven bank holding companies are BankAmerica, Bank of Boston, Chase Manhattan, Citicorp, First Chicago, NCNB, and Security Pacific. Office of the Comptroller of the Currency, *Quarterly Journal*, vol. 10 (March 1991), p. 13.

public affairs, and economic programs), review major initiatives before the chief approves them.

The separation of policymaking and operations reflects the autonomy granted to the OCC's field examiners. Policy is developed in Washington; most supervisory decisionmaking takes place in the districts. With the possible exception of those involving problem banks, actions taken against any bank with less than $1 billion in assets are handled at the district or even field office level. When a problem bank is involved or a particularly rigorous enforcement action is at issue, decisions are reviewed by the Washington supervisory review committee. But rather than handing down a formal approval or disapproval of the action, the review serves to check the consistency of a given decision with similar decisions in other districts.

Autonomy in field operations does not stop at the level of field office supervisor. OCC senior examiners in the field also operate with relative independence. "The OCC," commented one former examiner and current member of Washington policy management, "traditionally has put more control into the hands of its staff. . . . The field examiners (have) power to speak for the agency in the field." In contrast, "The FDIC has almost all the power in the hands of managers. . . . Their staff has almost no ability to make any decisions at all. . . . They are almost totally dependent on going back to the principals. . . . Whereas one of our senior examiners would render a decision without scrutiny." It is the OCC examiners' autonomy, he continued, that allows the agency to take action in the field to meet the changing needs and conditions of banks. It is an autonomy, however, that is formally granted from headquarters.

In addition to policy innovation, agency management in Washington has tried to rearrange functional responsibilities in headquarters and to adjust the location of operational authority to achieve better central direction. Before 1984, control over decisionmaking in the field depended on strict hierarchy. Operations were organized into fourteen regions headed by regional administrators. A regional office could not so much as enter a memorandum of understanding (an informal enforcement action in which a bank agrees to take particular actions to improve soundness) until the action was approved by Washington. The strain on operations began to show. "At one point," a field supervisor noted, "they loosened up and said we didn't need approval [for supervisory actions] for banks smaller than $50 million. . . . But for every other agreement we would write . . . we would have to send it to Washington, and there might be some interoffice negotiations, and then we would have to go back to the bank [with the decision]." The system was transformed in 1983 when the fourteen regions were collapsed into six districts, each headed by a deputy comptroller with significantly more decisionmaking power than the regional administrators had exercised.[4]

From this new district autonomy there has arisen a gradual delegation of responsibility to the field offices. Although districts still direct duty station activities, the oversight is much reduced. A duty station supervisor noted that "six or seven years ago, our district started to delegate to the field offices . . . and now most of the decisions pertaining to non-problem community banks are made out of this office." The duty station's independence from the district office and Washington should, however, not be overstated. Freedom varies with the seniority and experience of the duty station supervisor and his or her comfort with exercising authority. When I called them to set up interviews, for example, some supervisors agreed immediately, but others felt more comfortable checking with Washington before committing (and in some instances not committing). Nevertheless, the authority to make supervisory decisions for the smaller, nonproblem banks is there to be exercised as delegated from Washington and the districts.

This delegated autonomy for operations, however, was immediately followed by a strengthening of OCC headquarters' capacity to use policy innovation to assert central control. Before 1986, a single senior deputy comptroller for bank supervision was responsible for directing both policy development and operations for commercial examinations. A senior deputy comptroller for policy was responsible for research and economic programs, compliance programs, and coordination of the comptroller's ex officio responsibilities on the FDIC board of directors. The overwhelming responsibilities of the Operations Division overshadowed the policy function. In 1986 policy and operations were formally separated, which strengthened the policymaking ability of the agency.

The OCC's adoption of portfolio management and its new emphasis on paying more attention to the banks most at risk offers a good illustration of how centrally proposed policy innovations can strengthen headquarters' direction of operations and still give due consideration to supervisors' and examiners' judgment. As an OCC district supervisor described the agency's action:

---

4. Office of the Comptroller of the Currency, *Quarterly Journal*, vol. 3 (March 1984), p. 17; and *Quarterly Journal*, vol. 4 (March 1985), p. 9.

We adopted the concept of having an examiner in charge for every bank. . . . A portfolio manager was responsible for understanding the banks in his portfolio, and had to develop a strategy; maybe every twelve months [he] would check performance. . . . But [the policy] was based on the idea that if banks don't deserve a lot of supervision, don't give it to them. . . . Examiners . . . started to move away from operations and skewed more time to the lending in problem banks and in regional banks. . . . So we developed this hierarchy of risk for making resource allocations. . . . We would concentrate resources, and we accepted the fact that some banks fail.

Since passage of the FDIC Improvement Act in 1991, which requires annual on-site, full examinations for all but the smallest and healthiest banks, the OCC's hierarchy of risk is no longer used to prioritize examination resources, but portfolio management is alive and well. Portfolio management entails assigning a senior examiner based in one of the six districts to a portfolio of banks. Each of these examiners then determines a strategy for supervising each bank in the portfolio. The policy is committed both to the ideal of the good inspector and the delegation of examination authority, yet it is a centrally directed innovation that gives shape to district and field operations.

Before passage of the FDICIA, this tailored approach of portfolio management meant that some banks received only off-site monitoring of their financial activities if the manager considered them sound, while others (typically larger banks and banks in trouble) posing a greater risk to the banking system received concentrated and continuous on-site supervision. Portfolio management and targeting also entailed tremendous confidence in the judgment of the manager to assess how much supervision individual banks needed and confidence that the district supervisors would exercise sufficient oversight.

The OCC's use of policy innovation and procedural and organizational change illustrates the trade-offs that managers routinely confront. In separating the policy and management operations, for example, the agency tried to improve the professional capacity of the policy group to develop and oversee policy, but it sacrificed some of the close integration of operations and policy the two had when their work was more formally linked. One member of the policy group referred to the split as a "constant challenge." Nevertheless, she continued, "right now, for both sides the work is so demanding that it is a necessary split. . . . But if a policy is promulgated, it is difficult to ascertain if it is being implemented appropriately. In developing or identifying policy we need information from the field." Getting that information can be difficult given the separation. Similarly, by delegating broad responsibility for operations to the district offices, the agency gained flexibility at the expense of central control. "The policy-operations dichotomy in the OCC," argued a manager from the policy division, gives the headquarters staff "control over how policy is written, but not how it's implemented. . . . So we have some sense of accountability without control in practice."

The Division of Bank Supervision and Policy does attempt to achieve more control over (or at least contact with) field operations through various policy and technology innovations. When asked about the way he communicated with examiners, a manager from the policy division answered, "Through e-mail, anyone can write a question that they might have . . . and someone will answer." But the someone could be any employee (in headquarters or a district or field office) of the OCC who checks his or her e-mail and knows the answer to an inquiry, which typically comes from an examiner. A more direct form of communication is the bulletin board and the chief's wire, which transmit new policies, discuss policy development, and raise questions for examiners to help them monitor the industry and the challenges facing them. Examiners also, of course, have the OCC manual and the circulars that continually update OCC policy, but for questions that might not be addressed by existing policy or that present the examiner with a new problem, the ability of the policy staff to interact with the examiner in shaping a response is limited by the examiner's use of e-mail.

OCC training courses emphasize the need to call Washington when questions arise; but distance and a lack of central authority over the execution of operations makes the gap a difficult one to span. It is wider for those officials in the policy division who do not have bank examination experience. Several members of the policy management team have worked with the OCC's economic unit, for example, or with the Treasury on international banking issues, but are uncomfortable with visiting field offices or assessing the supervisory process. An OCC manager with responsibility for policy support contrasted the perspective of OCC employees who work their way up through field operations with what he contended was a distinctive emphasis on the part of Washington management:

The plain truth is, and some in this agency would take offense at this, most of the . . . OCC employees are primarily bank examiners with a business or math degree . . . and they have experience going out in the field . . . and they have a micro perspective. . . . To move up in the agency they do a stint in Washington. . . . But here what's important is not bank specific, but the broader issues.

Similarly, an OCC manager with policy responsibilities contrasted the vision he was seeking from his staff for policy development with the narrower focus that he believed accompanied a background in field operations:

> Examiners have a way to go at things. . . . They like to be told what to do, and go out and do it. . . . Then they come back and ask, "OK, what's next?" . . . I try to get them to become more visionary, to have a better sense of what's going on, and to ask why it's important for supervisory policy. . . . I don't have an examiner's background . . . but my deputy is good at making that jump for me. . . . He has an examiner's background and broad . . . experience in supervision and operations and administration, so he helps me look at the large questions and the small questions.

The Policy and Operations Divisions also reflect different operational styles. Since the reorganization of districts in 1984, the Division of Bank Supervision and Operations is more decentralized, not only from headquarters to districts but from districts to field offices and field offices to examiners. Once formal responsibility for basic operations was given to the districts, the districts delegated responsibility for supervisory decisions related to nonproblem community banks to the field offices. The supervisor of a field office in the OCC's central district identified the district management's interest in delegating authority to duty stations as representative of one individual's management style. It was a time, he argued, when "people were talking about empowerment at the grass roots" in management circles, and the deputy comptroller of the central district (a noncareer examiner with a Ph.D. from Northwestern), was interested in experimenting with delegating power. Beyond the delegation of basic supervisory decisions, field offices in the central district have experimented with teams to consolidate procedures or customize compliance policy procedures for small banks, for example, and with reviews of managers by subordinates. The techniques have facilitated management actions from time to time, but they have not been universally adopted. Offices have the flexibility to incorporate them if they choose.

In contrast, the policy management group in Washington operates in a more procedural and hierarchical fashion. "The way policy translates here," according to a key member of the policy management team, "is like a matrix. . . . I will take [an issue] to the policy group if it is important, and then it will go through what we call the borda process, through the legal division and I send it on to the economic people. . . . It might go back to the deputy comptroller, then I sign off on it." The day-to-day decisionmaking processes also unfold in a more hierarchical fashion. In reference to the constraints he faced as a manager of a policy support staff, an OCC official discussed the formality of operations that clashed with his own preferences for communication:

> This is a very hierarchical organization. . . . I do things by picking up the phone and calling someone who might be three or four levels above me, or if I run into someone in the cafeteria I'll bring something up with them . . . and that has gotten me into trouble sometimes. . . . Culturally, the OCC is not comfortable with that. . . . Hierarchy is pervasive and people are reluctant to talk unless you go through the right channels.

It is from this more formal system that the OCC's policy innovations flow. As a means of exerting management control over the district and field personnel, the system has the advantage of forcing people to turn to Washington for guidance, and it precludes or interrupts patterns in examination and supervisory methods that might be particular to a district or field office. It has also had the advantage of creating new opportunities for examiners to advance, either through specialization (with some specialties carrying more professional clout than others) or as a portfolio manager, and to abet examiner autonomy in the field. However, as a management technique, constant policy innovation has a serious flaw that can ultimately detract from the good inspector ideal: if examiner training fails to keep pace with the innovations or if the fundamentals of training are sacrificed in the continual effort to adjust courses to policy changes, examiners can become dependent on circulars, checklists, and job aids for implementing their task.

Developing an Examination Cadre

In a reorganization of the training program, the Department of Training and Performance Development was moved from the Division of Administration and placed under the supervision of the chief national bank examiner. The management of training now more closely reflects the use of innovation and organizational change initiated by the policy group, but management also illustrates the struggle to keep training and development on pace with the changes in policy. As supervisory and examination policy has changed, the skills required for examination have changed; and as the policy team attempts to bring about improved central direction, it has drawn on the Division of Training and Performance Development to help out by giving examiners a more centrally defined training experience.

A professional staff whose expertise is training and development rather than banking examination per se develops and implements a curriculum for OCC examiner training as well as management and executive training. In its current form training is, as a top manager from the division described it, "moderately centralized, and becoming more and more so all the time." For the Fed and the FDIC as well as the OCC, most training during an examiner's first three or four years takes place on the job. In the OCC about 60 percent of classroom training is conducted in Washington. To explain the OCC's emphasis on increasingly centralized training, a division manager commented,

> The [training] used to be decentralized, but it did not work. Decentralization in theory sounds good—to have the training out where the students are and the instructors are—but it didn't work. There was significant inconsistency in examination. . . . Today, while there are some inconsistencies, depending on which area of the country you are in—the Midwest [for example] does a lot of agricultural loans and the East Coast does big business loans. . . . there are some inconsistencies, but it should be consistent. There should not be a New York City way, or a Kansas City way. . . . It should be centralized.

Courses listed in a catalog each year are offered in the classroom with OCC instruction, through independent study and computer-based training, and on the job. They provide all OCC examiners with a core training and the opportunity to specialize in commercial examination, compliance, fiduciary (trust), and bank information systems (electronic data processing). After completing the core curriculum, typically within four to five years, all examiners must take the OCC's uniform competency exam (UCE) held and assessed in Washington. If they pass, they become commissioned examiners, known in the OCC as OC-12s.

This common training experience is the culmination of several changes in OCC policy in the past fifteen years. In the late 1970s and early 1980s, OCC policy emphasized specialization. An examiner was trained in consumer protection and compliance with civil rights laws, for example, and received little or no formal training in commercial examination. The compliance exam was conducted by a separate cadre that wore blazers of a color different from those of other examiners. A former OCC official discussed one of the reasons for dropping this highly specialized approach in the 1980s:

> What we found was that compliance specialists were treated as sec-
> ond-class citizens. . . . Some examiners wore red blazers and some
> green, and those wearing the green blazers were the black sheep. . . . I
> did not think it was an efficient use of examiner talent to have a crew
> trained in compliance, with nothing to do about safety and soundness.
> . . . What did make sense . . . [was] to have specialists who would
> augment the overall exam. . . . Let the compliance review process be
> part of the overall review.

A district supervisor offered another explanation for the change: "When you have specialists, such a distinct group, you have the potential for zealotry. . . . You can focus so much that the impact of that area on the ultimate concern, safety and soundness, might be lost."

Following a brief period in which all examiners were trained in commercial bank safety and soundness with supplemental training to allow them to conduct the specialized portions of a bank examination, the OCC now has a core curriculum that includes introductory specialty courses. An examiner must be proficient in the basics of commercial examination and pass the UCE before formally specializing, but specialty courses and on-the-job training are provided for examiners-in-training with an interest in specializing. OCC trainers now emphasize "cross-training" and equate specialization with selecting a college major in a general liberal arts program:

> We are changing from a generalist examiner who also looks at compli-
> ance to something like a college curriculum, where there are many
> standard or core courses, and then all of a sudden you decide "this is
> my major" and you go off and take electives. . . . You decide to special-
> ize just [before] passage of the UCE, then matriculate, but you don't go
> off until you are commissioned.

The current emphasis on centralized, professional, and systematic training also represents an attempt to compensate for the failures of the decentralized process in giving examiners only the basic preparation for field activities. Training, as a former comptroller and several members of the OCC management commented candidly, has not kept pace with the changes in supervisory techniques that occurred in the 1980s and early 1990s. A member of the policy division management team said, "Most people here will acknowledge that we are in the tail [of examiner training]." A former examiner and staff assistant to the comptroller reflected on her training on the job and in the classroom in contrast with current training:

> We received a formal six-month training program before we went into the banks, and we were assigned for several months to a seasoned examiner. . . . There were no time pressures; we would learn about [everything] from counting cash to the evaluation of loans. . . . There was also a lot of classroom training. . . . But now there are a lot of resource limits, and they throw you out there. . . . If you can find a mentor, great. . . . We had a chance to learn about the way a whole bank operates by starting with the little banks. . . . [But] if you are put in a multinational right away, you never have the chance to see how the whole bank works.

Many of the policy changes since the late 1970s were made with the assumption that examiners could exercise good judgment, that they understood the whole operation of a bank and the logic of the supervisory process. The new manuals issued to implement top-down examinations and the targeting of examination resources, for example, told the examiner what to do, but not why. "Our old examiner manual that we refer to as the 'brown mouse,'" noted one manager with examiner experience, "is focused on 'this is why you do something in the exam, and this is how.'" Without the manual and without sufficient training, examiners often come to depend on a list of procedures in conducting their examinations—a contradiction of the practice of a good inspector.

Many of the policy changes since the late 1970s were also made with the assumption that training would follow, but this has not always been the case. Consider the OCC's innovative approach to the examination report in the mid-1980s. Rather than focus on the production of an examination report to be read and used by agency supervisors, the OCC began to emphasize providing analysis and guidance for an individual bank to use to improve its condition. A somewhat critical observer from another agency commented that "their product [the report] was not paper-based, it was more abstract. In practice, they got away from an examination report, virtually no report at all." What the examiner in charge did produce was a more free-flowing narrative intended to be a useful source of information for a bank.

This innovation, however, led to another: the introduction of writing courses in the training curriculum (writing is now a standard course for all three agencies). While policy moved away from a standard report to be read by supervisors, what did not change was the need to alter the behavior of a troubled bank. That required an ability to communicate findings clearly. Referring to the immediate consequences of a more narrative report, a former OCC official said,

> I have sat down and read some of these reports, and I had to shake my head in disbelief. It was as if English was a second language. . . . I have told examiners that if they can't articulate their findings in a way that is meaningful for a bank's board of directors, and for management, they will have no effect on the behavior of the bank. . . . So we changed the format of the report; the important parts were pushed up . . . and we implemented writing courses for examiners.

The form of the examination report, as any OCC examiner with the agency in the past five years will testify, is not sacred. At a recent training session, an examiner with the agency for four years noted the use of three different examination reports. The recent adoption of a common report by the three agencies, a blending of each agency's style and format, has put a stop to changing the report, but it has not altered the OCC's emphasis on the report as a document for banks to use rather than one to guide supervisory decisions.

Despite the problems of keeping examination training current during the most hectic times of the banking crisis, the training staff and some supervisors in the field consider the OCC's training the most rigorous among the three agencies. One supervisor pointed out for example, that it "usually takes five to six years before [examiners] can pass the UCE, [and] our pass rate is not as high as the FDIC's." When asked why, he said there was "no comparison" between the levels of difficulty and the amount of pre-UCE work required of examiners in the two agencies. Voicing a similar (although clearly self-interested) sentiment, a manager from Training and Performance Development said, "We teach our examiners to be so self-reliant they think they can do anything. I guess an analysis between a racehorse and a plowhorse is appropriate. I'd rather have to hold them back than beat them to get them moving. Our examiners are thoroughbreds."

The comment reflects the heavy emphasis the OCC management places on the professionalism of the bank examiner and the prestige associated with the examination cadre. Although the Federal Reserve and the FDIC also emphasize professionalism, it is a central theme in the OCC's training courses. Along with offering the opportunity to specialize following passage of the UCE and to exercise autonomy as an examiner in charge of a portfolio of banks, management emphasizes the prestige of the profession as a way to promote career longevity. The OCC also differs from the FDIC, in particular, in its willingness to hire examiners with experience in the industry. Although most OCC hires are recent college graduates with a degree in business, accounting, or finance, an effort has been made to hire former bank presidents with expertise in small banks and people from other regulatory agencies with, for example, experience in agricultural loans to bolster its agricultural loan assessment capabilities.

Broad Delegation through Expertise at the Federal Reserve

"I think at first I had a problem of [the Fed's] believing on-site examination on a yearly basis was necessary. . . . And we have never deviated from that. . . . The OCC has always been more avant guard, trying to test new methods for supervision." This former OCC examiner, now associate director of the Fed's Division of Banking Supervision and Regulation, offered a striking contrast between the innovation in policy and organizational structure during his tenure at the OCC and the Federal Reserve Board's approach to supervision:

I used to say that if you took a trip to Mars for five years, when you came back the OCC wouldn't be the same. . . . It would be entirely reorganized. . . . But the Reserve Board organization chart wouldn't change. Getting this place to change is a draconian process. We are married to tradition and a conservative approach. . . . The OCC is more forward thinking, not in terms of trying to anticipate or plan, but . . . always doing something new. . . . It used to drive me nuts; they were always jumping into it. . . . They'd go off and develop some master plan changing the way we do things . . . and we only ended up confusing

ourselves about our mission. . . . Here we are harnessed to the past. . . .
If we could be like [Gregor] Mendel, if you could breed things like peas
and rosebushes, you could come out with something good.

A lack of a centrally defined top-down policy and organizational
change, however, does not imply inactive management. The Fed's management system builds upon a more subtle premise: a camaraderie of
expertise. It is a recognition of and a reliance on individual expertise
that defines the management in Washington, directs the broad delega-
tions of supervisory authority to the Federal Reserve banks, and guides
the development and promotion of examiners and their autonomy in the
field. The premise facilitates flexibility in the field, an efficient consen-
sus-building approach to new examination challenges, and confidence
among examiners. But it is of limited help in ensuring a consistent
training experience across the twelve Federal Reserve banks and limited
in its ability to bridge the gap (in all three agencies) between policy
development in the headquarters and the priorities of the operations in
the field.

Examination by Consensus

When asked about the way examiners used the Fed's examination
manual, a senior supervisor in a Federal Reserve bank explained that
new hires used it for basic information on conducting examinations.
When examination teams go into a bank, he said, "the chief examiner
will say, 'Joe, you have the investment portfolio; Mary, you're on fixed
assets.' For a new person, they can look at the manual to see what is
included in that. . . . [The manual] lays the groundwork and gives them
some vague idea of what's expected." But beyond presenting the nuts
and bolts of examination, the manual is not the definitive source for
examination questions and Fed policy. An assistant director in the Division of Banking Supervision and Examination referred to the manual as a
"resource research document" or an "encyclopedia" that would be used
to verify a fact or a procedure.

Examiners do receive periodic letters on policy from headquarters,
but this is in conjunction with a process one senior examiner referred to
as "examination by consensus." As new questions arise or as new Fed
policies are written, the information is distributed "on a district-by-
district basis. Someone with expertise in a particular area works on a
topic . . . and disseminates the information to others. . . . We will send
people, or loan people, to other districts to help with training. . . . It

becomes examination by consensus." A manager in Washington defined the process in a similar manner. Referring to the Fed's efforts to train examiners to address banks' handling of derivatives, both as dealers and as buyers, he commented, "What we are in the process of doing now is identifying those in the system who are experts with specialized knowledge, and we are developing course material. . . . It's like a pyramid structure. We take the knowledge we have, we take existing knowledge and leverage off of it. . . . One person teaches two, two teach four, and we grow it. We are growing that knowledge."

Fed representatives in the field and in headquarters emphasized that bank examination and the supervisory process are not the equivalent of an audit that can be conducted with checklists to make certain a bank is in compliance with regulations. A 1993 General Accounting Office report recommended that the Fed (as well as the OCC and the FDIC) standardize what bank examiners focus on in an exam, how they make their assessments, and how they record their activities.[5] Referring specifically to the GAO's recommendations for standardizing the examination of internal control systems, the Fed disagreed:

> The Federal Reserve concurs fully with the GAO on the importance of banks having effective internal control systems and on the need for the examination process to verify the existence of such systems. It is our considered view, however, that affording examiners discretion to decide on the scope of reviews to accomplish that verification is altogether appropriate. . . . Commissioned Federal Reserve examiners . . . have the training, the experience and the necessary information to enable them to make informed judgments regarding the appropriate scope of the internal control review.[6]

The GAO's approach, Fed supervisors argued, is the equivalent of using a checklist to conduct an exam. Indeed, with the model of the good inspector as the ideal, a checklist approach has the clear potential for "regulatory unreasonableness."[7]

---

5. General Accounting Office, *Bank Examination Quality: FRB Examinations and Inspections Do Not Fully Assess Bank Safety and Soundness*, GAO/AMFD-93-13 (February 1993).

6. GAO, *Bank Examination Quality: FRB Examinations*, p. 56.

7. The term is Eugene Bardach and Robert Kagan's in *Going by the Book: The Problem of Regulatory Unreasonableness* (Temple University Press, 1982).

Regarding a particular Federal Reserve Bank's working relationship with state member banks, one senior examiner argued that Reserve Bank leaders sought to be firm but fair. "We are not bankers. We're not going to tell the banks 'don't use this or do use that system.' . . . We ask, 'what are you trying to do?' and then we tell them where we see problems, and we give them forty-five days to respond, to say how [they] are going to fix the problems, or why [they] are not going to." It is this approach, straight out of the good inspector manual, that Fed officials believe builds solid working relationships with the banks. "Based on the comments we get, the banks like to deal with the Fed examiners, not because we're easy, because we're not, but because we listen to their case. . . . We are not a stone wall that always says, 'No, you will do what we said.'"

Of course, there is the very real possibility that banks tell their primary supervisor that they like dealing with the Fed the best in order to build a more compatible relationship. Nevertheless, it is a widely held perception by top management in the Fed that their approach is not only appreciated by the banks but that it produces more effective supervision. "We tend to have the best program," an assistant director of supervision said. "The general perception is that the quality is higher in our program. . . . Bankers tell me this."

This pursuit of the good inspector ideal is not, of course, unique. Examiners and supervisors in the FDIC and the OCC describe similar efforts to bring about solid relationships with banks to establish firm but fair supervision. What is distinctive is the way the Fed goes about trying to achieve the ideal.

Central Direction through Expertise

Fed management of the examination and supervisory process is built around broad delegation of responsibility to the Reserve banks and to the field, with central direction premised on individual expertise at headquarters, in the Reserve banks, and in the field. Quality control and some central consistency is maintained by a management system that emphasizes and rewards this expertise. In the Fed's headquarters, individual expertise and specialization is prominent. The Division of Banking Supervision and Regulation (BS&R) is responsible for supervisory policy and operations. As in the OCC's policy division, there is specialization, but the principle is emphasized at the Fed, even taking into account the combination of operations and policy within the same division reporting to the same director. The director of BS&R oversees a deputy director, three associate directors, three deputy associate directors, and numerous assistant directors, each responsible for a portion of the supervisory process. The organizational stability of the Fed's specialized units is much stronger than is the OCC's.

When organizational structure is changed, it is done to add another specialized task. For example, in 1977 the Fed created the Division of Consumer and Community Affairs to supervise banks' consumer and civil rights activities that were previously handled by the commercial supervision staff. Neither the FDIC nor the OCC has an entire division devoted to compliance policy and supervisory operations. More recently, the position of associate director of international supervision was created to manage the Fed's authority for the comprehensive supervision of the U.S. offices of foreign banks and U.S. banks' foreign operations, a power granted the Fed through the FDIC Improvement Act. Although the FDIC and the OCC have undergone several reorganizations of supervisory functions and regional and field office structures, the Fed has remained constant—as has its adherence to expertise to achieve accountability.

Throughout their interviews with me, Fed officials in Washington referred to the expertise of each employee and the Fed's collegial blending of the various types of expertise. As one member of the supervisory support staff said, "We take an academic approach.... It's very laid back, a non-cutthroat atmosphere. We have a great deal of respect for each other, and everyone has a great deal of expertise." Similarly, referring to the establishment of the Division for Consumer and Civil Rights Operations, one assistant director observed, "The board is not one to do a poor job.... Once it has a job, it wants to do it the best way it can." Another added, "Here, everyone pulls together. We draw on the strength of [each department].... No one has pride of authorship.... It's our strength." Referring to what he noted was a Fed policy to draw on the knowledge of those within the Federal Reserve System rather than go to consultants for management initiatives, for example, or course development, an assistant director stated, "The Fed employs a lot of Ph.D. economist types. I always figure someone in the system knows the answer." A financial analyst from the division referred to the specialization of the headquarters staff: "We stay on our own track.... There is little cross-training." Nevertheless, she said, people would come together to produce a high-quality project: "No one is hoarding information.... It doesn't happen here." And, referring to the proclivity toward specialization among field as well as administrative personnel, one regulator stated, "The Fed is much more compartmentalized. . . . If you want to be the top examiner for the top banks . . . you get formal training. . . . No one likes to be generic."

Expertise at the Fed is based on study and training, experience, and contacts and the ability to gather helpful information. It is routinely called upon for supervision of a new product, such as interest rate swaps or derivatives held by banks, or to deal with problems unique to one type of bank such as a multinational or a foreign branch operation. The various types of expertise held by the staff of the supervisory policy group are both experiential, including that of former bank examiners and commercial bankers, and technical, including that of financial analysts and economists. According to an assistant director, each type has a role to play in the evolution of policy. With reference to the often intangible basis for the supervision of risks yet to be taken by a bank, he noted, "To the extent that it is available, we will use empirical evidence to support our positions, but it is often not available." Instead, he continued, "we rely on our own background experience . . . [and we] rely on what we hear."

Expertise becomes a coordinating mechanism when Fed managers discuss their efforts to cooperate with the OCC and the FDIC in joint supervisory initiatives. "We will try to operate as a collegial body, collegial groups," said one assistant director. He noted the decorum common in interagency actions: "Occasionally an agency has particular expertise, and they will take the lead on the ministerial functions. . . . But the policy development function is done collegially." There was, nevertheless, a rivalry among the agencies in determining which had the expertise to take the lead. "Of course each agency has its own point of view and tries to lead, but [the Fed tries] to appear not to lead. . . . Other agencies often throw up that we do . . . but we try to appear not to." An analyst from BS&R made a similar comment: "It's not our philosophy [to act unilaterally]. . . . It's not the case. . . . We try to coordinate with the other agencies. We work with each other. . . . We have similar issues and interests."

Whatever the purported philosophies of the three agencies for cooperation and respect, the result is not necessarily well-blended interagency policies. The development of a common examination report is a good example. The result was an eleven-page form linking the OCC's report with the Fed's and the FDIC's. It is, according to Fed management, typical for the agencies to agree on the fundamentals of an appropriate regulatory response, "then bicker on superficial aspects."

An assistant director noted the standard inquiry by members of the board of governors when joint policy initiatives are on the table:

> The board will always ask, "Where are the other agencies? . . . Is the language identical? No? Why not?" Then we have to explain. . . . I can see [disagreements] justified if we really said, "no, there are differences in our view of safety and soundness." . . . But to say we want to do it as a regulation, someone else as a policy statement. . . . We want to write it up as a narrative, someone else as an outline. . . . It's insane . . . unless you believe the government that governs least is the best, a Jeffersonian republican view!

The Fed's emphasis on individual expertise and its systemwide application carries over to the Reserve banks as well. For example, the St. Louis Reserve Bank was able to apply its computer software expertise in the early 1990s to develop a program that enabled the Reserve banks to collect and aggregate data from commercial banks for the Home Mortgage Disclosure Act (HMDA) and to send the data to the Federal Reserve Board Washington staff for processing. Before 1990 bankers making or purchasing home loans or home improvement loans reported the type of loan and the census tract location of the home. In 1989 Congress amended the HMDA to require the additional reporting of the race, sex, and income of the applicant.[8] The new information required additional gathering and aggregating methods.

Similarly, the Boston Reserve Bank has research expertise in the area of housing discrimination. In autumn 1992 it completed a study on mortgage lending in the Boston area that provided additional data on the creditworthiness of mortgage applicants—their employment, credit history, debts, the property being sought, or other criteria that might be useful in the loan decision.[9] The study constituted a critical foundation for supervisors and policymakers working to bring banks into better compliance with the objectives of the Home Mortgage Disclosure Act.

Reserve banks can also specialize in dealing with a particular banking product or practice in their district that can then be shared with examiners and supervisors in other banks. The Chicago Federal Reserve Bank has developed an expertise in supervising derivative products, in part

---

8. Board of Governors of the Federal Reserve system, *77th Annual Report* (1990), p. 163.

9. See David K. Horne, "Evaluating the Role of Race in Mortgage Lending," *FDIC Banking Review,* vol. 7 (Fall-Winter 1992), pp. 1-15, for a critique of the study. See also *Community Reinvestment Act/Home Mortgage Disclosure Act Update*, vol. 3 (June 1992).

because of their early use by Chicago-area banks. As a derivative dealer, a bank will sell a contract to a customer interested in hedging against volatile long-term interest rates, for example, or to a customer interested in hedging a counterposition (or bet) on interest rate change. The bank will then warehouse the derivatives, managing the deals to maintain counterpositions so that on an aggregate basis, the bank knows where the various risks are. A bank might also purchase a derivative contract to hedge risk on its own balance sheet. Unlike a futures contract, derivatives need not be bought and sold through an exchange, and the buyer need not put up a set margin in the transaction. This often lucrative, yet high-risk activity entails many complexities for the dealing and purchasing banks, and the knowledge to supervise them is developing, as is formal regulation.[10]

Chicago's expertise in the capital market, however, is one that other Reserve banks may be less willing to acknowledge if it challenges their own, particularly since expertise per se is a difficult characteristic to contrast across banks. As one manager in Washington said, "In the core areas of Fed interest, no [Reserve] bank says that someone has more knowledge than they do ... and none of the areas we deal in lend themselves to a quantification of expertise." Occasionally there is some rivalry, however. When the New York Reserve Bank was planning to move staff to the Chicago area, it wanted to know if the staff in Chicago was capable of dealing with derivatives. An examiner based in Chicago not only assured the New York bank that there was sufficient expertise, but warned against tripping over the "cows and the pigs in the street."

The expertise of each Reserve bank reflects its organizational autonomy from the board. Each is technically owned by the member banks of the Federal Reserve system in a particular region that purchase shares in the institution. In turn, member banks help select Reserve bank directors and the president (see chapter 4). The staff of the Division of Supervision and Regulation develops policy, which is approved by a three-member subcommittee of the board responsible for supervisory policy, but the authority for exercising supervision is lodged with the Reserve banks.[11] Reserve banks generate their own income and finance

10. General Accounting Office, *Financial Derivatives: Actions Needed to Protect the Financial System*, GGD-94-133 (May 1994); and Albert R. Karr, "New Guidelines to Toughen Monitoring of Derivatives Transactions by Banks," *Wall Street Journal*, October 24, 1994, p. A2.

11. The board of governors conducts this more specialized level of subcommittee activity in groups of three to prevent the gathering of a quorum (four or more members, and thus an official meeting).

the board's operating activities through assessments charged by the board. In the context of American regulatory policy, the organizational arrangement is unique, but the organizational autonomy of the Reserve banks would not necessarily guarantee the operational autonomy that they have in practice. Although there are clear political reasons for the board of governors to support independent bases of power in the Federal Reserve system that help to maintain its carefully nurtured place within the political landscape, the commitment to expertise as a premise for central direction (or at least consistency) also results in the Reserve banks' exercising significant influence on the supervisory process—including training examiners and shaping Federal Reserve system policy.[12]

Policy is set in Washington, but initiatives can come from the bottom up and headquarters can provide a coordinating, sifting, and honing function in the evolution of any particular policy. As one manager described the process of "growing" expertise, systemwide policy can evolve from experience in the field that is communicated to the Washington-based staff. "Policy statements," said one supervisor from a Reserve bank, "usually come from the Reserve banks. . . . Then they will be reviewed in Washington, and [the staff there] will accept comments on the positions. . . . Some things get initiated in Washington, but they are not policy before it is sent out for input [from the Reserve banks]."

Training the Fed Examiner

A collegial partnership between the Reserve banks and the staff at the board of governors is also apparent in the training process. A top manager responsible for training in the Washington office emphasized the importance of the headquarters staff in coordinating training: "With training, policy is again set here, but we look at the entirety of what to offer, [from] whether or not to do a mix of classes, to getting a wide range of instructors, to coordination. . . . We set the policy, coordinate the resources, and it is delivered and received by the Reserve banks."

Like the OCC, the Fed uses on-the-job training, classroom work, and independent study to prepare examiners for commissioned status. And the Fed also requires its examiners, regardless of their eventual specialization, to take a set of core bank examination courses. As one manager said:

12. Donald F. Kettl, *Leadership at the Fed* (Yale University Press, 1986).

Our view has been, if [someone] is a Fed examiner, he should be a Fed examiner. There should be some basis of what you should know. Our compliance staff, in our view, cannot do a compliance exam without knowing the elements of safety and soundness, and our safety and soundness examiners cannot do a safety and soundness exam without knowing the elements of compliance. . . . There is a cross-fertilization. . . . They are on the same side and have the same interests.

Although the Fed's curriculum for specialization in compliance was developed much earlier than the OCC's, the concept of a core curriculum is the same. The two training approaches differ, however, in ways that reflect their agencies' premises for central direction. Approximately 60 percent of the classroom courses offered by the Fed are delivered in the Reserve banks rather than the training headquarters on New York Avenue in Washington. And although there are core courses, and syllabuses and outlines that are used throughout the system, the Reserve banks have some flexibility to add courses they would like their examination teams to take, and they can decide on how long the examiners are given to take the courses. Unlike the OCC, which emphasizes the gradual gathering in of the training experience to headquarters, the Fed's training program in Washington is settled in its policy, coordination, and occasional delivery of courses.

One effort to improve the connection between Reserve banks and the board, however, is in course development. The approach is very much in line with the camaraderie of expertise and very much in contrast to the OCC's centrally directed practice. In addition to the more informal gathering together of expertise at the various Reserve banks, management in BS&R works with committees that bring staff from the Reserve banks together with staff from the headquarters to develop courses. Reserve banks frequently turn to the board staff to address problems that a particular bank might believe requires a systemwide solution. But as a manager in the Department of Supervision and Regulation noted, "The Federal Reserve is not geared toward Washington issuing commands. . . . We're not going to get a response [from all the Reserve banks]." To address the situation, the Fed is using course development as a vehicle for bringing representatives from the Reserve banks into decisionmaking.

We have tried to make the Reserve banks more of a part of command and control instead of bouncing back and forth between the Reserve banks demanding things from Washington. . . . . We have tried to bring more people into command and control to see the position that we were in. . . . We have course committees, staffed by officials of supervision training and reserve bank representatives, people who have knowledge of the course, and it provides a link between the banks and Washington. . . . It's another element of decentralization, with more involvement from the Reserve banks so that they can have more of an understanding of how the board operates.

The management team at the board has the authority to make overall Fed policy, but it cannot direct operations of individual Reserve banks. At the same time, although the Reserve banks have responsibility for operations, there is a more regional focus in their demands on the board. The committees provide a bridge. "It has worked so well in so many areas," said a manager of training, "I don't know if the Fed could work any other way." It preserves, in other words, the camaraderie of expertise as a means to shape systemwide direction.

Finally, the Fed's training program differs from the OCC's in how its decision to award commissioned examiner status is determined. In the OCC the decision is made in Washington and based strictly on the successful completion of the final exam—the UCE. At the Fed the decision is left to the Reserve banks, and completion of the Fed's core proficiency exam is, as a manager of training said, "a necessary but not a sufficient condition." Each bank could, for example, have its own set of criteria, beginning with taking the core courses and passing the core proficiency exam, but incorporating performance on the job and the successful completion of additional courses. Examiners are then recommended for commission. "It's like anything else," said a training manager. "In academia, at some point, there must have been someone who completed their thesis, but for some reason, the school did not grant the degree. There is more to it than just passing the exam."

Both the Fed and the OCC have begun to draw examiners from the ranks of experienced bankers or those with special knowledge, although most are still recent college graduates. As one Fed official observed, "As products have developed, and the needs have become more specialized, we've gone for more experienced people."

But managers in Washington have encountered a significant problem in bringing in more senior professionals: getting those with experience to fit in with the Fed's approach to examination and supervision. An assistant director in BS&R explained, "Our staff has been expanded, staff that has to be trained. And we are not hiring college grads, we are hiring people with ten to fifteen years experience working with banking issues, but it takes time to get used to the culture of an organization, to fit in, to be fully productive. . . . So it has meant resource problems, time constraints, an enormous regulatory process." Some Reserve banks offer their examiners the opportunity to get a masters degree in business (and in some instances law) by providing tuition reimbursement and half the cost of books. It is not only a strategy for the expertise of the examination cadre, but also for building a loyalty to the Fed that might translate into a long-term commitment.

Common Training and Central Direction in the FDIC

In 1990, following an extensive review of its training program by an outside consultant, the FDIC placed it in a special Office of Training and Education. The office is responsible not only for training bank examiners, but also employees involved in data processing, support services for the agency's primary tasks, and the resolution and liquidation of failed banks. Initially the office was organized to reflect the agency's divisions. The Division of Supervision, for example, had a special training branch. But divisional organization now reflects functional organization based on specific types of training. There will be a unit for the development of programs for examiners, liquidators, data processors, and legal staff. Similarly, a special unit will address training operations. The new office, located in Arlington, Virginia, in a large, high-technology building with a sprawling lawn, long intersecting walks, and park bench seating, is very much like a campus.

The new facilities represent the most recent manifestation of a long-standing FDIC practice. There have traditionally been a core curriculum for examiners, centralized instruction, and a common testing and evaluation procedure. In contrast to practices at the Fed and even the OCC, all this classroom training is conducted in Washington. What has changed with the development of the new office is who, or what professional group, is responsible for developing courses. Traditionally, management in the Division of Supervision and the eight regional offices, in conjunction with senior examiners, developed and conducted the courses. The new office, as one of its managers noted, is intended to "professionalize the training of examiners with human resource professionals in participation with professional examiners." But the concept of centralized training, she said, "represents our philosophy that we have a real desire for consistency. We detail our examiners all over the country, and we want them to have a common view—not the Dallas [regional office] way, or the New York way."

Centralized training is part of the FDIC's method for balancing professional autonomy with the need for accountability to headquarters. As at the OCC and Fed, each examiner trainee must complete core courses and pass a final exam. But every aspect of the FDIC's classroom training and the decision to award the status of commissioned examiner are defined and executed in Washington. And unlike the Fed and OCC, the FDIC is much less likely to hire examiners with previous examination experience. Instead, according to a director of training, 90 percent are trained in Washington. There are also fewer positions in the commercial examination cadre for specialists.

Although homogeneity is recognized as necessary to facilitate central direction of field operations, its drawbacks are also acknowledged: "Homogeneity has its good and bad points. . . . You can't forget that every bank is unique and must be approached differently. If you want a force that you can ship across the country to meet changing needs, the question is whether you should know a little about everything or a lot about one thing." Examiners in all three agencies can be transferred from district to district to meet a particular demand, learn more about the problems facing banks in a region, or keep attuned to agency policy rather than the possible peculiarities of a particular district or region or the proclivities of a group of banks. The FDIC, however, formalizes its concern for common method to an extent not yet achieved by the OCC or attempted by the Fed.

The importance of common training for central direction extends beyond the use of common methods of bank examination. Fewer FDIC examiners specialize than at the OCC and Fed, but they do know a great deal about one thing: protecting the FDIC insurance fund and its importance in the conduct of an exam. Examiners in training receive "lots of cultural indoctrination," observed a training officer. In every course, the relevance of a particular procedure, or of conducting it with a particular objective in mind, is always defended with "Why? Because the FDIC cares about the insurance fund." For example, in one of the early courses examiners learn how to determine the overall value of a bank, a concern that might be less relevant for the OCC or Fed examiner. But in an animated voice anticipating a predictable answer from a class an official asked, "Does the FDIC care about the value of the institution? Yes! Because it affects the fund!" The more value left if it fails, the more the FDIC has to work with in the resolution process (see chapter 4). Each of the three agencies has a character that is part of the training experience and examiner development, but the FDIC's emphasis on the safety of the fund is recognized by managers in the other agencies as exceptional (or excessive). "I think they have a statue in the lobby," snapped an official from the OCC, "and every day they bow to the fund."

Centrally Integrated Policy and Operations

Centralized development of curriculum and course work reflects the FDIC's general reliance on top-down direction of the supervisory process. Whereas the Fed's policy group will adapt to changing situations through a supervisory letter to update policy, for example, the FDIC's Division of Supervision constantly updates the agency's manual of examination procedures as new developments in banking practices are addressed, new regulations fleshed out and translated into policy, and new interpretations of policy made. The manual is a binder notebook, and each new set of revisions comes with a front page telling examiners which pages should be removed from the manual and which inserted. Training officials in all three agencies noted the relevance of the manual as a reference for the examiner in the field, but FDIC instructors awarded it greater significance. "There are different reference materials," one said, "but the principal one is the manual. It's very important. There is a lot of self-study necessary beyond on-the-job training, and the manual helps to implement what you learn in the first year. The manual is very important reading to help you perform." The manual is not a binding set of rules that eliminates the exercise of judgment. Instead, the emphasis the agency places on it as a common source for examination guidance reflects the emphasis on central direction through hierarchy more generally.

Centralized direction has also meant that delegation of responsibility to regional and field offices is tighter in the FDIC. There is a daily flow of communication between regional and Washington officials, and there are formal meetings between regional directors and Washington management throughout the year. Even the Washington buzzwords that characterize policy changes are quickly transmitted to the field offices. "Recently," one field office supervisor said, "the word has been *flexible*. Before that, it was *speaking as one government* [referring to coordination efforts between the three agencies]. And there was a time before that when *proactive* was in vogue." These are more than fashionable slogans. They set a tone for regional and field office supervisors in directing their personnel—indicating when examiners should practice forbearance in order to address more serious concerns for safety, for example, or when more serious scrutiny should be used to prevent problems. "I used the word *flexible* in some connotation the other day," continued this same supervisor, "and I said that I didn't know if *flexible* was in, but *proactive* was definitely out." He said that one of his primary duties was to provide field examiners with an interpretation of the regular Washington directives giving meaning to a term such as *proactive*.

The closely integrated management staff in the FDIC's headquarters reflects its common training and central direction. In the Fed several people presented me with an organizational chart at the beginning of my interview with them. The chart detailed the particular expertise of each unit in the Division of Banking Supervision and Regulation. A similar organization chart for the FDIC's Division of Supervision is more difficult to come by. Every agency annual report offers a chart identifying the major divisions (supervision, resolutions, liquidations, and so forth) and support offices and the director or head of each unit. But the internal breakdown of functions is not noted. A glance at the *Federal Executive Directory* (the phone book for federal agencies) reveals a similar lack of emphasis on position within the division. The *Directory* lists four names associated with the Division of Supervision, three of which are identified by function but not by position or title. Flip pages to the Fed, and the Division of Banking Supervision and Regulation is noted as a separate listing in capital letters, followed by a detailed listing of the director, deputy director, and associate, deputy associate, and assistant directors—seventeen positions in all.

This exercise is not meant to show that the FDIC lacks or is not interested in expertise, but only that specialization is not as much a priority in an agency that addresses the challenge of far-flung field operations through central direction and training. If the Fed's inclination is to adapt to new supervisory responsibilities by developing a specialized unit, the FDIC's is to adapt new situations to fit with its centralized direction and the importance it places on protecting the fund. The Fed, for example, established a separate division, management, and corps of examiners in 1977 to supervise banks' consumer and civil rights responsibilities. The FDIC resisted separating this activity from commercial supervision until 1991. Until then, commercial examiners conducted consumer and civil rights compliance exams in conjunction with safety exams. When the FDIC did make adjustments, it created a separate corps of examiners trained in compliance matters but left the management of their operations within the Division of Supervision. "Specialization is good to a point," contended one member of FDIC management, "but it has its limits. . . . As you get more specialized, you can lose sight of the overall evaluation of the institution." And it is the overall evaluation that is the linchpin of the FDIC's efforts to protect the insurance fund.

Broad delegation of responsibility to examiners is one way to ensure flexibility when changes in banking practices and products might require alterations in agency policy or examination procedure. If a regional or district office can move quickly to address a situation without policy guidance from Washington, the ability to prevent problems might be improved, assuming the office has sufficient insight and information to make the right decision. Many banks are engaged in extensive unsecured lending to credit card holders, for example, while others are buying mortgage derivatives as part of their investment portfolio without much knowledge, according to supervisors, of the risk of rapidly falling interest rates. Still other banks are heavily involved in providing loans based on a borrower's home equity, but many of these loans are really second mortgages. A problem in any one of these situations could require an immediate change in examination policy. But central policy guidance, as one Fed official noted, is "like any bureaucratic structure, you allocate resources to the activity, draw up guidelines, and send it through the approval process, and by the time it hits the examiner in the field it is outdated and useless." The FDIC deals with the need for timeliness in part by giving its policymakers in the Division of Supervision broad flexibility in developing and approving policy. A member of management involved in policy development commented:

We operate very independently. . . . An organization chart is not a governing document for what we do. . . . The result is signed by the head of the division, sometimes the chairman [of the FDIC], sometimes the executive director of supervision and resolutions. . . . When there's something coming into my office, I'm like a tailgate. . . . I try to figure out who in senior management needs to be looped in, whose opinion is necessary. . . . Sometimes all, sometimes a few, it really depends on my perceptions. . . . I adjust or learn based upon negative feedback. . . .

If a question is raised about someone else's opinion, then I loop them in next time.

This approach keeps the manuals current, develops policies in response to changing circumstances, writes regulations, and sends guidance to the field offices. The policy team also drafts testimony for congressional hearings related to supervisory policy and conducts studies as requested by Congress or the FDIC Board of Directors. Its emphasis, however, is on practical applications rather than on the kind of research conducted by the Division of Research and Statistics. The team is interested in the effect of new regulations, policies, or industry conditions on the examination process. In many respects, this practical bent reflects the character of FDIC management more generally.

Central guidance does not, however, translate into a checklist approach to examination. A 1993 General Accounting Office report leveled the same criticism against the FDIC as a similar report had at the Fed.[13] The following excerpt is representative of the GAO's recommendations.

We continue to believe that FDIC examiners would be more effective in fully assessing bank safety and soundness if their work was guided by the minimum essential requirements we recommend. . . . We recommend that FDIC establish a policy for examinations that requires representative and adequate documented evidence to support conclusions reached by examiners for both passed [sound] and classified [problem] loans. . . . We do not believe that FDIC's current requirement for examiners to provide only summary comments indicating they have reviewed sufficient material to pass loans provides adequate documentation for loan quality review.[14]

The FDIC's response, like the Fed's before it, was polite disagreement with the checklist approach as an effective means of conducting an examination. The agency equated GAO's recommendations with an audit, not an examination. A "by-the-book" procedure would be "counterproductive," and would be implemented "at the expense of the scope

13. General Accounting Office, *Bank Examination Quality: FDIC Examinations Do Not Fully Assess Bank Safety and Soundness*, GAO/AFMD-93-12 (February 1993), pp. 26–29.
14. GAO, *Bank Examination Quality: FDIC Examinations*, p. 54.

and depth of examination coverage in areas that truly pose risk to the bank and the insurance fund."[15] With greater emphasis on flexibility in conducting an examination, the FDIC's policies require a final report to present evidence of a bank's condition—good and bad—but to "concentrate primarily on supporting findings relative to negative conditions that might adversely affect the insurance fund." In response to a question about the agency's possible use of checklists, a training official commented that they were used simply as rules of thumb and that examination instructors "caution that they are a good starting point, only. Each situation is unique, and you must develop judgment in the field." Yet it is important to remember that this flexible exercise of judgment is conducted within the context of an emphasis on centralized examiner training and promotion from within, a constant flow of policy guidance from Washington, and close communication between the field, regional, and Washington offices.

The FDIC's effort to develop an agency-specific pool of examiners rather than more advanced or specialized outsiders is facilitated by incentives for employees to commit to a long-term agency career. The first incentive, in contrast to the OCC and Fed, is the speed with which examiners can become commissioned. According to an FDIC instructor, the training period has been "pushed to the shorter side. Up until the 1980s, four years was standard. In the mid-1980s, three years, the minimum possible, became standard." The minimum he refers to is the least amount of time the civil service allows for a promotion from the rank of a new examiner to a GS-11, or a newly commissioned examiner. Although OCC officials will point to their more lengthy training period as a source of examiner commitment, the FDIC remains convinced its rapid training is a better route to ensuring long-term commitment. Nevertheless, turnover at the FDIC and OCC was comparable throughout the 1980s, while the Fed's turnover rate was the highest (see figure 2-1).

A second incentive for long-term commitment is that flexibility in the field is exercised primarily by the FDIC's senior examiners. When asked about the extent of autonomy among examiners, a manager in Washington replied, "It varies. They have to be able to support their opinion. Those with more experience write the report. They have to be persuasive . . . that their judgment or assessment of the condition of the financial institution is right." Still, even the most senior examiners must

15. GAO, *Bank Examination Quality: FDIC Examinations*, p. 55.

TABLE 3-1. *Management Systems of the OCC, Federal Reserve, and FDIC*

System characteristic	OCC	Federal Reserve	FDIC
Central direction	Top-down innovation	Camaraderie of expertise	Common training and hierarchy
Policy and operations	Separate	Combined	Combined
Field delegation	Changing (now broad)	Broad	Narrow
Training	Changing (now centralized)	Decentralized	Centralized
Hiring	Bottom-up and horizontal	Bottom-up and horizontal	Bottom-up
Professional motivation	Professionalization, specialization	Expertise and individual advancement	Career ladder, esprit de corps

ultimately convince several layers of supervisors that their judgment has been exercised wisely. This is a hurdle examiners in the Fed and OCC rarely encounter, in large part because of the broader delegation of authority to the field and district levels.

Common Ground, Varied Styles

Management in the OCC, Federal Reserve, and FDIC share a common premise: that the good inspector is a model of effective examination and supervision. Yet these agencies try to achieve this goal in very different ways. Table 3-1 summarizes the differences with respect to central direction, training, hiring, and the means of professional motivation.

If agencies charged with the same task behave differently, the question is why? Perhaps more important, why should we care? To answer both questions one needs to step back from the details of management structure and look at how autonomous the OCC, Fed, and FDIC are from the demands of political oversight. Each is exposed to political scrutiny from officials who want to ensure their accountability, but the agencies vary in the kind of scrutiny they receive and the extent to which they must respond to it. These variations are the subject of chapter 4.

4

Who Has Autonomy
and Why?

Every government agency is exposed to political scrutiny to hold it accountable for public mandates. But political scrutiny varies in its intensity, and agencies vary in their attention to its demands and expectations. In short, some agencies are more autonomous than others. The most important determinant of autonomy is an agency's formal position on the federal organizational chart: to whom must it report? What federal rules, if any, govern its management systems? How is it funded? How are its regulatory activities enforced? But structural autonomy does not guarantee an autonomous existence. Autonomy also turns on the consensus for and clarity of an agency's mandate, whether it has a monopoly on expertise valued by political overseers, and the presence of a clear measure of agency performance that motivates agency personnel. To the extent that agency autonomy is contingent upon these four factors, the Federal Reserve, Federal Deposit Insurance Corporation, and Office of the Comptroller of the Currency can be arrayed on a scale of high, medium, and low autonomy, respectively. Table 4-1 provides a summary of the scale indicators.

Just why some organizations are more autonomous than others, and more important, how the variations might affect bureaucratic performance, piqued the interest of scholars Herbert Simon, Donald Smithburg, and Victor Thompson in their text, *Public Administration*. They contended that organizations have varied levels of autonomy, varied abilities to reach and execute decisions without extensive contact with other "units."[1] The more autonomous the organization, the more likely it will have the flexibility necessary to conduct its tasks. But why were

1. Herbert A. Simon, Donald W. Smithburg, and Victor A. Thompson, *Public Administration* (Knopf, 1950), p. 268. The authors use the term *self-containment* rather than autonomy.

85

TABLE 4-1. *Autonomy Indicators for the Federal Reserve, FDIC, and OCC*

Agency	Formal autonomy	Clarity and consensus for broad mandates	Value for expertise	Presence of performance measurement	Self-containment
Federal Reserve	High	Low and high	High	No	High
FDIC	Medium	High and high	High	Yes	High to medium
OCC	Medium to low	Low and low	Medium to low	Yes	Medium to low

some organizations more autonomous than others? The authors suggested one reason: autonomous organizations typically possess "an organization goal that is thought of by many people as a worthwhile activity in its own right."[2] The goal will also likely be clearly defined and its attainment readily measured. Yet more than forty years later Simon and Thompson contend that little has been done in public administration to understand autonomy, to know what makes some organizations more autonomous than others, and to understand what the relationship might be between autonomy and performance.[3]

This chapter and the next argue that the extent of autonomy is crucial to understanding the evolution of the organizational character that integrates work within the agencies.[4] Character, represented by organizational commitments, provides guidance so that agencies can navigate the political environment and provides a sense of identification, purpose, and motivation for personnel. Most important, organizational character provides the context within which top managers make decisions to coordinate, direct, and develop an approach to the exam-

2. Simon, Smithburg, and Thompson, *Public Administration*, p. 268. The authors refer to such organizations as "unitary."

3. Herbert A. Simon and Victor A. Thompson, "Public Administration Revisited," *Society*, vol. 28 (1991), p. 42.

4. There are several ways to view organizational character or culture more generally. See Joanne Martin, *Cultures in Organizations: Three Perspectives* (Oxford University Press, 1992). Several prominent uses of the integration perspective (Martin, pp. 45–70) used here include Philip Selznick, *Leadership in Administration* (Harper and Row, 1987); Edgar H. Schein, *Organizational Culture and Leadership* (San Francisco: Jossey-Bass, 1985); and Thomas J. Peters and Robert H. Waterman, *In Search of Excellence: Lessons from America's Best-Run Companies* (Harper and Row, 1982).

ination and supervision of banks—thus the link between autonomy and performance.

Formal Independence: A Matter of Degree

Statutes define the structure that technically determines an agency's exposure to oversight by the executive branch, Congress, the courts, and constituent organizations. A regulatory commission, for example, is formally independent from the executive branch by its placement outside any executive department and the requirement that appointed officials serve for fixed terms that extend beyond the term of the appointing president. A government corporation is often provided an additional increment of formal independence as a self-funding entity, which removes it from the annual appropriations process (a feature of the OCC, Fed, and FDIC). Other organizations might have formal independence through exemption from centralized personnel and procurement regulations and decisionmaking criteria that apply to other government agencies.

Statutes may also provide for the formal dependence of an agency on other organizations for enforcing its mandates or approving its regulatory activities. It is not uncommon for a regulatory commission to rely on the Department of Justice to prosecute criminal violations or for a regulatory agency in the executive branch to rely on approval of its actions by a central decisionmaking body such as the Office of Management and Budget or a task force established to assess the benefits and costs of regulations.[5]

The Executive Branch Bureau

The Office of the Comptroller of the Currency was created in 1863 to charter, administer, and supervise a new national banking system through which the U.S. government could establish a standard currency by circulating national banknotes and provide for the government's own financing needs. The OCC is organized as a steep hierarchy with a single leader, the comptroller of the currency, at the top. The comptroller is appointed by the president and approved by the Senate for a five-year

5. Terry M. Moe, "The Politics of Bureaucratic Structure," in John E. Chubb and Paul E. Peterson, eds., *Can the Government Govern?* (Brookings, 1989), pp. 267–329; and George C. Eads and Michael Fix, *Relief or Reform? Reagan's Regulatory Dilemma* (Washington: Urban Institute Press, 1984).

term. As a bureau in the Department of the Treasury, the OCC has the least formal autonomy of the three agencies regulating banking.

Congress did not experiment with administrative entities that were independent of the executive branch until the establishment of the Interstate Commerce Commission twenty-three years after the creation of the OCC. Yet despite its technical status as a bureau of the Treasury, the OCC (the first regulatory agency in the national government) was provided some independence from the executive branch from its inception. The comptroller's five-year term allows some independence from the priorities of the White House, an independence strengthened by the statutory requirement that a president seek Senate approval to remove a comptroller before the expiration of that term.

The OCC's self-funding status provides additional formal autonomy. Its income is generated through fees paid by the national banks for supervision and administration of the national banking industry (approving mergers, branch offices, and other business combinations and expansions). The bureau is required, however, to report directly to Congress each year on its financial status and regulatory activities, and Congress can call upon it to testify before committees on matters related to the banking system.

Before 1989 the OCC operated under many of the same rules and policies of the Treasury Department as the Internal Revenue Service, the Bureau of Alcohol, Tobacco, and Firearms, and the Custom Service. For example, Treasury regulations on personnel caps and salary scales for department employees applied to the OCC, while the Fed and FDIC were not similarly restricted. In practice, this meant that OCC compensation practices were tied to the governmentwide pay ceiling, and annual increases for examiners and management were limited to what was permitted under the general schedule.[6]

Referring to the Treasury's opposition to a more autonomous personnel system for the bureau, a former OCC official commented, "For a long time Treasury frustrated the efforts because they didn't want pay disparities between [the OCC] and the other agencies in the department. . . . We were the dog in the manger, and if the rest can't have it, we couldn't." The pay cap was lifted in the Financial Institutions Reform,

---

6. Although the OCC long had the statutory authority to set compensation levels for its employees, it was restricted by Treasury Department interpretations of departmental oversight authority that resulted in the department's reviewing and approving OCC pay plans for examiners. In addition, the department determined that the OCC's top management was to be covered by the provisions of the federal government's Senior Executive Service.

Recovery and Enforcement Act (FIRREA) of 1989. The act required that the financial regulatory agencies offer salaries competitive with one another and establish salary bands between the agencies. Some flexibility has been allowed for the agencies' different employee needs, but the legislation nevertheless gives the OCC, in particular, statutory authority to keep examiner salaries commensurate with those paid by the Fed and FDIC.[7]

Despite this formal distancing of the OCC from Treasury regulations, the department and the Office of Management and Budget have exercised their prerogative for oversight of the bureau's activities, particularly during the 1980s banking crisis. The frequency of meetings between top OCC management, the comptroller, and Treasury officials increased, according to several managers, and OMB review of the agency's congressional testimony and regulatory actions became the norm.

The Government Corporation

More autonomous than the OCC, the FDIC was established in 1933 to restore confidence in the nation's banking system following the suspension of operations in 9,000 banks in the previous four years. The corporation was to provide insurance to banking depositors, resolve and liquidate failed institutions, and supervise state-chartered banks that did not join the Federal Reserve system but nevertheless received federal insurance.

Although the first government corporation, the Panama Canal Company, was established in 1904, one would be hard pressed to identify organizational similarities between it and the FDIC.[8] As the number of government corporations (some wholly owned by the government, such as the FDIC, others privately owned but insured by the government, such as the Federal National Mortgage Association, or Fannie Mae) has increased, so has the diversity of their autonomy from Congress and the president, the way they are financed, their balance between public and private ownership, and their policy functions. However, they can be loosely characterized by their legal status (they can sue and be sued without the government's consent, and they can borrow money without drawing on the credit of the government), the method of financing their

7. See Office of the Comptroller of the Currency, *Quarterly Journal*, vol. 8 (June 1989), pp. 56–57.
8. Harold Seidman, "Public Enterprises in the United States," *Annals of Public and Cooperative Economy*, vol. 54 (1952), pp. 3–18.

operations, the extent of their autonomy in making expenditures, and their establishment of boards of directors.[9]

Government corporations are authorized by law to bring about a public purpose, yet the supporting argument for their formal autonomy traditionally rests upon the need for greater flexibility in managing public responsibilities that are of a "commercial nature."[10] Despite the theoretical justification for creating a government corporation (which many argue is used inconsistently in practice), these public-private hybrids operate with varied degrees of autonomy from the political arena—too much autonomy for those concerned about accountability to elected officials.[11]

The FDIC is governed by a five-member board of directors whose composition provides some ex officio exposure to the executive branch. Until 1989 the board consisted of a chairman, a director, and the comptroller of the currency as an ex officio member—all appointed by the president and confirmed by the Senate. With passage of the FIRREA, the board was expanded to include an FDIC vice chairman and the ex officio membership of the director of the newly created Office of Thrift Supervision in the Department of the Treasury.[12] The FDIC's chairman, director, and vice chairman each serve six-year terms, but the duration of the chairmanship is five years (the chairman can continue to serve

9. Harold Seidman and Robert Gilmour, *Politics, Position and Power: From the Positive to the Regulatory State*, 4th ed. (Oxford University Press, 1986).

10. See Marshall E. Dimock, *Business and Government: Issues of Public Policy*, 4th ed. (Holt, Rinehart and Winston, 1961); Harold J. Laski, *The American Democracy: A Commentary and an Interpretation* (Viking, 1948); Lloyd D. Musolf, *Uncle Sam's Private, Profitseeking Corporations: Comsat, Fannie Mae, Amtrak, and Conrail* (Lexington, Mass.: Lexington Books, 1983); and William A. Robson, "The Administration of Nationalized Industries in Britain," *Public Administration Review*, vol. 7 (Summer 1947), pp. 161–69. Government corporations are different from government-sponsored enterprises, some of which are private nonprofit corporations (the Corporation for Public Broadcasting), while others are private for-profit enterprises (Amtrak, the Federal National Mortgage Association, and the Communications Satellite Corporation).

11. For discussion of inconsistent practices in creating government corporations, see Hal Rainey and Barton Wechsler, "Managing Government Corporations and Enterprises," in James L. Perry, ed., *Handbook of Public Administration* (San Francisco: Jossey-Bass, 1989), pp. 499–512. On the problem of accountability, see Lloyd D Musolf, "Government-Sponsored Enterprises and Congress," *Public Administration Review*, vol. 51 (March-April, 1991), pp. 131–37; and Ronald C. Moe and Thomas H. Staton, "Government-Sponsored Enterprises as Federal Instrumentalities: Reconciling Private Management with Public Accountability," *Public Administration Review*, vol. 49 (July-August, 1989), pp. 321–29.

12. The inclusion of the director of the OTS on the FDIC board reflected the responsibility given the FDIC to manage the Savings Association Insurance Fund for the thrift industry following the failure of the Federal Savings and Loan Insurance Corporation to cover depositor losses in the industry. The FIRREA also assigned the FDIC to oversee the activities of the Resolution Trust Corporation established to resolve the assets of failed thrifts.

one more year on the board if he or she is not reappointed by the president for another five-year term as chair).

Like any insurance company, the FDIC's income is from the premiums paid by banks and the interest earned on the management of its investment portfolio (primarily Treasury securities). Also like any insurance company, the solvency of its fund depends on setting the appropriate assessment rate and keeping claims at a manageable level. Unlike its private sector counterparts, though, the FDIC can make premium adjustments only after submitting to a process of accountability involving public comments and debate and a formal decision by the board. But the agency can interact directly with troubled or failing institutions to try to preclude the need to pay off depositor claims. This is an important element of autonomy. Although the FDIC depends on the condition of the banking industry or particular banks as part of its decisionmaking, it can intercede to alter that environment as a means to protect the solvency of the fund.

The Public-Private Regulatory Board

The Federal Reserve is also led by a board of governors whose members are appointed by the president and confirmed by the Senate. The agency's formal autonomy from the executive branch as well as Congress is, however, more explicit than the FDIC's. Most prominently, Fed board members are appointed to fourteen-year nonrenewable terms, and members of executive branch departments do not sit on the board. This aspect of the agency's formal autonomy is the result of the 1935 Banking Act, which eliminated the ex officio board membership of the secretary of the Treasury and the comptroller of the currency, boosted term length to fourteen years from twelve, and provided the president with the authority to designate a Federal Reserve chairman and vice chairman to serve four-year terms. The chairman's term begins midway through a president's term in office and extends for two years into the following presidential term. If the chairman is not reappointed, he or she can continue to serve the remainder of the fourteen-year term.

At the heart of the Fed's formal independence are its responsibilities as a central bank. Through the board of governors, the agency exercises the power of a central bank delegated by Congress in 1913 to coin money and control its value. It does so by issuing paper currency, creating bank reserves by purchasing government securities on the open market and lending to member banks from its discount window, providing services to other U.S. banks and the Treasury, supervising the activities of state member banks and bank holding companies, and administering particular government regulations.[13] The formal freedom of the Fed to exercise monetary policy is crucial to maintaining its ability to carry out its supervisory functions.

The board determines policy for the conduct of the central bank functions, but policy implementation is managed by the twelve Reserve banks in Boston, New York, Philadelphia, Cleveland, Richmond, Atlanta, Chicago, St. Louis, Minneapolis, Kansas City, Dallas, and San Francisco. These administrative arms of the Federal Reserve system represent another autonomous feature of the agency in that they have a unique public-private status. National banks and state-chartered banks that join the Federal Reserve system must purchase stock in the Federal Reserve banks. In return the member banks select six of the nine members of the boards of directors of their respective Reserve banks and have a representative say in the selection of the banks' presidents. Four Reserve bank presidents then rotate as members of the Federal Open Market Committee (FOMC), a twelve-member committee of the Federal Reserve system, consisting of the president of the New York Reserve Bank (a permanent member), the seven governors of the Federal Reserve Board, and the four rotating members. The FOMC determines board policy related to the purchase and sale of government securities. This arrangement gives the member banks some authority in central bank decisionmaking, and it gives the Reserve banks a somewhat autonomous role in implementing Federal Reserve policy, including banking supervision of member banks.

Like the OCC and FDIC, the Fed is self-supporting. The board assesses the twelve Federal Reserve banks for its operating expenses and capital expenditures.[14] The Reserve banks, in turn, earn their income from loans to member banks, holdings of Treasury securities, foreign currency transactions, and the provision of various services to Federal Reserve member banks. The Fed is audited by the GAO and a private accounting firm each year, and its monetary activities are reported to Congress twice a year.

Although provisions for formal autonomy grant the OCC, FDIC, and especially the Fed some reprieve from the pressures and expectations of

---

13. Thomas F. Wilson, *The Power "to Coin" Money: The Exercise of Monetary Powers by the Congress* (Armonk, N.Y.: M. E. Sharpe, 1992), p. 180.

14. The board also earns income from data processing services, subscription fees for its publications, and assistance provided to other federal agencies.

the political arena, especially the annual appropriations process, the agencies are not guaranteed operational freedom from it. The political and academic debate over the nature of the Fed's independence in setting monetary policy, for example, has been long and intense. One of its fiercest defenders argued that an "intelligent and fearless performance of its functions involves as much of sanctity and of consequence to the American people as a like discharge of duty by the Supreme Court of the United States."[15] But presidents and members of Congress frustrated by the institution's policies have often been less enthusiastic about its sanctity.

In fact, both Congress and the president have exerted significant influence over the content of monetary policy.[16] And, of course, a wide range of other individuals and institutions have been interested in doing so. The agency must also navigate the turbulent waters of opposing economic expectations. Fed leaders, anxious to find a balance between these competing interests and maintain the agency's ability to manage a stable economy, have long maintained the Fed is "independent within government, not independent of the government."[17] Others, struggling to reconcile the agency's broad grant of autonomy from Congress with congressional concern for responsiveness, suggest that it operates responsively to Congress with the anticipation that formal autonomy might be rescinded.[18]

Regardless of the Fed's formal autonomy, in other words, the political arena still strongly influences its behavior. For it to act as if it were independent of rather than independent within government could disrupt the delicate balance that prevents congressional definition of monetary and supervisory policy.

15. Senator Carter Glass, quoted in Wilson, *Power "to Coin" Money*, p. 187.

16. See, for example, Thomas M. Havrilesky, *The Pressures on American Monetary Policy* (Boston: Kluwer Academic Publishers, 1993); John T. Woolley, "Partisan Manipulation of the Economy: Another Look at Monetary Policy with Moving Regression," *Journal of Politics*, vol. 50 (May 1988), pp. 335–60; Nathaniel Beck, "Presidential Influence on the Federal Reserve in the 1970s," *American Journal of Political Science*, vol. 26 (1982), pp. 415–45; and Beck, "Domestic Political Sources of American Monetary Policy: 1955–82," *Journal of Politics*, vol. 46 (August 1984), pp. 786–817.

17. Donald F. Kettl, *Leadership at the Fed* (Yale University Press, 1986).

18. Nathaniel Beck, "Congress and the Fed: Why the Dog Does Not Bark in the Night," in Thomas Mayer, ed., *The Political Economy of American Monetary Policy* (Cambridge University Press, 1990), pp. 131–50; and Robert L. Hetzel, "The Political Economy of Monetary Policy," in Mayer, *Political Economy*, pp. 99–114.

Factors Influencing Informal Autonomy

Fundamental to the three agencies' efforts to maintain their respective levels of formal autonomy from political overseers and other interested institutions and individuals is a more informal assertion of independence. To varying degrees this informal assertion depends on the clarity of each agency's mandate, the extent of the political consensus supporting the mandate, the agency's distinctive areas of expertise, and clear ways of judging the success of its performance.

Consensus and Clarity

Within the entrance of the Federal Reserve building is a tribute to President Woodrow Wilson, founder of the Federal Reserve system, engraved with an excerpt from his first inaugural address: "We shall deal with our economic system as it is and as it may be modified, not as it might be if we had a clean sheet of paper to write upon, and step by step we shall make it what it should be."[19] Discussions of banking regulatory reform since the early twentieth century have bemoaned the complexities of a system including both state- and nationally chartered banks, distinctive regulations that limit or expand the powers of banks depending on their charter, and supervision by multiple federal agencies.[20] Yet this mosaic reflects the complexities of a federal political framework. From its beginning the federal government faced firmly entrenched state banking systems with their own regulations for chartering, branching, merging, and issuing banknotes. Gradually, it began modifying the economic system by confronting, compromising with, and dangling irresistible carrots such as access to the Federal Reserve discount window and deposit insurance before the state-chartered banks.

It is in this context that the OCC, Fed, and FDIC were established, each with broad statutory mandates that varied in clarity and the political consensus they elicited. Each was initially assigned regulatory responsibilities that spanned the banking industry as well as more specialized responsibilities for supervising a portion of the industry. The clarity of the broader mandate and consensus supporting it are two

19. Ross M. Robertson, *The Comptroller and Bank Supervision: A Historical Appraisal* (Office of the Comptroller of the Currency, 1968), p. 94.

20. For an excellent overview of these arguments, see Robert S. Pasley, "Consolidation of the Federal Financial Regulatory Agencies," graduate thesis, Stonier Graduate School of Banking, University of Delaware, 1989.

factors that contribute to the autonomy of each agency. To the extent that consensus for the broad mandate is strong and clearly stated, according to Herbert Simon and his colleagues, an organization becomes more autonomous in its ability to conduct other activities—in this case, banking supervision.[21] An agency navigating a political archipelago fragmented over its poorly defined mandate could have little opportunity to steer a straight course. But many congressional mandates *are* vague, poorly defined, and contradictory. Under such conditions, it is often up to the agency to determine its mission (or goals) from the statutory mandate and build a consensus supporting that mission. Its efforts will be promoted or restrained depending on how much conflict accompanies its defining efforts.[22]

PROMOTION WITH RESTRAINT. The OCC was created by the Currency Act of 1863 to charter, administer, supervise, and promote a national banking system and support a standard national currency. Its formal mandate was stated with clarity but nevertheless harbored an ambiguity and placed the agency squarely in the bloody debate between states' rights and the constitutional authority of the national government to establish a central bank. The OCC was expected to aggressively promote national banking as a challenge to the state banking system, while at the same time provide the restraint necessary for a stable and sound system that would facilitate the financing and regulatory needs of the national government (including a standard currency).

The Currency Act (later the National Bank Act of 1874) was passed in the midst of the Civil War with the primary purpose of establishing a national banking system to compete with, and eventually drive out of business, state commercial banking. It was a roundabout response to the national government's inability to finance its activities adequately and stabilize a currency in the wake of two successful challenges to the chartering of a Bank of the United States. The First and Second Banks of the United States, chartered in 1791 and 1812, served the credit needs of the national government, became lenders of last resort to many commercial banks, circulated banknotes throughout the country, and through

21. Simon, Smithburg, and Thompson, *Public Administration*.
22. Hal Rainey has made a similar argument with respect to the clarity versus ambiguity of goals set for public organizations. He contends that public organizations do vary in the extent to which their mandates are ambiguous, but that the greater the influence political authorities have over an organization, the less its autonomy in clarifying the mandate and providing clear goals to accomplish it. See "A Theory of Goal Ambiguity in Public Organizations," *Research in Public Administration,* vol. 2 (1993), pp. 121–66.

conservative lending policies imposed discipline on the less restrained and sometimes outrageous practices of state-chartered institutions. In the eyes of their opponents, however, who defeated proposals to renew their charters, the concentration of credit within one institution closely associated with the power of the national government was a usurpation of states' political and economic power.

But opposition to a national bank did not eliminate the federal government's financing needs nor the need for a stable currency. The 1863 act was therefore an effort to avoid concentrating monopoly power in a single institution, prevent the constitutional challenges evoked by the First and Second Banks, yet still create a demand and a market for treasury securities. The act charged the OCC with chartering national banks and administering a national banking system. Any five people who wanted to charter a national bank were required to put up $100,000 if the bank was to be in a city with a population of less than 50,000 and $200,000 if the population exceeded 50,000. The banks then had to purchase U.S. government bonds worth one-third of their capital and place the bonds on reserve with the Treasury Department. The requirement created a demand for federal bonds, which was essential for the government's financing needs.

Initially it was thought that a charter and notes backed by the full faith and credit of the federal government would convince new banking entrepreneurs to seek national charters and those holding state charters to switch. Once a bank was chartered, OCC supervision would ensure that it followed sound banking practices. Yet state banks continued to proliferate and compete with the new national banks. So in 1865 the federal government passed a 10 percent tax on all notes issued by state-chartered banks. The legislation eliminated the profitability of issuing state banknotes. As intended, the number of state-chartered banks immediately plummeted—from 1,089 in 1864 to 349 in 1865.[23] But state banks began to circumvent the law: instead of continuing to issue notes that would be taxed, they began to set up accounts for deposits on which customers could write checks. The innovation (soon adopted by nationally chartered banks) took the state banknotes, widely varied in value and often worthless, out of circulation and also allowed the state banking system to thrive once more.

The emphasis given to the dual goals of promotion and restraint by the OCC, as well as the meaning of those terms, varies with the condi-

---

23. Robertson, *Comptroller and Bank Supervision*, p. 53.

tion of the national banking system and the leadership of the agency. The very conservative administration of the national banking system during the agency's early years (1863–84), and from 1936 to 1955 (in which a scant 211 banks were chartered), stands in contrast to the aggressive chartering periods just before the Great Depression, throughout the 1960s, and during the early 1980s. It was also in these more aggressive periods that comptrollers, anxious to let the national banking system compete more aggressively with the liberally regulated state banks, offered lenient interpretations of the National Bank Act.[24]

LEANING AGAINST THE WIND. The creation of the OCC and its chartering of a national banking system did not eliminate the basic problems of the U.S. financial system. The national banking system provided some stability, but it was also inflexible. When an expansion of money was needed for short-term deposit demands or credit requests, the system tended to limit the issuance of additional banknotes and the extension of credit.

This is precisely what happened during the banking crisis of 1907. At the time, many banks held very small cash reserves, and many banks invested depositors' funds heavily in railroad and copper stocks; when the value of these stocks fell sharply, the banks experienced runs and could not meet depositors' demands for cash.[25] If any one bank failed to meet the demands and closed, confidence in other banks deteriorated and prompted runs on them, too. The system had no means to combat the spreading panic, nor even to provide for the normal variation in seasonal or regional demands for currency. A central bank would have been able to regulate the reserves, make short-term loans to banks facing abnormally high depositor demands, and expand or contract the supply of money based on the fluctuating needs of business for credit.

In 1908 Congress passed legislation establishing the National Monetary Commission, chaired by Senator Nelson W. Aldrich of Rhode Island, to examine the weaknesses in the financial system that produced episodic crises and determine how the economy might be better stabilized. In 1912 the commission recommended that a forty-six-member National Reserve Association with fifteen district branches throughout the country be created to mobilize cash reserves, issue circulating notes, increase

24. Office of the Comptroller of the Currency, *Quarterly Journal: Special Anniversary Issue, 1981–1991* (September 1992), pp. 3–8, 71–74.

25. Sandra B. McCray, *State Regulation of Banks in an Era of Deregulation: A Commission Report* (Washington: Advisory Commission on Intergovernmental Relations, 1988), p. 10.

the geographic flexibility of credit, and hold Treasury balances. It also recommended that political influence over the proposed association's activities be limited to five presidential appointments.[26]

Reaction to the commission's recommendations demonstrated clearly that system instability alone was not enough to eliminate opposition to a central bank. From within the progressive wing of the Republican party, and among Democrats, opposition focused on the worrisome concentration of power of the banks and the government's delegation of responsibilities to coin money and regulate its value to a board consisting of forty-one out of forty-six members selected by the banking industry itself. A modified version making the board the exclusive preserve of presidential appointees (including the ex officio membership of the secretary of the Treasury and the comptroller) and giving greater authority to reserve banks rather than branches of a central bank was able to pass both houses of Congress and meet with the approval of President Wilson.

Both the National Bank Act and the Federal Reserve Act faced advocates of states' rights and state-chartered banks who were opposed to a centralized system. However, the acts dealt with the existence of state-chartered banks and their role in a federally regulated system very differently. With the National Bank Act the government attempted to force state banks into conformity with national banking practices or even to eliminate them. By the time the Federal Reserve Act was passed, however, the dual federal-state banking system was well established and the government adopted carrot-and-stick tactics to achieve compliance. The carrot was the opportunity for state-chartered banks to join the Federal Reserve system. Membership brought them access to the Federal Reserve discount window for short-term lending needs, but it also gave the Federal Reserve Board the authority to determine reserve levels and to supervise them. National banks were automatically made members of the Federal Reserve system, but supervisory authority over them remained with the OCC. The Federal Reserve system was also made less intimidating to state interests by its regional structure. Twelve regions were established, each with a Federal Reserve bank. Although the Federal Reserve Board set systemwide policy, the Reserve banks maintained some autonomy that reduced the centralized appearance of the new system.

---

26. Wilson, *Power "to Coin" Money*, pp. 180–83. These included a governor, to be appointed by the president; the secretaries of the Treasury, agriculture, and commerce and labor; and the comptroller of the currency. Two department governors were to be elected by the entire board.

The sting of state competition having been resolved, the Fed was left to confront the Treasury Department and other detractors and hone its vague mandate into a workable mission. The Federal Reserve Act was clear as to the administrative functions of the central bank: "to provide for the establishment of Federal Reserve Banks, to furnish an elastic currency, to afford a more effective supervision of banking in the United States."[27] But its role in monetary policy was left open; the statute simply added that the system was also established "for other purposes." Nowhere did it direct that full employment, low inflation, stable prices, or other congressionally defined goals be achieved through monetary policy.[28] Rather, the system was given the murky guidance of conducting monetary policy "with an eye toward the needs of business and commerce."

Today, the Fed defines its primary mission as the application of discretionary monetary policy to stabilize the economy. Its role is to "lean against the wind."[29] When the economy heats up, the Fed acts to cool it down. When the economy slows, the Fed tries gradually to spur growth. Knowing when to lean one way or the other is the distinctive expertise it has acquired over the years, particularly by its leadership. But it is an expertise requiring constant vigilance to protect the system from the political pressures that would assert more control over the power to coin money and regulate its value. Unlike the OCC, the Fed's vaguely defined mandate embraces the interests of very diverse economic and political groups. Fundamental to managing the money supply is managing these conflicting interests, precluding their attempts to define the objectives of monetary policy more explicitly.

FULL FAITH AND CREDIT. Despite the incremental strengthening of the banking system, depositor confidence in it was not guaranteed. Nor did the OCC's supervision of national banks and the Federal Reserve Board's oversight of state-chartered banks prevent all unsound banking practices. Between October 1929 and the end of 1933 more than 9,000 commercial banks failed or suspended operations.[30] They were hit, first, by the seemingly endless free fall of the stock market in 1929. Most had invested

---

27. *Federal Reserve Act of 1913*, preamble, quoted in George L. Bach, *Federal Reserve Policy-Making: A Study in Government Economic Policy Formation* (Knopf, 1950), p. 5.

28. There were, however, several policy reforms after World War II, such as the Full Employment Act of 1946, that helped to better define the Fed's monetary role.

29. Kettl, *Leadership at the Fed*, p. 83.

30. Federal Deposit Insurance Corporation, *Federal Deposit Insurance Corporation: The First Fifty Years: A History of the FDIC, 1933-1983* (1984), p. 3.

depositors' funds heavily in the expanding market throughout the 1920s, and many banks or their affiliates had used depositor funds to underwrite new issues of securities. Much of this activity was speculative and at times criminal, but much was also legal and based on relatively sound management decisions to invest in the rapidly expanding market.[31] The concentration of investment in the stock market was in part precipitated by increased competition. By the early 1920s there were approximately 20,000 state banks and 8,000 national banks.[32] In this highly competitive environment, they turned to the stock market as an investment option.[33]

Banks also suffered from a loss of depositor confidence that took hold in one state or one bank and in a chain reaction expanded to others. As the economy collapsed after 1929, people began to demand their deposits from one bank, or banks in a particular region, in large numbers. In some instances they needed to cover daily living expenses; in others rumors that a bank was unable to meet depositors' demands prompted a run. Finally, in 1933 public confidence in the banking system as a whole was shattered as the outrageous practices by the nation's largest and most prestigious banks were revealed daily by the investigative staff of the Senate Banking and Currency Committee.

Confronting this general loss of confidence, President Franklin Roosevelt declared a national bank holiday on March 6, 1933. Congress enacted emergency legislation that provided for the immediate suspension of banking activities and for the Treasury and Federal Reserve Board gradually to reopen banks that were determined sound by their primary supervisors.[34] Senator Carter Glass and Representative Henry Steagall weighed in with their own method for restoring depositor confidence: a bill (which would become the Glass-Steagall Act) to provide deposit insurance and to prohibit banks from engaging in investment banking activities. Commercial banks were to stay out of the securities business as "principal" participants. The Federal Deposit Insurance Corporation was established to administer a temporary insurance fund (made permanent in 1935).

31. Susan Estabrook Kennedy, *The Banking Crisis of 1933* (University Press of Kentucky, 1973), pp. 13–14.

32. Robertson, *Comptroller and Bank Supervision*, p. 98.

33. The situation was not unlike that related to the collapse of real estate markets, particularly in the Northeast and Southwest, in the late 1980s. Although banks in these years usually made loans to commercial real estate projects based on appropriate assessments of risk, many of the loans turned sour when a regional economy weakened. And the real estate loans that were speculative or less than sound were in part the result of the increased competition banks faced as credit intermediaries.

34. Kennedy, *Banking Crisis of 1933*, p. 182.

Like the Fed and the OCC, the FDIC's mandate was twofold. First, it was to manage the insurance fund, which would protect depositors' savings up to $2,500 in commercial banks. It was to resolve and liquidate failed institutions in a manner that limited disruption of the financial system. Second, it was to supervise those state-chartered banks that did not join the Federal Reserve system but were the recipients of deposit insurance. It thus offered state banks deposit insurance at a time of debilitatingly low depositor confidence in return for another expansion of federal authority over the banking industry.

Like both the National Bank Act and the Federal Reserve Act, the Glass-Steagall Act was not without controversy, but it had much to offer. Deposit insurance muted debates within the banking industry over the efficacy of branch banking versus unit banking (a policy that disallowed branching to achieve geographic and portfolio diversity) and of government intervention in the industry.[35] The legislation offered a means to control the economic consequences of bank failures, particularly for advocates of unit banking, without changing the structure of the banking system. Thus, as Carter Golembe observed, the act "provided a rallying point for men formerly in disagreement and confounded in equal measure those who did not admit a need for government action and those who sought fundamental reorganization of the banking structure."[36] Rather than allow widespread branch banking as a means to prevent massive failures, the 1933 act permitted only limited national bank branching into states that permitted it and boosted investor confidence (through insurance) for unit banks, many of which were particularly vulnerable to bank runs.[37]

Once the law was in place, it seemed to prevent failures, whether of large or small banks, and minimized the conflict over the efficacy of federal insurance.[38] In the 1970s, when competition for deposits increased among depository institutions (credit unions, banks, savings and loans) with the growth of money market mutual funds, pension plans,

35. Under unit banking, any new banking entity must be a self-contained unit with its own capitalization rather than a branch of a parent organization that draws upon the larger capital base.

36. Carter H. Golembe, "The Deposit Insurance Legislation of 1933," *Political Science Quarterly,* vol. 75 (June 1960), p. 200.

37. Robertson, *Comptroller and Bank Supervision*, p. 132; and Gerald C. Fischer, *American Banking Structure* (Columbia University Press, 1968), pp. 51-52.

38. There was, of course, doubt about the wisdom of attempting to insure deposits, particularly given the failure of state insurance schemes in the past. Nevertheless, the banking crisis pushed the administration and Congress toward compromise. See Kennedy, *Banking Crisis of 1933*, pp. 214-23.

and other investment options, banks received a dramatic increase in deposit insurance coverage to better compete for funds. The Depository Institutions Deregulation and Monetary Control Act of 1980 liberated depositories by eliminating interest rate ceilings for savings and time deposits and increasing the insurance coverage from $40,000 to $100,000 per account. But the combination of higher coverage, volatile interest rates, regional collapses of real estate markets, and widespread defaults on loans to less developed countries pushed the insurance fund into the red by 1991 and prompted serious debates over the efficacy of deposit insurance and how it might be reformed. Although some observers proposed significantly altering the way insurance is provided for depositors (such as making the industry responsible for operating an insurance fund without a government guarantee or making depositors pay a deductible on their insured deposits), most of the proposals left government-backed deposit insurance in place with full coverage up to $100,000.[39] Banks depend heavily on the insured funds to attract and keep depositors, and the competitors of commercial banks depend on the restrictions placed on banks' powers when deposit insurance is in place.

Consensus among political officials and economic interests strongly supports the FDIC's clearly stated mandate to provide depositor insurance and protect the fund. The Fed, too, draws autonomy from the carefully nurtured consensus surrounding its mandate to lean against the wind with respect to monetary policy—a mission created by the agency itself out of vague congressional language. In contrast, the OCC's autonomy suffers from a mandate requiring the simultaneous exercise of promotion and restraint, and thus there is often intense controversy over how it carries out its mission.

Respect for Technical Expertise

Elected officials in Congress and the administration rely on the OCC, Fed, and FDIC to supervise the banking industry. This is the core of the OCC's expertise and the primary means it has to demonstrate competence vis-à-vis its sister agencies in promoting a safe banking system. To maintain its edge, the agency has been in the forefront of research and development on examination techniques. Its duties as the administrator of the national banking system, responsible for the chartering and ex-

---

39. See Philip F. Bartholomew, *Reforming Federal Deposit Insurance* (Congressional Budget Office, September 1990), esp. pp. 103–09, 147–57.

pansion of individual banks through merger and acquisition, are only minimally different from its supervisory mission. These are duties also carried out to some extent by the Fed and FDIC with respect to banks under their jurisdiction. The FDIC, for example, must perform an administrative function in approving bank applications for insurance, and the Fed administers the merger and acquisition activities of bank holding companies.

The additional types of expertise exercised by the FDIC and the Fed, however, require integration with bank examination and supervision. To the extent that their political overseers depend on the agencies for these additional tasks, the agencies exercise their supervisory activities under a broader umbrella of autonomy.

RESOLUTIONS AND RECEIVERSHIPS: WHITE KNIGHTS AND AUCTIONS. As manager of the bank insurance fund, the FDIC is responsible for the resolution of failed banks; as the appointed receiver of a failed bank, it also handles the liquidation of assets. Just as effective supervision entails careful timing and the balancing of risks and safety, resolution and liquidation require coordination between several regulatory agencies (including state supervisory authorities) and the ability to handle the risk that a particular resolution process or the timing of a liquidation could send shock waves through financial and lending markets connected with the failing bank.

Resolutions are handled by the FDIC's Division of Resolutions. The process involves establishing a "deal structure" that determines the way funds will be disbursed from the bank insurance fund to protect the depositors of a failed institution. When a bank fails, the agency has several ways to meet this obligation. First, it can arrange to have all the bank's deposits (those that are insured up to $100,000 and those that are uninsured or that exceed $100,000) purchased by a healthy institution that then assumes responsibility for the obligations. The agency has used this kind of transaction, known as a purchase and assumption (P&A) with increasing frequency: out of 168 bank failures in 1990, for example, it resolved 148 this way.[40] Not only does this method prevent the need to pay off depositors out of the insurance fund, but it also limits the disruption of financial services to a community. Depositors simply have their accounts switched to another bank. It also limits (but does not eliminate) the expenses required to protect depositors. Often the

40. Federal Deposit Insurance Corporation, *1990 Annual Report* (1990), p. 24.

deal in a P&A will include a loss-sharing provision that makes the FDIC responsible for as much as 95 percent of the potential losses associated with a purchased loan portfolio from a failed bank.[41]

Another resolution technique is to establish a bridge bank until an institution willing and able to assume responsibility for the deposits of the failed bank can be found. Under these circumstances the FDIC provides the capital to operate a bank under a national bank charter by using the deposits of the failed bank. The procedure therefore provides a bridge to maintain financial services for a community without having to liquidate the assets of the failed bank and pay off depositors.

Finally, the FDIC can write checks for insured depositors of a failed institution when no other bank is available for a P&A or a transfer, or when a bridge bank is too costly. Depositors whose accounts exceed the insurance coverage, shareholders, other creditors, and the FDIC are reimbursed as funds become available.

Each method of resolution requires the "disbursement" of insurance funds, some more than others. Before 1991 the FDIC was permitted to pursue any resolution option, as long as it was less costly than a payout to insured depositors and a liquidation of the assets (of course, the final option was and is permitted; it is simply not preferred because of the expense). Since 1991 the FDIC Improvement Act (section 141) requires the Division of Resolutions to select the least costly resolution. Simply put, the agency must compare all proposed bids from banks to other alternatives, and it must require the bidding banks to provide proposals that incorporate the assumption of all deposits as well as those that include only insured deposits.[42] Ideally, the resulting arrangement will also be good in the long term for the banking system as a whole—a balance of two concerns (cost of the resolution and the soundness of the industry) that can be at odds.[43] In achieving this balance, the FDIC can pursue one other option: open bank assistance. Rather than allow a bank to fail, the agency can provide a troubled bank with assistance from the insurance fund to keep it solvent. The assistance, however, must be less costly than liquidation.[44]

---

41. Federal Deposit Insurance Corporation, *1992 Annual Report* (1992), p. 35.

42. FDIC, *1992 Annual Report*, p. 32.

43. Frederick S. Carns and Lynn A. Nejezchleb, "Bank Failure Resolution, the Cost Test, and the Entry and Exit of Resources in the Banking Industry," *FDIC Banking Review*, vol. 5 (Fall-Winter 1992), pp. 1-14.

44. For a discussion of the policy implications for the various resolution methods, see John F. Bovenzi and Maureen Muldoon, "Failure-Resolution Methods and Policy Considerations," *FDIC Banking Review*, vol. 3 (Fall 1990), pp. 1-11.

The resolution process is precarious. Deciding when it ought to begin is a judgment call. The Division of Resolutions gets involved with the bank "when it appears more likely than not that failure is imminent," commented one official connected with the DOR. "It's usually . . . just prior to an anticipated failure." Resolution requires a sound grasp of the banking needs of a community and the condition of potential white knights that might purchase portions of a failed bank. It also requires careful coordination between the FDIC and the primary supervising agency, coordination that often is not easy to achieve. Before passage of the FDICIA the FDIC could not begin resolution until the failing bank's chartering agency (either the OCC, in the case of a national bank, or a state chartering authority) revoked the charter. If it was a state-chartered member of the Federal Reserve system, the Fed would enter the equation.

The central problem, as an agency official described it, is that the chartering agencies "have a proprietary interest in the people they charter . . . so there is a natural tension between the OCC [for example] . . . and the FDIC." The process can go smoothly if the supervisors in each agency cooperate; but it can disintegrate into near futility if they do not. Although the FDICIA gives the FDIC the authority to close a bank and appoint itself as receiver, it is a power that agency officials are reluctant to use. Cooperation between the chartering agency, primary supervisor (if it is not the same agency), and the FDIC is preferred for packaging the best possible resolution. "I can't define my job without talking about coordination," commented the same FDIC official. "Without coordination, I would fail."

Once a resolution is complete, the FDIC's Division of Liquidations takes away the remaining assets: it manages the receivership of a failed bank. If the resolution entails a purchase and assumption, the division will oversee the process. If there is no purchase, it provides depositors with their insurance checks. The division is also responsible for selling any assets of a failed bank that are assumed by the FDIC; the proceeds go toward those creditors not insured by the agency. Over the years the agency has been the receiver of typical and atypical banking portfolios, from real estate loans for homes, businesses, and churches to fleets of taxi cabs, distribution rights to a pornographic movie, and tuna boats.[45]

Many assets are difficult to sell, and often it is in the interest of the receiver and creditors to wait until real estate values, for example,

45. FDIC, *First Fifty Years*, p. 103.

rebound before an attempt is made to liquidate large loan portfolios. In the agency's 1992 *Annual Report* the division states that its objective is to

> maximize the recovery on assets from failed financial institutions at the earliest possible time and in the most cost-efficient manner. To accomplish this, the Division converts assets into cash . . . through loan collections and asset sales. In this regard, bulk sales of assets have proven to be an excellent method for converting assets into cash quickly and returning them to the private sector.[46]

Knowing when to sell in order to maximize the return on the assets without causing disruption in local markets is the key to a successful liquidation.

It is difficult for Congress to know how to assess the FDIC's performance of its liquidation and resolution activities. When there were few bank failures, it was content to leave the agency to exercise its expertise. But when the bank insurance fund ran into the red in 1991, this autonomy was circumscribed by the FDICIA's provision that resolutions be conducted at the least possible cost and liquidations in a manner that meets a variety of policy goals in addition to achieving the greatest return to the fund. In addition to the least-cost provision, for example, the act requires a set percentage of homes held as assets by failed banks to be sold to low- and moderate-income families.

MANAGING THE ECONOMY. As the federal debt grows and budget-deficit politics defines the fiscal options politicians have available to manage the economy, the Fed's special expertise has become increasingly important. Because presidents and Congress cannot make the economy grow through fiscal stimulus packages, they depend on the Fed to stabilize real incomes and prices by regulating the supply of money and credit. It is an expertise that, despite routine calls for making the agency more accountable in its definition and execution of monetary policy, and despite evidence of congressional and presidential influence from time to time, has received much deference from political officials in the past fifty years. Observers have tried to predict the application through formal economic models, political assessments and the political pressures to which they

46. FDIC, *1992 Annual Report*, p. 40.

must occasionally attend, and any possible nugget of insight provided by former insiders—which way will the Fed lean this time?

The Federal Reserve Board of Governors uses several tools to influence credit conditions. Through its Federal Open Market Committee it can decide to sell government securities from its portfolio to soak up money in the economy or purchase securities from investors to put more cash into it. The Federal Reserve Bank of New York does the actual buying and selling. Credit conditions can also be influenced by Federal Reserve Board decisions to raise or lower the discount rate—the rate that the Federal Reserve banks charge member banks for short-term lending—and to raise or lower the amount of reserves that banks are required to hold against deposits. Finally, the Fed has the authority to increase or decrease the margin levels required to purchase stocks and bonds.[47] Currently, investors must provide at least 50 percent of the value of securities to secure ownership, a level maintained since 1974. If the Fed were to reduce the margin, the action would facilitate the purchase of additional securities, but it would also free investment dollars that were no longer required to secure stocks and bonds and would thus increase the supply of money.

The Fed's monetary and supervisory powers are closely related. On the one hand, the board claims its examination and supervisory efforts are integral to its efforts to influence credit conditions, providing important information for decisionmaking and evidence of the effects of monetary policy. On the other, the autonomy the agency derives from its monetary powers provides significant room for exercising its supervisory powers.

Political scientist Francis Rourke has argued that expertise will provide an agency with political power if political overseers depend on that expertise and the agency is able to deliver tangible, meaningful results.[48] When there is competition from other able agencies or from the private sector, or when the agency fails to deliver tangible benefits, its expertise

47. The Fed was given authority over margin requirements in 1934 when legislation was passed to regulate the buying and selling of securities. Before 1929, investors were allowed to obtain securities through their brokers by paying as little as 10 percent of the value of the stocks or bonds. Brokers in effect loaned their customers the remaining 90 percent by borrowing from banks that were anxious to cash in on the growing market. When the value of stocks plunged, the loans made to brokers went sour. A higher margin for the purchase of stocks was seen as a way to limit speculation; and because margin was directly related to the supply of credit, the job of regulating the margin was given to the Fed.

48. Francis E. Rourke, *Bureaucracy, Politics, and Public Policy*, 3d ed. (Little, Brown, 1984).

ceases to provide as much political clout or as much reason for it to be allowed to remain so free of political scrutiny.

In the case of the Fed, Congress and a host of economic interests not only depend on the agency's expertise in managing the money supply, they depend on its interpretation of the status of the economy for determining whether Federal Reserve policy is working. This is not to ignore the vast number of institutions and economists competing to examine and give meaning to complex economic indicators, but it is precisely because of the competing sources (and the resulting noise) that the Fed's opinion carries the most weight.

The Fed's definitiveness, however, rests on a competence more complex than the technical expertise required to read and manage the economy. It is a competence carefully managed by the Federal Reserve Board, one that thrives precisely because there are powerful competing economic interests with a stake in shaping decisionmaking.[49] The Fed's careful management of the money supply and the economy under the political guidance of its chairmen and its cultivation of the argument that political intervention from one or many interests could have disastrous economic consequences, have provided the agency great autonomy. A reservoir of support from competing economic interests for the Fed's having a freer hand has also helped maintain the agency's autonomy. Better for the Fed to set policy than leave it to an economic competitor.

Clear Indicators of Performance

An agency with straightforward goals supported by broad public consensus and with an unambiguous measure of how well it has achieved the goals is likely to have greater autonomy than an agency that labors in a less defined context. Political oversight will be less intrusive to the extent that elected officials and the public can refer to an immediate barometer of performance. If that indicator should point to mediocre results or failure, however, there would probably be a challenge to the agency's autonomy. And other agencies might very well impinge on its territory by claiming to be able to perform the task more effectively.

THE DEPOSIT INSURANCE FUND. Among the three banking regulators, the FDIC has the most concise, readily interpreted performance indicator: effective management of the Bank Insurance Fund. Performance is readily assessed by the solvency of the fund. If depositors are protected when

49. Kettl, *Leadership at the Fed*, pp. 15–17.

banks fail, and if the fund remains sufficiently solvent to protect against projected levels of failure, political overseers will leave the agency to make the decisions necessary to manage its responsibilities. This includes its supervisory activities intended to minimize the need for disbursements by maintaining a safe and sound state nonmember banking system as well as resolution and liquidation responsibilities.

In the one instance when the FDIC projected a deficit for the fund, autonomy was quickly reduced by congressional hearings and investigations, studies of the agency by the General Accounting Office, and press probes. The need to borrow from the Treasury Department to meet deposit protection liabilities eradicated a long-standing autonomy from the political process and heightened dependence on the decisionmaking and priorities of other organizations—especially the GAO.

There was no effort by either the Fed or the OCC to assume the FDIC's responsibilities for insurance. Nor was there an effort on the part of the Resolution Trust Corporation (RTC), created to resolve and liquidate the assets of failed savings and loans, to take over any of the FDIC's resolution and liquidation duties. Not only was the RTC slated to go out of business once its responsibilities were complete, but the excellent record of the FDIC in maintaining a solvent fund up to that time no doubt provided it with some defensive capital in Congress to ward off any poaching. Indeed, in 1989 Congress gave the FDIC responsibility for managing the newly established savings and loan insurance fund to protect depositors in the remaining savings institutions, rather than place that responsibility with the S&L resolution agency.

Nevertheless, the FDIC's clean record up to that point was again not sufficient to eliminate the intrusive actions of congressional probes and GAO investigations. In fact, the GAO investigations took on such a high profile in the legislative debate over how the system of deposit insurance and accompanying supervisory efforts ought to be fixed that the audit bureau itself became a constraint on the agency's autonomy. When the FDIC advocated a more flexible approach to the resolution of failing banks as a means to leverage dwindling deposit insurance funds, the GAO's argument for imposing a least-cost test on all resolution activities introduced a constraint (eventually stated in the FDICIA) on the agency's resolution options. And when the FDIC (and its sister agencies) made a case for flexible, informal enforcement actions as a means to improve supervisory rigor and ensure that banks were complying with supervisory demands, a GAO report on the need for more formal and timely enforcement actions again set the parameters of the debate against which the FDIC had to argue—again, unsuccessfully. Provisions for formal, automatic enforcement actions were mandated by the FDICIA.

THE HEALTH OF THE NATIONAL BANKING SYSTEM. Indicators of the OCC's performance are more diverse and more difficult to interpret. The health and stability of the national banking system provides something of a measure for assessing the agency's supervisory and administrative activities. Yet the terms *health* and *stability*, or similarly, *safety* and *soundness*, can be defined in various ways. For example, industry growth could indicate competitiveness and thus health. As the number of national bank charters increases, the size of assets held by national banks increases, or the annual profits for national banks grow, an argument might be made for the industry's health.

The OCC's periodic efforts to push for more charters as a means to establish a more dominant national bank presence in the industry vis-à-vis the state banking system and to increase the competitiveness of the banking system suggest the importance the agency has placed on growth as an indicator of its performance. Yet rapid growth in the number of charters or the concentration of banking assets in a few large institutions could easily be an unstable situation if many banks failed in a more competitive environment or a large bank with concentrated assets failed and brought disruption to its business partners (including other banks) as well as depositors.

The highly criticized policy of "too big to fail" that was practiced by all three regulators throughout the 1980s was a direct reflection of the financial market disruption and the high cost (in terms of disbursements) of protecting depositors in large banks. Instead, efforts were made to find buyers for large banks on the brink of failure or to inject cash and work out oversight agreements to ensure the return to solvency under FDIC disbursement support and careful monitoring on the part of the banking regulators.[50]

Indicators of poor health in the national banking industry are also relevant and perhaps more readily interpreted by political overseers. The number of national bank failures and the cost of those failures for the Bank Insurance Fund have served as critical indicators of the OCC's performance, particularly in the wake of the 1980s banking crisis. These

---

50. L. William Seidman, *Full Faith and Credit: The Great S&L Debacle and Other Washington Sagas* (Times Books, 1993), pp. 145–59.

failures, which accounted for 67 percent of the losses in the insurance fund between 1986 and 1991, intensified the scrutiny of the agency by political overseers and increased its dependence on the other two agencies. Just as GAO reports served to set the parameters of congressional debate for defining what ought to be done to correct the deposit insurance system, GAO scrutiny of the OCC's supervisory and enforcement techniques became the argument for which the agency had to present a convincing rebuttal. Some autonomy was also conceded to the Treasury Department and the Office of Management and Budget. Both of these took greater interest in the internal operations of the Treasury bureau and in its communications with Congress as the banking crisis took on more significant proportions and as Congress became increasingly interested in defining a solution to the problem. All the OCC's testimony before Congress was routinely scrutinized by OMB and Treasury officials, and once-rare meetings between Treasury officials and OCC staff became common occurrences.

THE HEALTH OF THE ECONOMY. Reading the Fed's performance indicators is as tricky (or perhaps as simple) as interpreting the health of the economy. The rate of inflation, long-term interest rates, unemployment figures, and various other measures can be used to assess the agency's performance and that of the banks and bank holding companies for which it is responsible. Yet the interpretation of each indicator depends heavily on the Fed itself. As vulnerable as the agency might be to competing interpretations of its mandated task and the controversy surrounding its actions to regulate the money supply, its efforts to sustain autonomy hinge on its ability to interpret its performance.

Degrees of Autonomy

In contrast to most agencies headquartered in Washington, the OCC, Fed, and FDIC have high levels of autonomy. Their isolation from political overseers is built from formal structure (particularly self-funding), the clarity of and consensus for their mandates, the extent to which political overseers depend on their expertise, and the availability of a clear way of assessing performance. None of these factors guarantees autonomy. But they do interact in ways that create some distance between each agency and the political arena.

The OCC's exposure to the Treasury Department and executive branch offices, a primary expertise shared with both the FDIC and the

Fed, and its difficulty in generating a meaningful (and noncontroversial) way to assess its performance have made it less autonomous than its sister agencies and more dependent on the general political mood for its ability to control internal operations.

The more formal isolation of the FDIC from both the executive and legislative branches, its clear and broadly supported mandate to insure depositors in the banking system, its expertise in the resolution and liquidation of banks, and the presence of a simple performance indicator have together maintained a more substantial autonomy for the agency, but one that is vulnerable to falling economic indicators.

Finally, the Fed's mandate places it squarely between powerful and competing interests represented by various elected officials that disagree over its economic mission and the way it exercises its authority. The agency also lacks a simple means of assessing its performance. Yet political officials' dependence on the Fed for managing and interpreting the health of the economy have provided it with an informal autonomy that will likely not be breached as long as competing interests hold each other in check from direct intervention in its activities.

5

Character Building

The sociologist Philip Selznick contends that organizations develop "ways of acting and responding that can be changed, if at all, only at the risk of severe internal crisis. . . . [A] wise management will readily limit its own freedom, accepting irreversible commitments, when the basic values of the organization and its direction are at stake. The acceptance of irreversible commitments is the process by which the character of an organization is set."[1] Organizational commitments established at the Federal Reserve, the Federal Deposit Insurance Corporation, and the Office of the Comptroller of the Currency have evolved as means to integrate the expectations and demands of complex political settings with internal operations, professional ambitions, and agency objectives. Together, these commitments help the management guide each agency through the political environment and provide a sense of identification, purpose, and motivation for agency personnel. These commitments also define what is distinctive about the work of each agency, which can provide an organi-

---

1. Philip Selznick, *Leadership in Administration: A Sociological Interpretation* (Harper and Row, 1957), p. 40. What Selznick identifies as "commitments," the basis of character, another student of organizations identifies as the "basic assumptions and beliefs that are shared by members of an organization, that operate unconsciously, and that define in a basic 'taken-for-granted' fashion an organization's view of itself and its environment"; see Edgar Schein, *Organizational Culture and Leadership* (San Francisco: Jossey-Bass, 1985), p. 6. Gary Miller in *Managerial Dilemmas* (Cambridge University Press, 1992), pp. 12–13, calls them the "mutually reinforcing expectations" that can "induce the right kind of cooperation—defined as voluntary deviations from self-interested behavior" to give a firm a "competitive edge over other firms." And David M. Kreps in "Corporate Culture and Economic Theory," in James Alt and Kenneth Shepsle, eds., *Perspectives on Positive Political Economy* (Cambridge University Press, 1990), p. 121, describes them as "focal points" that "individuals [in an organization will] use naturally to select a mode of behavior."

zation with an identity that communicates competence to political over-seers.[2]

But why do these organizations have the characters they do? It has much to do with autonomy. The greater the autonomy, the more likely organizational commitments will reflect concerns for performing a task, usually defined by the professional groups within the agency. As an agency becomes more exposed to external demands, commitments will reflect the effort to integrate internal concerns with external expecta-tions. Organizational commitments are also intricately bound with an agency's efforts to maintain autonomy. The levels of autonomy at the Fed, FDIC, and OCC are contingent, in part, upon the agencies' per-formance. Poor performance, or outsiders' perception of poor perfor-mance, will intensify political scrutiny. Commitments, then, will reflect an effort to do a consistently good job.

How do organizational commitments manifest themselves in practice? Consider a bank whose operations are routinely exposed to the scrutiny of government supervisors. According to bankers interviewed for this study, government expectations for fuller disclosure to customers and for active reinvestment efforts in low- to moderate-income neighbor-hoods were forcing technical changes in their operations. But these conditions were also forging new commitments within organizations. Some bankers spoke primarily of "getting a handle on" statutory require-ments for community reinvestment, identifying boundaries and struc-ture for the legislation, jumping through "fifty hoops," getting "the pieces in the right place," and they described the functional operations that were in place to demonstrate compliance. Others spoke of a new awareness of their community, of cultural differences they had not been sensitive to in the past, and the excitement of their bank's first success-ful effort to work with community groups to build homes in low- to moderate-income neighborhoods. The reflections of a vice president for compliance in a large regional bank are representative:

> We are doing more than we would have even though we have always been a community-minded bank. . . . We have more of an awareness of the groups out there, the needs of low- to moderate-income groups. . . . We are more aware that there are people who don't want to darken the doors of the bank because they don't understand the language, for example.

2. Selznick, *Leadership in Administration*, p. 40.

Another vice president, who used the term *responsible banks* to refer to those banks that had made community reinvestment an organizational commitment, discussed his excitement in working with community groups he previously never knew existed: "It's an evolutionary process that makes [the Community Reinvestment Act] very exciting." He discussed the overlap in community leaders and the way they could now routinely communicate to his bank the needs of a particular area or the type of financing that would facilitate completion of a new home or weatherization or other improvements to an existing home. The banker elaborated on his evolving working relationship with a leader who served as the director of one organization and the founder of another dedicated to housing for low-income families: "He will bring projects to the attention of public and financial institutions, as we have an ability to help meet those needs. . . . We are constantly in contact with these groups. . . . You find organizations you know and trust, there is discussion that is ongoing, back and forth. If it is a good project, we get involved."

For an organization empowered or created by the political process to carry out functions of government, the expectations of politicians are more explicit and demanding than the pressures felt by even heavily regulated private organizations such as banks. The political process specifies an organization's mandate, formal structure, and the resources and types of authority with which it can pursue the mandate. The political process will also greatly influence the context within which the public organization operates. A government agency's jurisdiction will define the groups, individuals, industries, or countries with whom it will routinely interact as well as the nature of the contact and the location in which it will occur. The mandate to manage the forests, for example, puts rangers of the Forest Service in contact with logging companies, loggers, logging towns, ranchers, and environmental advocacy groups. It requires the rangers to be located across the country, often in remote locations. And when interests collide over the competition between environmental preservation and jobs, rangers are required to operate amidst conflict.

Government-empowered organizations, like their more market-exposed counterparts, develop a character that helps them contend with the context in which they operate in a manner that meets officials' expectations and pressures for performance and helps integrate the work internally among varied functions, professional groups, and points of friction.

The organizational characters of the Fed, FDIC, and OCC, each reflecting varied degrees of autonomy, are the key to explaining the translation of mandates to examine and supervise banks into management styles by the top managers in each agency. In Selznick's terms, management has been wise to use organizational character as a constraint within which decisions are made to coordinate, direct, and develop an approach to the examination and supervision of banks.

Defending the Fund

The primary commitment of the FDIC is to defend the Bank Insurance Fund. Defense of the fund is the core of its organizational character. The defense defines how well the agency meets expectations for performance and provides an internal focus for motivation, identification, and the integration of complex functions. For the agency's political overseers, maintenance of the BIF's solvency guarantees depositors that their accounts will be protected up to $100,000 in any banking institution and assures American taxpayers that the resolution of failed banks and the protection of depositors will draw on a bank-financed insurance fund.

In 1984 an FDIC publication commemorating the agency's fifty-year history noted, "Public confidence in the banking system has been maintained without the expenditure of one penny of taxpayer money. The FDIC's insurance fund . . . has grown rapidly from $11 billion at the beginning of 1981 to over $15 billion today."[3] By 1991, following a decade in which more than 1,000 banks failed, the insurance fund projected a $7 billion deficit and was authorized to borrow $30 billion from the Treasury to meet its obligations. Yet by 1993 the fund was not only solvent, but the FDIC had repaid, with interest, the loan.[4] Its competence, in short, had been reasserted.

Maintaining a commitment to a solvent insurance fund serves as a source of professional identification within the agency and a means to integrate its complex functions. A solvent fund allows the autonomy in which the responsibilities of bank examination and supervision, resolutions, liquidations, and management of the corporation can be profes-

---

3. Federal Deposit Insurance Corporation, *Federal Deposit Insurance Corporation: The First Fifty Years: A History of the FDIC, 1933–1983* (1984), p. iv.
4. Federal Deposit Insurance Corporation, press release 14-94, February 22, 1994.

sionally exercised. It is an autonomy, however, that began to erode when the BIF first projected a deficit.

Asked about the impact of the Federal Deposit Insurance Corporation Improvement Act of 1991 on the corporation, an assistant to the board of directors focused on the refinancing of the fund and the function of fund solvency: "We were going broke fast, and we needed to ensure the public's confidence with the system." Others focused on the FDICIA as a threat to the corporation's autonomy because the legislation placed taxpayer money at risk to defend the insurance fund. One division director commented,

> If you need to go back to your friends in Congress for money, they can put more reins on you. It can affect your independence. . . . [We have always] been opposed to attempts to minimize the discretion of an independent agency. . . . With FIRREA and the FDICIA they began to micromanage us, not directly, but by telling the agency how to micromanage the industry . . . limiting our discretion.

Another division director was more explicit in his opposition to the loss of autonomy that accompanied public funding, although he struggled with the balance that nevertheless needed to be maintained to provide accountability:

> Agencies [that regulate banks] ought to be independent, they ought not have to go to Congress for funding. . . . There ought to be oversight, I'm not saying we should or could avoid oversight, but there should be balance. . . . There should be independence of the function of having to get money appropriated, independence of being hired and fired by Congress or the administration. . . . There must be checks and balances, and you are independent to a point, but there should be avoidance of undue influence.

The commitment to maintain a solvent insurance fund also serves to integrate the FDIC's functions by giving them a common measure of the success of their performance. For example, the solvency of the fund ultimately rests with the health of banks. To the extent that failures can be prevented through effective examination and supervision, the fund will remain sound. Thus the success of the FDIC's supervision of state nonmember banks can be represented in the solvency of the fund. Indeed, examiners closely identify their work with the protection of the fund. When asked about any potential loss of autonomy in the field because of the strictures of the FDIC Improvement Act, one senior examiner commented that his job had not changed because "the nuts and bolts of our job doesn't change. There is a balance sheet and we determine the condition of the bank. We want to know, does it protect the fund? We are very protective of our fund. . . . When it's all said and done it's the financial institution versus any loss to our fund." Similarly, to the extent that the FDIC finds the least costly and least disruptive manner in which to resolve failing banks, there will be a smaller drain on the fund. And if the agency's liquidation activities as receiver are conducted in a manner that maximizes the return for assets, the final toll on the fund might also be minimized. Finally, because the agency draws upon the fund for its operating costs, effective management with low overhead will also be reflected.

Changes made in the management of agency affairs late in the banking crisis when fund solvency was threatened reflect the primacy of the agency's commitment to preserve its mission. The agency changed the way the fund was managed to guide it from projected deficits to long-term solvency and in doing so to reestablish some autonomy in managing agency responsibilities. The FDIC's management of bank resolutions and procurement of litigation services (both directly related to liabilities placed on the insurance fund) were centralized, and the agency was committed to conducting both activities in-house (for litigation, a greater percentage of the cases were pursued in-house). The training program was centralized in a new office with an emphasis on a common curriculum across regions and professional human resource management. And the agency began to bolster its capability to manage communications with political overseers, banks, and the public to carry out its responsibilities under more intense outside scrutiny of its activities.[5]

These changes have all helped protect the fund. First, they were made despite the potential for strong opposition. For example, the decision to regulate more closely the fees charged by legal firms under contract with the FDIC and the decision by the agency's legal division to reduce the reliance on contracting challenged economic ties between the corporation and an important constituent group. Within the corporation the decision to create the Division of Resolutions took important authority from the Division of Supervision and placed it with one now equally prominent. And the effort to manage the corporation's communications with political overseers more centrally (primarily by bolstering the resources of its Office of Legislative Affairs and the Office of Corporate Communications) and to manage its image more carefully required its staff to change long-standing patterns of behavior. In short, the obstacles that can make public organizations impervious to change were overcome.[6]

Second, changes in the agency's management of bank resolutions and its legal activities contradicted conventional wisdom for "reinventing" government performance. In both instances it pared down the delegation of activity to private sector contractors—it chose, in the image used by reformers of government, to do more "rowing" and less "steering."[7] And the changes emphasized greater central control over the agency's activities or a standardization of activities rather than broader grants of discretion to employees and the regional offices. FDIC managers were innovators in seeking ways to use the agency's expertise and resources more effectively, but they also reinvented their management of the BIF by invoking some traditional administrative techniques.[8]

Both tactics can be explained by the emphasis the agency placed on preserving the fund. Potential internal opposition to the loss of turf and the severing of ties to important constituents was less important than changes aimed at preserving organizational autonomy in the long run. Similarly, concerns for professional empowerment were less important than achieving tighter management that would also bolster organizational autonomy. Temporary professional empowerment might have been realized at the expense of organizational autonomy.

6. A large interdisciplinary literature addresses the question of organizational flexibility and change. See Herbert Kaufman, *The Administrative Behavior of Federal Bureau Chiefs* (Brookings, 1981); Kaufman, *Red Tape: Its Origins, Uses, and Abuses* (Brookings, 1977); Kaufman, *The Limits of Organizational Change* (University of Alabama Press, 1971); Donald P. Warwick, *A Theory of Public Bureaucracy: Politics, Personality and Organization in the State Department* (Harvard University Press, 1975); Anthony Downs, *Inside Bureaucracy* (Little, Brown, 1967); and James G. March and Herbert A. Simon, *Organizations* (Wiley, 1958). For an important exception, see Daniel A. Mazmanian and Jeanne Nienaber, *Can Organizations Change? Environmental Protection, Citizen Participation, and the Army Corps of Engineers* (Brookings Institution, 1979).

7. The phrase "row rather than steer" is used by E. S. Savas in *Privatization: The Key to Better Government* (Chatham, N. J.: Chatham House, 1987); and David Osborne and Ted Gaebler, *Reinventing Government: How the Entrepreneurial Spirit Is Transforming the Public Sector* (Reading, Mass.: Addison-Wesley, 1992).

8. See Khademian, "Reinventing a Government Corporation," for a more thorough discussion of the changes.

The FDIC's competence in managing the fund is also sustained by some lesser organizational commitments that define the way work is integrated at headquarters and throughout the regional and field offices and provide the framework for management decisions on the supervision and examination of banks.

Workable Solutions

Work in the FDIC is performed by a variety of professionals. Economists, attorneys, and accountants, for example, participate in supervision, resolutions, and liquidation. But the dominant professionals are the bank examiners, and it is their pragmatic search for workable solutions that serves as an integrating commitment in the FDIC's headquarters. One manager pointed out what he saw as the importance of maintaining the client-counsel relationship between the Division of Supervision and the Legal Division. Rather than giving the attorneys a more prominent role in the enforcement of bank supervisory actions, supervisors and examiners work best with the advice of the Legal Division:

> With a client-counsel relationship we may make a business decision to pursue some action, and we would ask Legal, how good is our case? The counsel then says, if you do this, there is a 60 percent chance of success. . . . But then we'll make the decision. But if you leave that decision to lawyers, they always want a better and better case before it moves, and you may not get anything done. They always want more and more information. We say, well here's our case, it has a few warts, but let's go. It's more timely that way.

This same manager contrasted the FDIC's approach to dealing with problem banks, or banks engaged in high risk (or illegal) activities, with that of the Office of Thrift Supervision (the supervisor of federally chartered savings and loans and its predecessor agency, the Federal Home Loan Bank Board: "[They] strangled on moving enforcement [that was] controlled by lawyers."

Like lawyers, economists are viewed as support staff. When asked how the Division of Resolutions used the work of the Division of Research and Statistics, a top manager paused and said, "They have economic models to estimate the cost of bank failures that we use. . . . And for background for decisions that we make." What made the research division valuable for this manager was the "balanced and wise judgment" that the division's senior official brought to decisionmaking. Noting their consultation on a failing bank, the manager emphasized, "It made a difference to me that [we] reached the same conclusion."

The agency values the practical, the knack of comprehending a complex situation and making wise and timely decisions to achieve workable solutions. To the extent that economists and legal staff can contribute, their advice and counsel is embraced. Staff in the Division of Research and Statistics and the Legal Division have no pretensions about their role in the integration of work within the FDIC. They describe themselves as advisors and counselors, contributing to ease the main functions of liquidation, supervision, and resolutions. In the words of a manager from Research and Statistics:

> We get our duties as assigned. . . . The primary role of the FDIC is supervision, ensuring safety and soundness. Banks take on risk to make money, and we want to control that risk. [Research and Statistics brings] different views to the process, primarily economic decision-making, just as lawyers bring a legal perspective, and accountants and supervisors their own perspective. . . . In essence, we bring a different viewpoint to public policy issues that affect the insurer. . . . We try to bring a prospective view. . . . We support the other division in their activities. . . . [Basically] we support the organizational mission of the FDIC.

Perhaps the most obvious manifestation of the commitment to workable solutions is in the Division of Resolutions. Situated between the work of supervision and liquidation, the division's task has no clear boundaries. Similarly, with the exception that the division is charged with adopting the least costly means to resolve a failing institution, no specific procedures or guidelines define the way in which resolution is to be conducted. The work is carried out through coordinated efforts with other federal and state regulators, and its success often turns on the ability of the regulators to be able to achieve a quick consensus and move forward. "The process works well, currently," commented one division official, "because it is well coordinated." It works, he continued, because the officials in the various agencies were willing to "take the heat" that might go along with breaking away from the constraints of some "impeccable process," particularly "with high-visibility events, some large bank closures."

Although hardly an "impeccable process," the conduct of resolutions was at one time more systematic than it is today. A formal meeting would be held in which banks (traditionally rated 1 or 2 on the CAMEL scale), bid for a failed, usually small, institution's deposits and assets. But this procedure failed when Continental Illinois, Penn Square, Butchers, and other large banks began to fail in the late 1980s and the number of potential bidders dwindled. As the official from the Division of Resolutions said,

> If 40 instead of 140 banks failed a year, maybe we would feel differently, but with so many failures to resolve, restrictions have eased. . . . Who's allowed to buy, and are they strong enough? We used to only allow 1- and 2-rated banks to bid for a failed bank, but there are not a lot of those around. . . . Resolution is tough. . . . It's designed to minimize risk. . . . We go to the Fed, to the OCC, and ask them to let so-and-so participate in a bid. In some cases they are accommodating; other times there might be too much risk.

Officials will argue that the exercise of judgment is crucial in resolutions and, as in the case of bank examination and supervision, that there is more art than science involved. Referring to Congress's demand that the agency conduct resolutions as inexpensively as possible, a division official noted, "It's also in the minds of the people who wrote the legislation that we have better information than we do. A key thing we have to do is exercise our judgment. . . . And there are no statistics to make judgments; it's anecdotal. . . . Which deal structure to push for is perhaps the most important decision we make." After it arrives at a deal structure, the agency is required by the FDICIA to state the assumptions that went into the selection and to justify the choice. For example, the Division of Resolutions must make an assumption about how much a deal will cost the insurance fund. Referring to a legislator's frustration with the division for stating conclusions rather than assumptions in the documentation of a resolution, the official responded, "Well yes! . . . But we had documented our judgment, and it was the best we can do. . . . They seemed to think that if we couldn't *prove* [the deal] was cheaper, we should have burned down the bank." Instead, the division is committed to finding workable deals for a large number of failing banks and a limited pool of healthy ones at the least possible cost and disruption to the financial markets.

Anecdotally, this pragmatic approach is evident in the operating environment of the Division of Supervision and throughout the FDIC. Work on each floor of the agency is arranged around open hallways with a constant flow of staff and information from office to office. One need spend only ten minutes in front of the copy machine on any given floor to recognize the rapid exchange of information between offices and divisions and between staff, associate directors, and division directors. Day-to-day business is run efficiently but informally. Sleeves are rolled up, jackets are left in the closet, ties are loosened, shoes are comfortable.

The primary professional group in a public organization can be dominant in determining the way organizational commitments are defined, particularly when the professional group develops in connection with a particular government mission.[9] A profession, in a very general sense, derives clout from its claim to a jurisdiction. As the sociologist Andrew Abbott observed, a profession will "perform skilled acts and justify them cognitively," but it claims *jurisdiction* when it asks society to "recognize its cognitive structure through exclusive rights."[10] Professionals make these claims to exclusive jurisdiction, Abbott argues, in a variety of arenas, such as the legal system (which can control entry and practice of the profession's particular expertise), or within the realm of public opinion to carve out a niche among consumers of health care, for example, or legal services. Most relevant for the discussion here, professions also make claims in the workplace, or within organizations—perhaps the most difficult arena, Abbott said, within which to make the claim.[11]

Yet professions do make the claim successfully, particularly in government organizations. Professional groups make claims on an organization and its elite management and line positions during its formative years, in the midst of a reorganization or crisis, or simply through a small claim that grows incrementally as the group is able to facilitate decisionmaking in the organization or help it adjust to a changing political and economic environment.[12]

---

9. Frederick C. Mosher, *Democracy and the Public Service*, 2d ed. (Oxford University Press, 1982); Robert A. Katzmann, *Regulatory Bureaucracy: The Federal Trade Commission and Antitrust Policy* (MIT Press, 1980); Anne M. Khademian, *The SEC and Capital Market Regulation: The Politics of Expertise* (University of Pittsburgh Press, 1992); and Herbert Kaufman, *The Forest Ranger: A Study in Administrative Behavior* (Boston: Resources for the Future, 1960).

10. Andrew D. Abbott, *The System of Professions: An Essay on the Division of Expert Labor* (University of Chicago Press, 1988), p. 59.

11. Abbott, *System of Professions*, p. 65.

12. Mosher, *Democracy and the Public Service*; Charles Pruitt, "People Doing What They Do Best: The Professional Engineers and NHTSA," *Public Administration Review*, vol. 39 (July-August 1979), pp. 363–71; Khademian, *SEC and Capital Market Regulation*; and Herbert A. Simon, "Birth of an Organization: The Economic Cooperation Administration," *Public Administration Review*, vol. 13 (Autumn 1953), pp. 227–36.

The ability to capture part of an organization as a profession's jurisdiction means the profession can influence the way decisionmaking procedures are structured, the criteria used for decisionmaking, the priorities given to particular matters, and the criteria for advancement and evaluations of performance within the agency.[13] It is the ability, in short, to define organizational commitments. For those professions that develop in the context of a particular government mandate and implementing organization, professional and organizational priorities can be synonymous.[14] Such is the case with the examination profession in the FDIC because it promotes not only the defense of the fund as basic to the profession's autonomous exercise of expertise, but also the commitment to workable solutions and the subordination of legal and economic contributions to a supportive function.

The Conservative Approach

Contrasting the emphasis of the FDIC with that of his own examiners, a field office supervisor from the OCC pointed to the FDIC's "more traditional" approach. "They are concerned about loan quality, fraud, and violations, and they react accordingly. We tend to get away from that approach and focus instead on the systems of the bank and how well they are managed." This difference is one readily recognized by FDIC examiners as well. Contrasting the OCC's emphasis on process and why a bank was "doing what it was doing," a senior examiner in the FDIC argued that his agency "is more objective. It is interested in the condition of the bank, not the processes, the condition of the bank." The FDIC's more traditional or more objective approach is represented in its greater conservatism in supervising banks' risk taking.

Decisionmakers at the FDIC believe in promoting a competitive banking industry, yet agency examiners take pride in their insurance mission and their consequent willingness to restrain banks from taking on too much risk. Part of that pride is represented by comparisons made between the FDIC, on the one hand, and regulators with the authority to charter banks. Both the OCC and the Office of Thrift Supervision, for example, are bureaus in the Treasury Department with responsibility for supervising as well as chartering national banks and national thrifts, respectively. Contrasting the OTS with the FDIC as an insurer, one

13. James Q. Wilson, *Bureaucracy: What Government Agencies Do and Why They Do It* (Basic Books, 1989); and Mosher, *Democracy and the Public Service.*
14. Mosher, *Democracy and the Public Service*; and Kaufman, *Forest Ranger.*

member of management said, "The FDIC view [is] flavored by safety and soundness above all else. . . . That's different from the OTS . . . which is told to *promote* home lending. . . . The FDIC didn't have promotion in its statute for anything, and so it is less aggressive. . . . The FDIC is not a chartering authority, it is an *insurer*."

It is the concern for protecting the fund that fosters the FDIC's commitment to a conservative supervisory approach, and that is seen as providing examiners within the agency an independence from banking interests. Not only is it essential for FDIC examiners and management that banks not fail, but the diversity of banking interests that receive insurance from the agency makes it less likely that any one interest such as state nonmember banks will dominate the decisions of the examiners. And the agency is the backup supervisor of all federally insured institutions, including federally chartered savings and loans. This is in contrast to the OCC, for example, whose primary mission as the supervisor for national banks gives it just one constituency: banks with the most assets and with strong interest in branching and product diversification.

The FDIC's tendency toward risk aversion is also apparent in the unease of some of its managers with the diversification of commercial banks that require supervision and request insurance. Most Division of Supervision managers in the agency's headquarters have been bank examiners and have served in some management capacity in one of the regional offices. Consequently, they bring with them an understanding of the needs and concerns of state nonmember banks. Although the agency does not promote community banks, it does appreciate the dual banking system and the role that community banks play in the system. One might argue that the traditional FDIC professional is a firm believer in federalism in which communities and regions have diverse needs and interests that only a mix of national and state-chartered banks can meet. Reflecting on the trend toward consolidation of smaller institutions, one division director said,

> I think there is a place for the small community bank . . . and government ought to be careful it doesn't choke them. They are the heart-line for the rural structure of America and we ought to nurture the entrepreneurial bankers in small communities. [The community bank] knows the community better than any branch. . . . Don't create all branches. . . . There must be a balance. . . . Big banks need to diversify their product base. . . . But you don't want to eliminate small banks.

Concern over the diversification of financial intermediation reflects the FDIC's preference for less risk. The typical commercial bank is represented by the community bank, a single-unit institution dealing in community commercial and residential loans and offering checking accounts, savings accounts, certificates of deposit, and safety deposit boxes. But many of the community banks, whose lending activities bind them to particular geographic areas, have been the most vulnerable to failure in the event of regional downturns in commercial or farm real estate prices.[15]

Analogies routinely used by members of the agency illustrate its commitment to a conservative approach. The most frequently offered is made not only by FDIC officials but by managers in its sister agencies (although in a somewhat derogatory tone).

> If [the FDIC] was in charge of setting the speed limits for the national highways, the speed limit would be thirty miles an hour because that would cut down the drawing on the FDIC fund. . . . Accidents at thirty miles an hour will not be as serious as accidents at sixty-five miles an hour. . . . The FDIC has a tendency to go slower . . . to keep the industry in tow, not as anxious to compromise the bottom line. . . . Anything with the potential to deplete the FDIC fund is bad.

The second analogy, used less frequently, illustrates the frustration experienced by conservative FDIC supervisors in trying to cope with changes in the industry that challenge conventional wisdom about what constitutes a bank. Referring to the difficulty his office had in determining whether a particular depository institution was indeed a bank and thus qualified to receive federal deposit insurance, an associate director commented,

> First you have to figure out, what in the hell is a bank? And what is the intent of deposit insurance? It's a far cry from when they set it up. A typical commercial bank was one that made agricultural loans, commercial loans, and held demand deposits. . . . Congress had in mind

---

15. House Committee on Banking, Finance and Urban Affairs, *Analysis of Bank Deposit Insurance Fund Losses*, 102 Cong. 1 sess. (September 9, 1991), pp. 10–11. But see James R. Barth, R. Dan Brumbaugh, and Robert E. Litan, *The Banking Industry in Turmoil: A Report on the Condition of the U.S. Banking Industry*, Report of the House Subcommittee on Financial Institutions Supervision, Regulation and Insurance of the Committee on Banking, Finance and Urban Affairs (December 17, 1990), p. 25, for a discussion of the possible longer-term health of the smaller banking institutions.

what a bank was. . . . Now, you may have a furniture company and they may say, "we will sell a lot of couches on credit, and we borrow money to do that. We could [finance the credit] with commercial paper, but by and large we use a commercial bank for our needs. . . . Why don't I establish a bank and get insurance. . . . I could go out and sell CDs. . . . Then I've got back up, and my financing rates go way down. . . . Now I am a lender for couches; instead of selling the loans to the bank or borrowing, I just put the loans on my books." Well that isn't what anyone was thinking of or imagined at first. . . . They get deposit insurance and they play on the federal guarantee to reduce interest costs and financing.

Common Training and Central Direction

It is in this context of organizational commitments to protect the deposit insurance fund, find workable solutions for troubled banks, and practice conservative supervision that the FDIC's management style of standardized training and central direction can be understood. The agency's autonomy is highly dependent on the preservation of its mandate and is bolstered by its formal statutory status. Its organizational commitments reflect not only maintaining a solvent fund, but also maintaining the autonomy that has come with keeping the fund solvent. The professional priorities of its examination and supervisory staff have shaped organizational commitments that define the way its goal is achieved—through workable solutions. Both the common training of examiners and the reliance on central direction reflect the primacy of examination professionals whose autonomy depends heavily on a consistent approach to examination that ensures the primacy of the fund.

A Safe and Sound System

The OCC defines its competence as maintaining banking safety and soundness through its administration and supervision of the national banking system. It is a competence given formal definition through the effort to strictly enforce national banking laws, promote national bank competitiveness, and ensure stability in the system.[16] Yet promoting competitiveness could threaten industry stability, and practicing by-the-book enforcement of the national banking laws could limit industry

16. See Office of the Comptroller of the Currency, *1983 Annual Report* (1984); and OCC, *Quarterly Journal: Special Anniversary Issue, 1981–1991* (September 1991).

competitiveness. As one administrator in the Fed commented, "We have teased the OCC in the past because they can't figure out what [their primary duty] is." It is this dual mandate that often exposes the agency to conflicting political demands, an exposure made more difficult by the agency's direct links with the executive branch and its need to compete with the Fed and FDIC to demonstrate its expertise. It is in this exposed organizational position that the OCC's character is best understood.

A Shifting Commitment to Clientele

The OCC has emphasized banking industry stability at some points in its history and competitiveness at others. The changes certainly reflect conditions in the banking system or policy preferences of particular comptrollers, but perhaps most of all they reflect the agency's need to preserve some autonomy. If autonomy can be increased by bolstering the strength of the national banking industry, a prudent OCC will pursue more aggressive administrative policies (more rapid approval of mergers, acquisitions, and new charters) and supervisory policies aimed at increasing the competitiveness and profit margins of national banks. Otherwise the agency would miss an opportunity to provide political overseers with powerful indicators of its effectiveness and build a consensus for its emphasis in a particular political climate.

Competitiveness might also be pursued when the industry is suffering from bank failures caused by increased competition among commercial banks and other financial intermediaries. The OCC would need to orchestrate a turnaround in the industry to demonstrate its own administrative and supervisory expertise. Comptroller philosophies also help determine whether competition will be pursued during times of national banking crisis or impending crisis or whether industry strength is defined as a smaller, more conservative set of banks that reverse a trend of failure.

Regardless of the emphasis on stability or competitiveness, OCC personnel consistently show commitment to a primary clientele, but one that changes with changes in organizational emphasis. Employees today speak of their commitment to national banks rather than, as they once did, to depositors as clients. "We see our work as a consultant," a field office supervisor said, "in that we are more willing to work with a bank. . . . We could go into a bank that overall might be fine, but we might see something that we don't see in other banks, such as very high overhead. We might make a recommendation as to how they could lower their overhead. The FDIC would be less likely to do that."

Similarly, an OCC assistant director praised the willingness and discretion of the agency's examiners to take quick action for the sake of the banks: "To serve the needs of the banking community, you have to take action. . . . It might not always be the best action . . . but had you waited and done nothing, the consequences could have been worse." And in reference to the growing complexity of regulations, an OCC director discussed working with banks to reduce the time and effort associated with compliance.

> One benefit of technology sharing is relations improve. . . . Bankers tell us, for example, that the risk-based capital ratio [the necessary capital given the level of risk associated with assets] is so hot, they are told to report to the bank board every meeting what that ratio is. . . . The application that we supply allows them to produce that ratio in fifteen minutes. Prior to that it took four hours, and that had to be done monthly. We don't know how long it takes each bank, in reality, or if they have to report each meeting, but we had 5,000 banks request it after notifying about 3,700 nationally chartered banks.

In contrast, a long-time examiner and current director reflected on the OCC's previous commitment to depositors as the agency's primary clientele.

> There have been major changes. . . . It used to be that when we trained examiners we said, "when you go in [the bank], think of them as using your money to play with." The depositor was the focal point. . . . Then the bank became our client, and we became the advocacy group for banks. . . . You can't supervise and be an advocate. Banks are not the only client. . . . We used to focus on safety and soundness, compliance with the law, to ensure the benefit to the depositors. . . . We didn't prioritize the risk to shareholders. . . . The concern was depositors because they assume no risk with deposit insurance.

To cope with the shifting emphasis between stability and competitiveness, the agency's commitment to "a" clientele has evolved. However, it is as much a commitment to any clientele that is unique to the OCC. Although employees who have a history with the agency that predates the 1980s speak somewhat disdainfully of the recent catering to banks, it is not a reorientation that has weakened the organization. In fact, it initially strengthened the OCC's clout among political overseers, who were unable to stem the agency's broad interpretation of its powers to charter a wide range of institutions as national banks.[17] And even with an emphasis on national banks as clients, the agency maintained significant autonomy in its supervisory efforts. At the height of the 1980s banking crisis, national banks routinely characterized the OCC as the "regulator from hell," not the regulator of forbearance.[18] Its rigid supervision of the national banks in New England, especially, was blamed for curtailing too many loans and creating a severe credit crunch. And at the time, Comptroller Robert Clarke spent a great deal of time testifying before Congress and meeting with representatives of the national banking industry to explain the *need* for increased supervisory rigor.[19]

A Commitment to Constant Change

A central feature of the OCC's management style is also a primary organizational commitment: change. Just as a commitment to clientele allows for alterations in focus, a commitment to altering organizational design and policy as necessary provides the agency a built-in means to adapt to a sometimes volatile environment.

FDIC employees cite their conservative efforts to protect the fund; OCC personnel cite their agency's inclination toward innovation. In its supervisory responsibilities, the OCC competes with the Fed and FDIC. Distinguishing itself from these two is accomplished in part through a commitment to innovation in its supervisory policy, examination techniques, and organizational arrangements. Typically, current and former OCC employees review the agency's work in pointed contrast to the less than innovative supervisory efforts of the other two. A former executive assistant described the 1979 creation of the multinational group for examination and supervision:

> The multinational unit, that was an innovation. . . . We decided we needed to address the needs and concerns of the largest banks . . . and that was fairly innovative. . . . No other regulators had begun to look at

17. John T. Woolley, "Conflict among Regulators and the Hypothesis of Congressional Dominance," *Journal of Politics*, vol. 55 (February 1993), pp. 92–114.

18. Jim McTague, "Feeling Good about Feeling Bad," *American Banker*, October 13, 1986, p. 10; Joel Glenn Brenner and Carlos Sanchez, "D.C. Knew Firm Had No Bank Charter," *Washington Post*, December 7, 1990, p. A1; John M. Berry, "Regulators to Ease Up on Banks," *Washington Post*, December 15, 1990, p. A1; and Fred R. Bleakley, "Tough Guys," *Wall Street Journal*, April 27, 1993, p. A1.

19. Remarks of Robert L. Clarke before the Consumer Bankers Association on the supervision and examination policies of the Office of the Comptroller of the Currency in OCC, *Quarterly Journal: Special Anniversary Issue* (September 1991), pp. 91–93.

systemic risk . . . and the approach taken by the OCC hung upon the whole notion of systemic risk. . . . It was an effort to look at the cause of problems. . . . You have to get at the macro issues and focus resources where there is the greatest risk. . . . Since that time, other agencies have caught up.

It was the OCC, she remembered, that initiated the examination of the health of the banking system as a whole. But this emphasis placed the agency in the line of critical fire from Congress when banks began to fail regularly. As part of a new multinational focus and emphasis on the hierarchy of risk and portfolio management, the agency took the chance, according to a former examiner, that "a bunch of little banks [could] fail, but nothing [was] going to happen . . . to the system as a whole." However, it was precisely the large number of failures among small national banks that drew congressional scrutiny in the 1991 House staff report. Nevertheless, the willingness to experiment defines the way work is done in the OCC, and it is recognized and at least sometimes appreciated by the other agencies. An FDIC administrator admitted, "The OCC is out in front on a lot of things. Leadership [of a bank], risk-based capital. . . . It's difficult to be out in front in theoretical areas . . . [but] then we can sit back and second-guess them."

The commitment to change, however, is not without detractors in the agency. For example, although changes in policy and examination techniques are often recognized as ways to increase examiners' autonomy, they can also be unsettling for those who are affected by a reorganization or are the targets of a new policy. Reflecting upon his time as an examiner with the agency, the administrator of another agency said, "The OCC is in constant change. . . . I remember a big reorganization when I was there. . . . At the end I received a letter saying I had been pushed up and I had a raise. I said, 'great!' and put the letter away. . . . Later someone told me, 'congratulations on surviving.' I didn't even know I was in jeopardy." The rapidity of change and its unpredictability, he added, were very much the result of the leadership structure of the OCC—a single comptroller, rather than a board of directors. "If the comptroller is walking down the hall one day and he says, 'it's too dark in here, the walls should be blue,' tomorrow they are going to be blue." But a commitment to change is not merely the influence of the comptroller and the external pressures for performance he or she might represent, but a recognition by all employees of the need to stay on the cutting edge of examination techniques and policy as well as a need to facilitate a concern for professional discretion that fosters the commitment to change.

In 1988 the OCC once again employed its systemic view of the industry to identify policies and examination techniques aimed at preventing the conditions that had led to the banking crisis. An OCC internal study of the industry from 1979 to 1987 identified poor management as a primary cause of the failures.[20] The report was innovative in encouraging people to think more systematically about the assessment of management techniques independently of examiner assessments of capital, assets, liquidity, and earnings. As described by a regional OCC director,

> We threw out the management chapter of the handbook, and we have replaced it with "Board and Management Processes." . . . This thing for once tried to focus on the processes of management. We are always assessing ourselves on the fundamentals of management, so why not use the same criteria for banks? . . . It is more a set of questions, not examination procedures . . . designed to get examiners away from results [the CAEL assessments] and to give them some comfort level in pushing [on management assessment].

The report has also altered long-standing patterns of behavior in the agency that had prevented a systematic examination of management assessment. The regional director continued,

> It has been an evolution. . . . We finally had everyone on board. . . . Before, it was easy to talk about [management assessment] and hard to practice. The culture wasn't there to encourage it. People would talk about it, but if someone rated a bank a 3 without high loan problems, the report would be sent back [to the examiner]. . . . But it is now a product of more and more people saying, "let's not talk about it, let's do it, and let's give the examiners something in writing." . . . People

---

20. Office of the Comptroller of the Currency, *Bank Failure: An Evaluation of the Factors Contributing to the Failure of National Banks* (1988). There are, of course, other causes cited for the large number of bank failures during this period. Kenneth J. Meier and Jeff Worsham, "Deregulation, Competition, and Economic Changes: Assessing the Responsibility for Bank Failures," *Policy Studies Journal*, vol. 16 (Spring 1988), pp. 427-39; and George A. Krause, "Economics, Politics, and Policy Change: Examining the Consequences of Deregulation in the Banking Industry, *American Politics Quarterly*, vol. 22 (April 1994), pp. 221-43, present evidence that the deregulation introduced by Garn-St. Germain and the Depository Institution Deregulation and Monetary Control Act of 1980 played a key role in the large number of failures.

were looking at history and saying, "we could have stopped this, and I knew it was a problem, and I wish I could have said it."

The point of the report—that poor management rather than economic conditions was the primary cause of most banking failures—according to supervisors helped focus the agency on the importance of independent management assessments. In conjunction with procedures and guidelines drafted by the Washington and regional offices, it also provided examiners with ammunition to conduct management assessments. As noted in chapter three, the OCC's Division of Supervisory Research has been developing examination techniques to facilitate assessments of management in the field. "There were cracks in the foundation before [the economic bust]," noted one supervisor. "We're trying to look at the little cracks before the mess, to start being more preemptive." Although a preventive approach to supervision is embraced, theoretically, by all three agencies, it is the OCC that experiments most persistently with it.

A Commitment to Professionalism

The OCC's need to demonstrate competence in supervision and examination is also manifest in an organizational commitment to professionalism among examiners. It is not uncommon for field office supervisors and those involved in training examiners to contrast the rigor of the OCC's training program and requirements for becoming a commissioned examiner with what they believe to be a less rigorous process at the Fed and FDIC. In addition to longer training, the program emphasizes the professionalism of the bank examiner, the capacity to exercise independent judgment. The FDIC also refers to the professionalism of its examination cadre, but professionalism is not an organizing commitment for the agency nor is it a core emphasis in its training curriculum. In the FDIC, preservation of the fund, not commitment to professionalism per se, is the source of autonomy. A professional examination cadre is a feature of the organization that is allowed to flourish under more autonomous conditions. But the OCC, lacking the measure of performance and the widely supported mandate of the FDIC, must emphasize its professionalism in the conduct of supervision as a feature of its competence.

The OCC's commitment to professionalism does not, however, always mesh well with the agency's need for central control and direction. In fact, the exercise of professional autonomy often creates a tension between Washington and the field offices that is not necessarily reconciled through the stream of policy innovations and alternative ways to exercise autonomy that comes from headquarters. Commenting on the constraints he faced overseeing the supervisory process from the OCC headquarters, one manager said he had difficulty securing additional staff because of the "strong anti-Washington bias in this agency. . . . Washington is seen as a waste of bureaucracy . . . and so it's hard to demonstrate that two more people would allow us to do so much more when there is such opposition from the field. . . . There is a lot of power housed in the districts of this agency." But it is a housing of power that is essential for the organization. To suppress the independence of the examiners would be to risk losing them to another agency and being unable to attract new ones. Without an additional source of motivation, such as the protection of an insurance fund, examiners must look to their own professional identity and autonomy. And because the OCC relies entirely on its supervisory and administrative activities as the source of its competence, a less-than-professional examination cadre that is tightly controlled from Washington would diminish the importance of the agency as an expert on supervision and examination to whom political overseers might defer.

The tensions between Washington and the field reflect a common resistance to central direction among field agents. The FDIC controls this resistance in part through a common career path—most managers are former examiners. In the OCC, however, many managers (although not all) have not served as examiners. They are economists, for example, or former Treasury Department officials responsible for domestic and international finance. There are former examiners in top management positions for operations, but their numbers in Washington are small.

The tension between the field and Washington also represents a formal separation between the Division of Bank Supervision and Operations and the Division of Bank Supervision and Policy. "The policy-operations dichotomy in the OCC," noted one manager on the policy side, causes problems. "The staff has control over how policy is written, but not how it's implemented in the field. . . . So we have some sense of accountability without control in practice." This tension does not confront Fed managers, who also emphasize professionalism. The Fed does not attempt to control the urge for autonomy in field operations through policy directives from Washington, but instead uses the urge for professional autonomy to create a camaraderie of expertise in which field behavior is coordinated through peer expectations for professionalism.

The most prominent challenge to the OCC's commitment to professionalism is the growing importance of the Treasury Department as an overseer of the agency's broad policy initiatives. This oversight is a threat to the ability of field personnel to exercise judgment and of the policy staff to use rapid innovation to direct a powerful professional examination cadre. An OCC staff member involved in policy development commented that in the past decade banking issues had become "so much more important and politically charged. . . . It's not just [the OCC's] project. Now Treasury comments constantly and limits OCC's flexibility. . . . There has been a decline in the independence of the OCC. . . . Being part of the Treasury adds lags to our process; the time it takes us to respond is greater, so it slows the process." A similar sentiment was expressed by an assistant director:

> We are under the thumb of Treasury. . . . Everything we write or publish, before we say it or do it, we have to pass it by Treasury. . . . Before there was so much publicity surrounding banking supervision, Treasury was not in the least interested. . . . Now everything we do every day gets scrutinized by Treasury. . . . It is a detriment to regulators having the administration on our back.

Top-Down Innovation

Commitment to a clientele, to innovation, and to professionalism provides a context in which OCC management takes on its supervisory and examination challenges. Without a clear way to measure its performance or a goal that is clearly stated and evokes broad support, and with its formal placement in the Treasury Department, the OCC experiences a greater struggle for autonomy than do the Fed and FDIC. It is autonomy maintained through an effort to demonstrate expertise that exceeds the efforts of its sister agencies, manifest in its continuous innovation with policies, organizational design, and examination procedures. The agency's hierarchical design in Washington reflects not only its greater exposure to political overseers in the Treasury and the administration, but the divisive expectations among elected officials for how the OCC ought to ensure a safe and sound banking system.[21]

21. In "Accountability in the Public Sector: Lessons from the Challenger Tragedy," *Public Administration Review,* vol. 47 (May-June 1987), pp. 227–38, Barbara S. Romzek and Melvin J. Dubnick discuss a similar organizational phenomenon in NASA. Without clear consensus on its mission following the successful moon landings, a very decentralized, professional organization became hierarchical with a rigorous effort to exercise central direction over field operations that had previously been professionally run.

Without the freedom to pursue a clearly defined and broadly supported mandate in a more decentralized manner, OCC officials must
balance the importance of demonstrating the agency's expertise with its
ability to provide centralized accountability to its divided overseers—all
without stifling the good examiner ideal. As a result, the agency depends
on continual policy innovations from headquarters that keep field personnel tuned to Washington for guidance and on broad delegation of
responsibility to the field in executing the policies.

The Reasonable Approach

Unlike the OCC, the Fed's commitment to professionalism is less
inhibited by political pressures for centralized accountability. The Fed's
high level of autonomy depends in large part on its expertise in managing the economy. Without the need to consistently defend its expertise
before political overseers, the agency can build on its expertise throughout its supervisory and examination system to ensure consistency in its
policies. The agency's autonomy is, nevertheless, not invulnerable, and
organizational commitments have evolved to maintain it. These commitments, in turn, provide the context within which supervision and examination are managed from the central offices of the board of governors.

A Commitment to Reasonableness

A commitment to reasonableness at the Fed manifests itself in two
forms: it weighs the consequences of its actions both for the banks that
will be affected and for the depositors, consumers of banking products,
and the communities from which banks draw deposits; and it maintains
some consistency in its policymaking by adhering to internal standards
such as management's definition of "doing the right thing" rather than
definitions of good policy determined by the current political climate.

Contrasting the regulatory initiatives taken by the Fed and its sister
agencies, a Fed assistant director responsible for supervisory policy
related to consumer and community affairs said:

> If you took a broad historical view . . . the Fed has been very steady on
> the course. . . . We have not been hog wild, but we have not been
> sloughing off either. . . . Others are more responsive to the political
> winds. . . . There will be some sloughing off, and then [the other
> agencies] will get religion. . . . When they have fallen off, we get
> questioned about why we are more demanding, and when they are

more intense, we get asked why we are sloughing off. . . . We tend to have the best program . . . [but] consistency is difficult.

An organizational commitment to consistency and a measured approach to the development of policy and the conduct of examinations is a hallmark of the way work is done at the Fed. For example, more so than the people in its sister agencies, Fed employees spoke not only of the regulatory burden borne by banks and the agency's responsibility for preventing its unreasonable growth (particularly in the wake of the FDICIA and its many new regulations), but the challenge of determining the actual extent of that burden for banks as well as the cost of trying to make that determination. An assistant director described the calculation:

Everyone and their Uncle Charlie have been involved in initiatives to reduce the regulatory burden. . . . Not too many people know what the burden actually is. The irony is that we don't have the data to measure burden, but to collect the data is a burden. . . . So we wrestle with the burden issues. . . . Nevertheless, one of the things we have always striven for is to do what we think is right.

To the extent that assessing the regulatory burden was not attainable, the Fed would nevertheless incorporate internal standards based on available data, examiner experience, and communications with banks to enforce those regulations deemed necessary.

As part of its effort to maintain consistency, Fed policymakers commented that they almost never initiated anything with Congress. Not only would initiatives for new legislation bring legislators more squarely into the agency's daily activities, but such activity would force it to negotiate routinely with Congress over the definition of reasonable policy. Furthermore, legislative activism would detract from the Fed's standards of reasonableness, which are intended to provide some consistency in its regulatory approach. Instead, as one assistant manager responsible for consumer and community affairs said, "We have a strong reputation, and contact is usually based on Congress's initiation. . . . They might have a glimmer of an idea and want us to come and talk to them, or a draft of a bill from a lobbyist and they want to ask us, 'what do you think?' . . . We had one initiative in 1980, but it was for a reduction in regulation."

When members of Congress (or more likely, congressional staff) do approach the Fed for advice on an initiative, the agency attempts to work with them to make the legislation as reasonable as possible. The 1991 FDICIA, for example, included a provision titled "Truth in Savings." It mandated the development of regulations to be enforced by all supervisory agencies that required banks to disclose information on fees, interest rates, and other terms related to deposit accounts before consumers opened accounts. It required banks to provide periodic statements to consumers about fees associated with a savings account, interest earned, and the annual percentage yield. It also restricted the way interest could be calculated on account balances and the ways banks could advertise. One Fed employee responsible for drafting the regulations described the agency's calculation this way: "Our view with Truth in Savings was, don't try to derail it. It's going to happen, so make it as good as possible." As part of the Fed's efforts to remain dissociated from regulatory initiatives, this effort was conducted "in a semiofficial way, informal . . . staff to staff. . . . We will do things in a confidential manner." Despite the low-profile effort, this same person lamented that inevitably someone on the Hill would announce that "the Fed thought this is the way to go" to provide additional clout for the legislative position.

Regulators in the FDIC and the OCC also speak of the need to achieve a balance between the needs of banks to be competitive, the need to protect the deposit insurance fund, and the needs of consumers and depositors—in other words, to be reasonable. But the routinely rapid changes in policy and examination techniques at the OCC and the FDIC's weddedness to a conservative, fund-first approach to supervision replace the quest for reasonableness and consistency as an organizational commitment. At the Fed, whether the issue is a legislative or regulatory initiative, an interagency collaborative effort, or decisions made by an examiner, the commitment to reasonableness is primary. Policymakers in Washington contrast other agencies' habit of jumping the gun on policy initiatives and failing to consult with other regulatory entities with the Fed's commitment to "try to operate as a collegial body, collegial groups." And field supervisors talk of the effort to be firm but fair in dealing with individual banks and bank holding companies. It is an organizational commitment not only to professionalism and expert judgment in making decisions, but to the preservation of the agency's autonomy.

The Respect for Expertise

To convey what she considered the Fed's devotion to each staff member's expertise, a financial analyst in supervision related the following story:

The other day I organized a meeting of Norwegian bank regulators. . . . They were here to talk about how we close banks. . . . I stayed for the meeting, and I ran into [one of the Fed participants] after the meeting and I told him, "I learned so much." And he said, "I'm so glad you were there because you could answer that question [on a foreign bank issue] that we didn't know about." . . . We're all highly specialized, and we recognize each other's expertise. . . . I have worked in the private sector, and I think the reason for [the mutual respect] is because none of [the working groups] is a profit center. . . . I could write part of [a recent paper] about German banking, and then the people on the domestic policy side can provide their expertise, and someone else can provide the gossip about a particular provision, why certain things were thrown in. . . . I could bring a global approach to bear. . . . We were working together, and it was a high-quality project. . . . No one was hoarding information. . . . It doesn't happen here. . . . Their bonus is not based on how well their section did.

Perhaps more so than the lack of a profit motive, however, the Fed's commitment to expertise reinforces its primary source of autonomy—the exercise of that expertise in a manner that produces sound policy. The obverse of the commitment is that Fed employees are able to engage in the give-and-take among well-trained experts precisely because the agency's considerable autonomy allows for it. Whether the expertise of the Fed in matters of supervision and examination is greater than that of the FDIC or OCC is debatable. Indeed, OCC professionals cite a laxity in the training of Fed field personnel. Nevertheless, the general perception that the Fed's expertise in managing the economy carries over to supervision and examination is the reason the agency enjoys less scrutiny from political overseers.

References by OCC and FDIC personnel to the Fed's less intense interest in supervision and in its task are common. Yet one need only observe the agency's vigorous defense of its supervisory authority in the 1993 debate to consolidate supervision in a new agency (stripping the Fed of its supervisory responsibilities) to see its clout with Congress, in particular.[22] What was described by observers as "an unusual public

22. The proposal, "Consolidating the Federal Bank Regulatory Agencies," was put forth by the Treasury Department on November 23, 1993, as part of the Clinton administration's efforts to reinvent government. Specifically, Under Secretary Frank N. Newman proposed creating a new, independent agency built from the merger of the OCC and the OTS that would also assume the supervisory responsibilities of the Fed (for state member banks and bank holding companies) and the FDIC (for state nonmember banks).

attack" by the Fed against the proposal was effective in halting what many considered an inevitable consolidation in the name of both government and industry efficiency.[23] In its place the Fed offered a plan that split supervisory authority between it and an agency created out of a merger between the OCC and another Treasury bureau, the Office of Thrift Supervision. The Fed's action was not unique. Other efforts to achieve consolidation or some type of regulatory reform have been derailed by the Fed's arguments to the contrary.[24] Similarly, it was the Fed's supervisory policy emphasizing full-scope, annual, on-site examinations that was heartily endorsed by Congress in the FDICIA, an endorsement readily noted by Fed supervisors. As one Fed policymaker said, "Congress would appear to have endorsed the traditional approach by requiring full-scale exams [in the FDICIA]. . . . That approach is seen as the most reliable for identifying problem banks . . . to take problem banks to sound bank status and to mitigate losses to the insurance fund."

On those rare occasions when the Fed does approach Congress with a regulatory initiative, it is typically to fix or consolidate a regulatory responsibility not fully under the agency's control. Such proposals are often accepted without a great deal of debate or compromise. In 1991, following the major international banking scandal known as BCCI (for the Bank of Commerce and Credit International), the Fed proposed and received an expansion of its jurisdiction to approve applications by foreign banks to operate branch or agency offices in the United States and to examine those entities annually.[25] Before this legislation, responsibility for chartering and supervising foreign bank operations was shared between the Fed and the states from which most foreign operations received authority. Many of the banks' activities were conducted without direct Fed oversight—thus the difficulties in preventing BCCI's violations of U.S. banking laws. One Fed analyst described the agency's initiative to strengthen a weak link: "We had a certain amount of leverage with our position in Congress to get primary responsibility [for

23. Keith Bradsher, "Fed Assails President's Bank Plan," *New York Times,* January 5, 1994, p. D1.

24. See, for example, statement by Arthur F. Burns, chairman, Board of Governors of the Federal Reserve system, before the Subcommittee on Financial Institutions Supervision, Regulation and Insurance of the House Committee on Banking, Currency and Housing (March 18, 1976), folder "Banking Reform," box 122, Burton Malkiel Files, Gerald R. Ford Library; and memorandum to the chairman, Council of Economic Advisers, from the chairman of the Board of Governors of the Federal Reserve System, regarding the Financial Reform Act of 1976 (March 8, 1976), folder "Banking Reform," Box 122, Burton Malkiel Files, Gerald R. Ford Library.

25. See *Federal Deposit Insurance Corporation Improvement Act,* secs. 202-04.

foreign bank operations].... We asked for a whole lot, and we got everything.... A charter for a foreign bank now requires Federal Reserve Board concurrence, which essentially gives us full veto power."

Congressional respect for the Fed's expertise does not come automatically. The agency must nurture it constantly. To do so, it uses congressional actions and reactions as a barometer. The status of its expertise is also routinely measured in terms of its ability to change the behavior of supervised banks before it must bring an enforcement action. The term *moral suasion* describes the Fed's influence over banks. Supervisors in the Federal Reserve banks comment that their ability to work with banks in a relatively unconstrained manner to achieve safety and soundness is due in large part to the Fed's power of moral suasion, a power reinforced by the tremendous confidence of Fed examiners. Reflecting both the agency's good inspector approach to bank examination and his own confidence, a Reserve bank supervisor described the way he used mistakes made by a bank:

> When a bank makes a mistake, it provides part of the learning process. ... We can look at one of the problems, and ask what prompted the problem, and how did the organization protect itself, for the next time. ... We can always tell banks to make sure they are running a parallel system.... We learn from banks' mistakes and our own, but we don't make mistakes!

Autonomy of the Reserve Banks

Finally, the Fed's character is represented by a commitment to the Reserve banks' autonomy in supervision. Studies of the Fed typically assume that the Reserve banks implement policies determined by the Federal Reserve Board of Governors. But in matters of supervision, there is a distinctive autonomy that is carefully respected by managers at the board, and is viewed as a serious commitment by the agency. The independently governed and privately owned Reserve banks are essential to the Fed's formal statutory autonomy. "The operation of the FDIC and the OCC," said one member of the Federal Reserve Board, are more similar.

> They operate through regional offices with regional directors [who report to the Washington offices]. We have regional Federal Reserve banks and the approaches of the different regions are not uniform. There is differentiation even in examination standards between the

different Federal Reserve banks. . . . The policymaking is a board function and supervision is a delegated authority, but [the Reserve banks]
will still fight conformity. In the FDIC and the OCC the field officials
don't have dual loyalties. But the head of supervision in the New York
Reserve Bank works for the Fed president [of the New York bank] and
[the manager] who heads up supervision and regulation [in Washing-
ton].

The autonomy of the Reserve banks constrains the exercise of centrally directed initiatives and Fed examiners' training, yet it is viewed
more as a strength of the Fed's supervisory operations than a limitation.
In chapter 3, the board's effort to construct committees made up of
representatives of the Reserve banks as well as staff from the Washington headquarters was discussed in conjunction with the development of
training policies and techniques. As a director in the training program
noted, "The Federal Reserve is not geared toward Washington's issuing
commands. . . . We're not going to get a response." Rather than demand
conformity from the Reserve banks, a demand that would likely be
evaded, the board has sought to include the Reserve banks in
decisionmaking. Although the agency's commitment to Reserve bank
autonomy creates difficulties in maintaining consistency across the Federal Reserve system, strict consistency is readily forgone in exchange for
the varied types of expertise the banks bring to the system and the
additional autonomy they provide. The arrangement also reinforces (if it
does not inspire) the Fed's commitment to manage through reliance on
the expertise of each component of the system.

Character and Management Styles

Agency autonomy is directly linked to the development of character.
Character is best understood as a set of organizational commitments that
define the way work is done within an agency. The commitments represent efforts evolved by the organization to integrate external political
expectations for performance with internal needs to motivate employees and direct their behavior from a central headquarters. Together, the
commitments work to preserve or improve elements of the organization's autonomy, which is contingent on formal statutory independence, the clarity and consensus for broad organizational mandates,
respect for (and dependence on) the agency's expertise, and the presence of a clear measure of organizational performance.

For the Fed, organizational commitments to reasonable policymaking and examinations, the promotion of individual expertise, and recognition of Reserve banks' autonomy are as much a product of autonomy as they are means to protect the agency. Within a highly autonomous organization, expertise can flourish. Political expectations (often conflicting) are muted, and political overseers' dependence on the organization's expertise precludes the need for a highly centralized system to account for individual actions. Yet the consistent, reasonable exercise of that expertise is essential for maintaining autonomy. If policy changes were inconsistent and not incremental, conflict not only over the way the Fed manages the financial system, but the way it carries out its supervisory responsibilities would likely lead to stronger outside attempts to influence its decisionmaking and limit its freedom to operate. Reserve banks' autonomy is in large part a feature of the Fed's statutory structure, but the agency's commitment to their autonomy is critical for maintaining their power as independent, hybrid (public-private) participants carrying out financial policy. It is in the context of these commitments, in turn, that the Fed's management style—broad delegation of responsibility and autonomy to examiners—is best understood.

The OCC's commitments to innovation and change, its focus on a clientele, and its professional cadre of examiners result from its greater exposure to political oversight and are means to prevent further erosion of its autonomy. Dependent on the exercise of supervision and examination as its primary source of expertise, the OCC must compete with its sister agencies in demonstrating a particular competence for the task or maintaining a particular level of respect for its expertise. The agency's commitment to innovation and change reflects those conditions, as does its emphasis on professionalism. Recall the reference by an OCC administrator to agency examiners as race horses rather than plow horses: "We teach our examiners to be so self-reliant they think they can do anything. . . . I'd rather have to hold them back than beat them to get them moving." Part of that professional training, and part of the professional motivation, is the agency's emphasis on serving a particular clientele. In a minimally autonomous organization, however, that clientele can readily change as the organization attempts to give definition to a mandate lacking clarity and consensus. Commitment to flexibility in choosing which clientele to serve, however, allows the agency to cope with the changes. Together, these commitments provide the context within which the OCC's management strategy—top-down changes in policy and innovation in organizational design—has evolved.

Finally, the FDIC's centralized direction and minimal delegation of responsibility to the field offices is best understood in the context of its commitments to the insurance fund, workable solutions, and a conservative approach to banks' risk taking. The overwhelming importance of the solvency of the fund in ensuring the agency's autonomy makes preserving the fund a basic organizational commitment. Flexibility within the Washington headquarters to achieve workable solutions for supervising, resolving, and liquidating banks represents the commitment among the dominant professional staff members to preserve the fund in the most effective way possible, as does the conservative approach to banks' risk taking. With such a clear means of preserving the agency's autonomy, FDIC managers practice centralized direction and rely on centralized training to promote the organization's commitment to the fund.

6

Organizational Character and Bank Compliance

Since 1969 the supervisory responsibilities of the Federal Reserve, the Federal Deposit Insurance Corporation, and the Office of the Comptroller of the Currency have expanded. In addition to overseeing and examining banks' commercial activities, the agencies now supervise banks' statutory obligations to do business in a manner that is equitable for their customers and communities. Banks must disclose information to their customers on lending and savings policies, lend fairly, and invest in the communities from which they draw deposits. Statutes such as Truth in Lending (1969) and Truth in Savings (1991) are intended to protect the rights of borrowers and depositors. The Community Reinvestment Act of 1977 and the Home Mortgage Disclosure Act of 1977, among others, are intended to encourage lending in low- to moderate-income neighborhoods that might otherwise be neglected and ensure that discriminatory lending practices are identified and corrected through supervision (see box 6-1).

These statutes, referred to collectively by agency managers as compliance mandates, represent the expanding scope of special interest groups that have sought to define banking policy and the representation of their interests on the congressional banking committees in the past twenty years. Although banks claim that compliance mandates place a burden on their commercial lending and borrowing activities, particularly during difficult economic times, well-organized consumer and community groups advocate active enforcement of the statutes.[1] Their objective is to ensure that consumer and community responsibilities are not forgone when the commercial viability of a bank or a cluster of

---

1. See General Accounting Office, *Regulatory Burden: Recent Studies, Industry Issues, and Agency Initiatives*, GGD-94-28 (December 1993), esp. pp. 48-51.

BOX 6-1. *Major Consumer Protection and Community Rights Statutes Defining Compliance Obligations of Banks*

Truth in Lending (1969)

Requires banks to disclose information to customers regarding the extension of credit (from credit cards to mortgages) prior to or at the time of application. Consumers should be informed of the bank's use of fees, finance charges, and calculations of interest; their own obligations (such as the number, timing, and amounts of payments required to fulfill an obligation); and their rights related to the transaction.

Truth in Savings (1991)

Requires banks to disclose to consumers information on fees, interest rates, and other terms related to deposit accounts before opening accounts, and requires banks to provide periodic statements to consumers about fees, interest earned, and annual percentage yield. Restricts the way interest may be calculated on account balance and the way banks can advertise to consumers.

Home Mortgage Disclosure Act (1977)

Requires disclosure (to the bank's primary supervisor) of the loan type and census tract location of building for mortgages or home improvement loans and applications. The law was amended in 1990 to require disclosure of a loan applicant's race, sex, and income. Data are used by supervisors to ensure compliance with the Fair Housing Act and the Equal Credit Opportunity Act and part of the compliance obligations.

Community Reinvestment Act (1977)

Requires supervising agencies to "encourage" banks to meet the credit needs of the communities in which they are chartered, including low- and moderate-income neighborhoods, but in a manner that is "consistent with the safe and sound operation" of the bank. CRA ratings are disclosed publicly and can be used to challenge bank applications for expansion or merger.

---

banks is in doubt.[2] A coterie of representatives and senators from the banking committees have provided congressional support for these groups.[3] They and their staffs have been adept at using the federal

---

2. See, for example, GAO, *Regulatory Burden*, esp. pp. 51, 55, 59, 61. See also the testimony of community group representatives, *The Implementation and Enforcement of the Community Reinvestment Act of 1977*, Hearings before the Senate Committee on Banking, Housing and Urban Affairs (Government Printing Office, March 22, 1988), pp. 10–95.

3. The 1992 congressional elections bolstered the number and positions of representatives and senators interested in "a socially aggressive agenda" with respect to banking. Representative Joseph Kennedy became the chair of the House Subcommittee on Consumer Credit and Insurance, an important venue for initiating compliance legislation. Four new members of the House Banking Committee in 1992 expressed an interest in community development, and Senator Carol Moseley Braun also brought a strong interest in compliance to the Senate Banking Committee. John H. Cushman Jr., "Banking's New Bosses in Congress," *New York Times*, January 17, 1993, sec. 3, p. 5. However, previously strong supporters of the banking industry retired or were defeated in the 1992 elections, and the transition to Republican control of both the House and Senate committees might well restrict the influence of the strong-compliance advocates. Representative Jim Leach, chairman of the House Banking

provision of bank deposit insurance as the necessary leverage to attach consumer and community responsibilities to the regulations governing banking activities.[4] As these groups and their supporters in Congress see it, compliance obligations are a price banks must pay for the federal guarantee of deposit insurance.

Managers in the Fed, FDIC, and OCC confront the task of integrating compliance expectations with other agency concerns and professional priorities. The challenge is particularly difficult given the conflict between banks and consumer groups in framing the mandates and the hostility toward the statutes from commercial examiners in all three agencies who quickly relegated the programs to stepchild status. In addition, the mandates clashed head-on with organizational commitments and management systems designed for traditional commercial supervision.

Each agency has nevertheless created a distinctive program for meshing compliance responsibilities and other organizational commitments. Crucial to the programs' operation has been the character in each organization. The result is three programs that vary in the extent to which integration of objectives is achieved. The more closely integrated the compliance programs are with commercial supervision and examination responsibilities, the more readily priorities and resources can be balanced, particularly when banks are commercially troubled. But the more isolated a compliance program is, the more likely it is to foster examiner expertise in compliance and to compete for organizational resources.

Four dimensions define compliance programs, each with a counterpart in the commercial programs: policy development to guide compliance examiners, the deployment of examiners and supervision of their activities, training of examiners who conduct the exams, and establishment of an examination cadre for compliance (table 6-1).[5]

Committee, does not list compliance among his priorities for the committee. Jonathan D. Glater, "Incoming House Banking Chairman Praises Fed," *Washington Post*, November 12, 1994, p. C1.

4. For example, the *Federal Deposit Insurance Corporation Improvement Act of 1991*, which provided for the refinancing of the bank insurance fund, contained the consumer initiative, Truth in Savings. It sets forth restrictions on bank advertising of deposit accounts, disclosure of account information on a periodic basis, and civil liability provisions for lack of compliance (title II, subtitle F).

5. Management in each of the agencies distinguishes between policy and regulations. Regulations are mandated by statute, developed through a formal rulemaking procedure, and require enforcement by a supervising agency. Policies are developed within the agencies to guide the examination process, and examiners in the field have some flexibility in applying them.

TABLE 6-1. *Bank Compliance Program Characteristics and Relationship to Commercial Programs, by Agency*

Characteristic	Federal Reserve	OCC	FDIC
Compliance policy[a]	Developed by policy team in Division of Consumer and Community Affairs, separate from the commercial Division of Banking Regulation and Supervision	Developed by compliance policy team within the commercial Division of Bank Supervision and Policy	Developed in commercial Division of Supervision with support and oversight from the Office of Consumer Affairs
Operations[b]	Overseen by management in Division of Consumer and Community Affairs and Reserve bank supervisors	Overseen by management team in commercial Division of Bank Supervision and Operations and field supervisors	Overseen by management in commercial Division of Supervision and field supervisors. OCA as watchdog
Examiner cadre	Separate and specialized	Generalists	Separate and specialized
Training	Core training in commercial examination with specialized advanced training in compliance	Training in commercial examination with supplemental courses in compliance	Minimal commercial training, primarily compliance. Many examiners hired with previous compliance experience

a. Provides examiners in the field with guidelines for implementing mandated regulations and assessing consumer protection and community rights activities of banks.

b. Entails the deployment of examiners to the field and supervision to improve banks' consumer protection and community rights activities or to ensure adherence to previous supervisory orders.

For the FDIC and OCC, resolution of external expectations with internal resistance has produced compliance programs somewhat integrated with the management of commercial supervision. In 1990 the FDIC began to train special compliance examiners rather than rely on commercial examiners to conduct compliance examinations. A compliance examination is conducted separately from the commercial examination of a bank; however, compliance policy is developed and operations overseen by managers in the agency's commercial division. A support staff in the Office of Consumer Affairs is charged with providing policy guidance and acting as a watchdog over compliance operations.

In the OCC compliance has been completely integrated with the commercial examination program since 1982.[6] Commercial examiners have been trained as generalists with training in compliance; they conduct the compliance exam in conjunction with (or at the same time as) the commercial exam and under the direction of the agency's commercial operations division.[7] An important change, instituted in 1992, has been the addition of compliance training to the examiners' core curriculum, with the opportunity to specialize after a commercial examiner has become commissioned.

In both the OCC and FDIC the integration is as yet uncomfortable. Employees still consider compliance examination a distraction. Its marginal inclusion in the business of the agency is an organizational adjustment to integrate new expectations with existing operations in a manner that does the least damage to organizational characteristics. An integrated approach to compliance provides the opportunity to give priority to commercial examination when the safety of the bank insurance fund or the national banking system is jeopardized. Only the OCC has made negligible changes in its actual organizational commitments to accommodate external expectations—owing in large part to its less autonomous status.

In the Federal Reserve the compliance program has fitted comfortably among existing organizational commitments while remaining relatively isolated from commercial supervisory activities. Examiners in the Fed were no more enthusiastic about compliance mandates than their counterparts in the OCC and FDIC, but the character of the Fed's organization proved accommodating in a manner that minimally disrupted commercial activities and fostered the evolution of compliance examiner expertise. Beginning in the late 1970s the Fed chose to make its compliance program autonomous in policymaking, operations, and training, and created a separate cadre of examiners. The program was placed in a separate division with its own management and specially trained compliance examiners.

---

6. See written testimony of Comptroller Robert Clarke, *Implementation and Enforcement of the Community Reinvestment Act*, Hearings, p. 251.

7. Unlike its sister agencies, the OCC implemented a stratified random sampling process in 1986—what its critics called Russian roulette—as a means of selecting banks for a compliance examination; rather than a consistent one- to two-year interval, the probability that a bank supervised by the OCC would be selected for a compliance exam in any given year was 0.16. See Office of the Comptroller of the Currency, *Quarterly Journal*, vol. 7 (June 1988), p. 39. The process applied, however, only to banks with $1 billion or less in assets. The largest banks received more routine attention.

Mushy Mandates and Combative Politics

Like their counterparts in commercial examination, examiners charged with implementing compliance policy conduct on-site examinations of banking activities. But instead of emphasizing the components of the CAMEL rating, they focus on a bank's efforts to protect consumer rights and serve its community. Compliance reports serve as evaluations and as the basis for changes that agency supervisors might seek to enforce formally or informally. Compliance examinations present agency management with the same challenges as those posed by commercial examinations. Examiners must be selected, well trained, and encouraged to pursue long-term careers. And compliance examination crews must receive some central direction to ensure consistency in applying agency policies.

Yet compliance examiners, supervisors, and the management in Washington face additional political and policy dynamics that make their task more difficult. For example, like many pieces of controversial legislation, the Community Reinvestment Act is unclear. As one compliance manager in Washington said, "CRA is mush." It does not specify what the banks must do to meet community needs, but "it tells us, the federal regulators, to do something . . . to encourage banks to do lending in their own communities." The banks do not want regulators telling them where to make loans, nor have they wanted their lending activities restricted by explicit rules to guide community reinvestment, particularly in low- and moderate-income neighborhoods.

In contrast to the banks' opposition, vocal community and national consumer groups seek to ensure that banks are respecting the rights of customers and are reinvesting in their communities.[8] Faced with picketing, negative publicity, and the possibility of unfavorable examination reports, banks have sought some guidelines from the regulators—on the CRA in particular. In fact, the assertive activities of community groups can provide examiners with an important source of leverage to make banks more responsive to compliance mandates. A bank might prefer to respond to supervisory suggestions to modify its lending practices rather than face public criticism. Nevertheless, with more explicit guidelines for the CRA now in place, many banks complain about the burden of compliance while community and consumer groups typically accuse

8. Fred R. Bleakley, "Cracking the Vault: How Groups Pressured One Bank to Promise More Inner-City Loans," *Wall Street Journal*, September 22, 1992, p. A1.

them of dodging the law and complain that the regulating agencies are not doing enough to enforce it.[9]

Banks not only consider compliance regulations restrictions on their commercial activities, but they also view efforts by bank examiners to enforce compliance as an affront to their integrity. One supervisor responsible for compliance policy in the Fed commented:

> Consumer compliance is burdensome. . . . It's technical and hard to get the details right. . . . And it's so annoying and insulting to bankers. To be mandated to disclose information to customers suggests you are not relating the information to customers in the first place; to demand community reinvestment suggests you are not reinvesting in the community in the first place.

The point is not that regulators and bankers should have a kindred relationship, but as various studies have shown, some form of cooperation and trust gained through routine changes is essential to reduce information asymmetries and monitoring problems.[10] Yet the often contentious dynamics of compliance supervision limit the potential for these relationships to evolve. As one compliance policy manager said, "Bankers don't mind when you tell them, 'you messed up your APR [annual percentage rate] calculation.' . . . But if you say 'discrimination,' that gets their dander up."

The adversarial quality of compliance supervision was compounded in 1989 when Congress passed the Financial Institutions Reform, Recovery and Enforcement Act of 1989 requiring public disclosure of the CRA ratings of individual banks (banks are rated "outstanding," "satisfactory,"

---

9. On attitudes of banks see GAO, *Regulatory Burden*, esp. pp. 49-51. On consumer group attitudes see *Discrimination in Home Mortgage Lending*, Hearings before the Subcommittee on Consumer and Regulatory Affairs of the Senate Committee on Banking, Housing and Urban Affairs, 101 Cong. 1 sess. (GPO, October 24, 1989), pp. 140-277; and *Provisions Aimed at Strengthening the Community Reinvestment Act*, Hearings before the Senate Committee on Banking, Housing and Urban Affairs, 100 Cong. 2 sess. (GPO, September 8, 1988), pp. 305-67. See also testimony by representatives of various consumer groups in *Implementation and Enforcement of the Community Reinvestment Act*.

10. See John T. Scholz, "Cooperative Regulatory Enforcement and the Politics of Administrative Effectiveness," *American Political Science Review*, vol. 85 (March 1991), pp. 115-36; Eugene Bardach and Robert A. Kagan, *Going by the Book: The Problem of Regulatory Unreasonableness* (Temple University Press, 1982); Steven Kelman, *Regulating America, Regulating Sweden: A Comparative Study of Occupational Safety and Health Policy* (MIT Press, 1982); and Ian Ayres and John Braithwaite, *Responsive Regulation: Transcending the Deregulatory Debate* (Oxford University Press, 1992). See also chapter 2.

"needs to improve," or "substantial noncompliance"). And also in 1989 an amendment to the Home Mortgage Disclosure Act (HMDA) required banks to release data on mortgage loan applicants' race, national origin, and sex as well as the census tract location of any property related to a loan application. The data (released in aggregate form) are used by agencies to alter practices that might have discriminatory consequences for particular neighborhoods. The first annual release of the aggregate HMDA data with the new information in 1991 created a tremendous uproar that, as one manager understated, was "unflattering for banks."

Perhaps because the HMDA data have serious limitations, they have added fuel to the antagonism between banks and consumer groups.[11] Revealing the information has heightened public awareness of banking practices and encouraged consumer action to bring about greater community reinvestment or to eliminate discriminatory lending. For example, if a bank wants to merge with or acquire another bank, it must file an application with its primary federal regulatory agency. If its community investment practices have been poor, community groups (or an individual) can file a protest while the application is under consideration, and the process could be halted until an agreement is reached.[12] Despite the combative environment that makes their jobs more difficult, the agencies might use it to bring about bank responsiveness.

Agency managers who translate compliance legislation into guidelines for examiners are very sensitive to its burdens. They recognize that a balance must be maintained between addressing the legitimate concerns of the community and allowing banks enough flexibility to run profitable operations.

In their efforts to achieve that balance, each agency uses a variety of mechanisms to include consumer groups and banks in the policymaking process. And each conducts liaison activities between the public and the banks it supervises. Although much of the contact entails receiving and responding to complaints from banking customers, each also tries to coordinate communications between consumers, banks, and regulators to encourage more diverse types of lending. For example, in the early

11. The data do not provide information on the creditworthiness of applicants, the type of property being sought, or other criteria that might be used in the loan decision. *CRA/HMDA Update*, vol. 3 (June 1992). See David K. Horne, "Evaluating the Role of Race in Mortgage Lending," *FDIC Banking Review*, vol. 7 (Spring-Summer 1994), pp. 1–15, for a critique of efforts to assess the HMDA data.

12. For example, see Neal R. Peirce, "Neighborhood Challenges to Big Bank Mergers," *National Journal*, July 18, 1987, p. 1862.

1980s the OCC encouraged the development of bank-sponsored community development corporations as a private sector initiative to build cooperation between banks, community groups, and businesses to address problems of unemployment, disinvestment, and poor development.[13]

Compliance managers also recognize their dependence on the cooperation of the banks they supervise to improve consumer protection and community lending practices. As in the case of commercial supervision, this requires examiners to be flexible and to consider the individual circumstances of each bank. Many large banks, for example, have elaborate compliance programs with their own officers overseeing community reinvestment, mortgage lending patterns, and consumer affairs. Many small banks, however, fret about the cost of such programs. Examiners recognize that every financial institution is not Citibank, yet each needs to have a process to integrate community needs with commercial activities.[14]

The ability to evaluate and work with different compliance programs also requires that examiners have sufficient expertise to judge their effectiveness. Indeed, as with commercial examination, most banks prefer seasoned examiners; new examiners might depend on a checklist of compliance indicators or have to be tolerated in other ways while they learn on the job.[15] An inexperienced examiner might also misinterpret or miss altogether a bank's important compliance initiatives.

Without a significant body of legal precedent to draw on when conducting examinations (particularly for the more recent compliance statutes and amendments), examiners' experience is all the more critical. They must often rely on what seems logical or what appears to work. Particularly in interpreting the statutes of the CRA, they must judge the evidence and make the enforcement call. The challenge is similar to that facing a commercial examiner attempting to assess the competence of bank management without relying on indicators of capital, assets, earnings, and liquidity. For inexperienced examiners the lack of solid criteria complicates monitoring and enforcement. The people in the field, one compliance manager said, "have to find the evidence, make sure it's the right stuff, and make the call. . . . That's a lot to put on people. . . . Many

13. OCC, *Quarterly Journal*, vol. 1 (December 1982), p. 1.

14. Benjamin B. Christopher, "Recent Developments Affecting Depository Institutions," *FDIC Banking Review*, vol. 5 (Spring-Summer 1992), p. 51.

15. See, for example, GAO, *Regulatory Burden*, p. 39. This observation was also made by several private bank officials in interviews with the author.

of these people are young [and] it's not an easy call to make. It's not crystal clear when you've got the wrong answer."

Significant cooperation already exists among some banks, examiners and supervisors, and community groups, but it is for the most part an aspect of the good inspector ideal—allowing for the uniqueness of each bank, its clientele, and the community from which it draws deposits— toward which to strive. Consumer and community groups and their supporters in Congress would like the examiners to be more aggressive in enforcing compliance, but banks complain about the increasing regulatory burden. The goal of compliance policy is less clear than that of commercial examination. Without a better sense of what works and what is appropriate, examiners have a more difficult time making decisions. And as in any area of regulation where the costs of noncompliance are high, bankers say they want concrete guidelines; yet, because of the burden, as one regulator commented, "it's the hardest nut for banks to eat." Compliance remains "something they have to do, not . . . what is the *right thing to do*."

At the core of the problem is the question of whether banks should be required to help bring about social change—a role imposed most clearly by the CRA and HMDA. Bank managers routinely point out that "social legislation" imposes "social obligations" on banks that their nonbank competitors do not face.[16] The difference, as regulators also point out, is that banks receive federally guaranteed deposit insurance at a relatively cheap price. This is the hook that Congress uses for requiring them to meet particular consumer and civil rights obligations.

Compliance Management and Organizational Character

Compliance mandates clash with the priorities of commercial examiners in each agency. In interviews, references to commercial examination as the priority were common; compliance examiners were referred to as "second-class citizens" and "stepchildren"—often by those themselves involved in compliance management. In the history of the OCC, a former official noted, "examiners were held accountable for safety and soundness but not for compliance." And a regional supervisor said with some condescension, "With safety and soundness, it's all numbers . . .

16. Banks compete with insurance companies, pension funds, mutual funds, finance companies, money market mutual funds, mortgage companies, credit unions, and other financial intermediaries. See Robert E. Litan, *The Revolution in U.S. Finance* (Brookings, 1991), for a discussion of the increase in the numbers of banks' competitors.

the whole focus is on the numbers. With the consumer group, it's other things. They are less analytically oriented . . . more, well, compliance oriented. . . . They focus on things like percentage of completed forms that are incorrect." Even in their dress, OCC compliance examiners are set apart: they wear green blazers when conducting an exam; commercial examiners wear red.

The extent and consequences of this perception of compliance programs' secondary importance have been shaped, however, by each agency's organizational character. In the OCC, organizational commitments have made the concerns of commercial examiners and the financial interests of the banking industry primary, increasing the challenge of meshing compliance with traditional programs. There has also been professional opposition in the FDIC, but the emphasis on protecting the deposit insurance fund has suggested ways to implement compliance examination that have marginalized commercial examiner opposition. In the Fed, organizational commitments suggested a solution that isolated compliance activities from commercial activities without compromising (indeed, by embracing) Fed commitments to expertise and reasonableness.

Clashing Responsibilities at the OCC

Implementing compliance policy has posed the greatest challenge at the OCC. The success of its commercial supervision is crucial to defining the OCC's competence. Its overwhelming commitment to promoting a sound national banking system places compliance supervision in direct competition with commercial supervision for resources. The competition is made stronger by the agency's commitment to the professional development of commercial examiners, who have traditionally defended their autonomy and priorities, and to a clientele—most recently defined as the banks composing the national banking system. Together, these commitments have fostered a compliance program that is integrated with but subordinate to commercial supervision to ensure commercial activities receive priority.

During the past fourteen years, compliance policy, operations, and examiner training have been absorbed into the OCC's commercial program. Compliance policy, for example, is developed within the Division of Bank Supervision and Policy. The management and field supervisors in the Division of Bank Supervision and Operations oversee compliance examinations. Examiners responsible for conducting the examinations are trained in commercial examination and must pass the OCC's uniform competency exam before specializing in compliance through additional course work.

Before 1992 most courses in compliance were not part of the common curriculum offered by the OCC. Today, in the words of one OCC field supervisor, "We have a whole new compliance program, with a lot more training up front." Most examiners are now exposed early in their training to both independent study and classroom courses in consumer compliance and fair lending and have a wider variety of independent study courses available for later specialization. The cadre of compliance examiners, however, is not separate from the commercial examiners—except for the jackets. Only senior examiners have the choice of focusing solely on compliance. In fact, many compliance examiners (who might now specialize after several years as commercial examiners) will continue to conduct commercial exams from time to time.

The elevation and institutionalization of compliance training is a recent change in the OCC. During the 1980s and early 1990s, compliance training was given short shrift, primarily because there were limited organizational incentives for commercial examiners to specialize in compliance examination. The reason was simple: a generalist staff, trained primarily in ensuring bank safety, provided the agency with more options for allocating examiners to different areas when necessary. With banking crises erupting in the Northeast and the Southwest and general concern for stemming the flow of bank failures, a highly mobile examination cadre was desirable. Nevertheless, Congress, as one OCC compliance manager noted, did not "make distinctions between commercial and compliance. . . . We can't ignore an area because it is the least likely to make a bank close." Compliance examinations had to be conducted, but with commercial examinations as the priority, the agency's compliance training was insufficient to prepare a new examiner to exercise compliance judgment and did not provide appropriate incentives to develop expertise.

> There must be the right number of people with the time, the knowledge, who can spend a small amount of time and get the very best . . . product. . . . Right now we are spending a lot of money training examiners over and over again that is being frittered away because they only ever get a smattering of understanding [before they focus on safety and soundness].

At the height of the banking crisis in the late 1980s and early 1990s, compliance exam procedures were in fact given a lower priority by the more experienced examiners—those with a career stake in their commercial expertise. According to one manager,

> In the past, as people became more and more seasoned, they were tapped to do higher priority work [in commercial examination]. . . . Others were left behind to do the less desirable work . . . always the new group. . . . They would get one dose of [compliance] training and never go back for more, and consequently they would never get the exposure necessary to be efficient.

Referring to external critics of the agency's integrated approach that placed compliance responsibilities in competition with commercial duties, one OCC compliance manager pointed out that the agency had "taken criticism by Congress for not doing enough. . . . They say that just because of the slump [in the banking industry], it doesn't excuse [us] from enforcing the CRA." At the time, not only was the OCC relying on generalist examiners to implement compliance, but resources were less available because of the use of stratified random sampling—what its critics called Russian roulette—to select banks for a compliance examination. Rather than a consistent one- or two-year interval for conducting a compliance exam at a given bank, the probability that a bank supervised by the OCC would be selected in any given year was 0.16.[17]

The compliance manager cited above, however, also emphasized that as examiners become more specialized in compliance, "you can't lose sight of the overall evaluation of the institution." To do so, another manager said, would be to risk allowing failure: "I can see that a bank is not likely to close if it is not in compliance . . . but it will close if it has bad loans and we are not there to supervise." From this perspective, treating commercial concerns, when necessary, as more important than compliance would more likely be achieved with an integrated program such as the OCC's. If a bank has a strong potential for failure, a trade-off could be more readily made between commercial and compliance priorities with a compliance program that was subordinate to, or contained within, the commercial program. Furthermore, it is less likely that commercial examination needs would have to compete for scarce agency

---

17. OCC, *Quarterly Journal*, vol. 7 (June 1988), p. 39. The process applied, however, only to banks with $1 billion or less in assets. The largest banks received more routine attention.

resources if compliance remained an integrated part of commercial supervision, rather than a separate entity.

One compliance manager in the OCC was acutely aware of the pressure to keep compliance in a subordinate position: "If I was someone on the safety and soundness side, I might resent compliance. . . . I might think that compliance can wait. . . . If we have to make a hard decision, I would want the best examiners [for commercial]. Not to have the best available might be short-changing the banking system." Throughout the agency a concern for balance was prominent. "Examiners must know how compliance fits in overall," one regulator stated.

> They can't be a zealot on compliance and ignore all else. . . . We will sometimes make trade-offs. . . . If a bank is rated a 5, we might skip the CRA exam, or if it's a 4 headed for a 5 . . . we might give them a break. . . . But for 4s [moving toward health], we don't let them get out of it.

It was only the record profit years of 1992 and 1993 that allowed compliance managers to advocate putting greater organizational effort into compliance training.[18] The result was the formation of the Consumer and Compliance Training Task Force, which provided the blueprint for developing courses at the introductory and intermediate levels. One senior member of the training staff remembered:

> We brought compliance managers together . . . and we sat down and asked "what would you consider basic management skills in the compliance area?" . . . Then we said, "what are the skills? Be more specific." . . . Based on that roadmap, we developed a self-study course. We use those as much as possible . . . to minimize travel and time off the job. The self-study course is about eighty hours long. From that we have also developed a basic consumer compliance school, and we are developing an intermediate-level course. We also have a CRA and fair lending seminar.

Compliance mandates have presented an obvious problem for OCC examiners. Like their counterparts in the FDIC and Fed, they have not

---

18. The industry had record net income in 1992 of $32 billion, more than double the net income earned in 1982. Federal Deposit Insurance Corporation, *Statistics on Banking* (1992), p. A4.

welcomed the additional mandates. Compliance examination distracts examiners from fulfilling their traditional mandate. But to create a separate program that relieves them of the compliance burden would also draw resources away from commercial examination, a concern that is very important for the OCC, which relies on supervisory fees rather than, as does the FDIC, insurance premiums. A separate program would also make reducing the importance of compliance concerns more difficult when the banking industry is weak. Thus one might expect that when the industry is in good health, as it is today, resistance to a distinctive program or more institutionalized training would be much reduced. And in fact, not only did the OCC bolster its commitment to the development of compliance training in 1993, it also initiated a program for sending testers into the field to identify discriminatory lending practices.[19]

With this broader commitment to compliance, some within the agency would argue, has also come some change in the primary organizational commitment. As one senior staff member said, "We are interested in the safety and soundness of banking, and *that it is done fairly and equitably.*" It was a change, he argued, that could be brought about rapidly in a hierarchical organization with a single leader. "[Comptroller of the Currency] Ludwig says we should give more attention to CRA and that springs us to action. Policies are developed, and we figure out how to train for it."[20]

But mandated changes in policy do not necessarily alter long-standing organizational commitments that define the way external expectations are integrated with internal concerns. As the least autonomous of the three banking regulators, the OCC maintains a tenuous balance between intrusive, often divided political overseers and agency autonomy. Although concern for the quality of compliance training has increased, it is not clear whether the concern would evaporate in the face of a crisis in the national banking industry. As of now, however, balancing compliance priorities with the commercial needs of banks remains important. "When you have specialists," said one district supervisor, "you have the

19. Office of the Comptroller of the Currency, *Examining Issuance*, 93-3 (1993); and Office of the Comptroller of the Currency, "Statement by Eugene A. Ludwig, Comptroller of the Currency, news release 93-38, April 5, 1993.

20. Eugene Ludwig was appointed comptroller of the currency by President Clinton in 1992.

potential for zealotry. . . . You can focus so much that the impact of that area on the ultimate concern, safety and soundness, might be lost. . . . That drove us . . . to try to look at the big picture."

Integrating Compliance While Protecting the Fund

When asked whether compliance examiners could become stepchildren in the FDIC, a member of the training staff replied,

> It's more likely to occur for the FDIC than for the other agencies, because of the fund. Congress has mandated it, and we are interested in compliance to the laws in all areas, but compliance is not directly related to protection of the insurance fund. . . . Compliance is hot now, and people in Congress are excited, but it will pass.

This attitude reflects perhaps FDIC examiners' greater confidence (or greater autonomy) than their counterparts in the OCC.

Before 1990 the FDIC's approach to carrying out the compliance mandate resembled that of the OCC. Compliance policy was developed in the Division of Supervision, where supervision of compliance operations was also housed. Examiners with a smattering of compliance training carried out most compliance examinations in conjunction with a very small group of specialists.[21] As one FDIC manager observed, "Compliance training was offered to everyone, but not everyone got training." Much of this optional training was left in the hands of the regional offices.

In 1990, however, the FDIC established a separate corps of compliance examiners. It also upgraded the importance of the Office of Consumer Affairs to serve as watchdog over the compliance activities of the Division of Supervision and provide policy and training guidance. But unlike the OCC, the agency did not thoroughly revamp its training program. Instead, it has relied heavily on hiring examiners who have had compliance experience working in a bank or at the OCC or the Fed (a large pool of compliance examiners was hired away from the Fed in 1990). This practice would be unheard of in the ranks of commercial examiners, where long-term training and development is emphasized. Training in both commercial and compliance examination, which has become OCC policy and is a long-standing feature of Federal Reserve policy, is not FDIC policy. The agency pays little attention to training

21. Federal Deposit Insurance Corporation, *1990 Annual Report* (1990), p. 19.

commercial examiners in compliance, while compliance examiners receive little commercial examination training.

Hiring a specialized compliance cadre has proved a very workable way for the FDIC to maintain its commitment to the fund. As in the OCC, managers had feared "zealotry" might take hold among specialized compliance examiners. To supervise a bank's compliance responsibilities aggressively, the argument went, might be to lose focus on its soundness and the threat it might pose to the insurance fund. "You do not want Nader's Raiders," said one manager. "You want them to be able to understand where the banker is coming from."

Although the initial effort to maintain such a focus meant little attention to the cross-training of commercial examiners or the specialized training of compliance examiners, the situation created by the passage of the Financial Institutions Reform, Recovery and Enforcement Act in 1989 required a quick, workable solution for addressing the expectations for compliance. The act increased the FDIC's workload tremendously by making the agency the backup supervisor of savings and loans and giving it oversight of the Resolution Trust Corporation, the agency created to resolve the assets of insolvent thrifts. In addition, the number of banks the FDIC had to resolve or liquidate and the number of problem institutions that needed greater supervision increased during the late 1980s (approximately 1,000 federally insured banks failed between 1985 and 1990).[22] Consequently, to allow commercial examiners to concentrate on commercial supervision of state nonmember banks and the safety of the bank insurance fund, a separate corps of compliance examination specialists was established. Again, it was protection of the fund that provided the incentive, but it was the agency's commitment to workable solutions that produced the needed examiners without having to train them.

Compliance Supervision and Expertise at the Fed

When asked why the Fed had established an autonomous compliance program rather than one integrated with the commercial division, one regulator replied, "In a way there was some sort of self-interest. The board is not one to do a poor job. . . . Once it has a job, it wants to do the best it can." As the central bank, the Federal Reserve Board had the resources to do the job right, and with an organizational commitment to the development of expertise, Fed management and staff had the incen-

22. FDIC, *1992 Annual Report* (1992), p. 168.

tive. By creating the Division of Consumer and Community Affairs to handle compliance, the agency acted to protect the prestige identified with its expertise and to maintain its ability to carry out its commercial supervisory activities. Both concerns are central to maintaining confidence in the Federal Reserve Board as the nation's central banker.

The decision to support a separate compliance division complete with a policymaking team, managers responsible for overseeing operations, and a separate cadre of examiners has allowed for the development of compliance expertise in two ways. First, the division has developed a knowledge base in the past eighteen years. The Fed has taken the lead among the three agencies in developing compliance policy. The Washington-based management group has counterparts in each of the Reserve banks, where a focus on compliance has translated into particular expertise. The Federal Reserve Bank of St. Louis was able to develop the software program necessary for all the Reserve banks to collect data on applicants for home mortgage loans and send it on to the Federal Reserve Board staff in the Division of Consumer and Community Affairs for processing. The Reserve Bank of Boston gained expertise in research into housing discrimination. Its 1992 study on mortgage lending in the Boston area provided information on creditworthiness—employment, credit history, and debts of loan applicants—that is not part of the data collected under the Home Mortgage Disclosure Act.[23]

Second, the compliance division has fostered the development of an expert staff—an expertise recognized by the FDIC when it hired so many Fed compliance examiners from the Reserve banks—and offers examiners a greater incentive to choose compliance as a career. The Division of Consumer and Community Affairs creates a clear career path for compliance examiners. Like commercial bank examiners, compliance examiners can eventually take management positions with the Reserve banks and the board in Washington. Nevertheless, as the opening interview comment in this section indicated, the most prestigious positions (as in the OCC and FDIC) are associated with commercial supervision. If examiners perceive that the best positions in the agency (including management positions in the field and regional offices) are associated with commercial exam expertise, compliance may not attract many examiners or the best may not stay with compliance for the long term. A separate management hierarchy, however, provides compliance

23. See *CRA/HMDA Update*, vol. 3 (June 1992). However, see also Horne, "Evaluating the Role of Race in Mortgage Lending."

examiners with the opportunity to advance through the agency as supervisors and managers, an advancement not as likely for compliance examiners in a commercial examination hierarchy.

Just as the resources for compliance supervision (and general operations) were strained at the FDIC during the late 1980s, the Fed's responsibilities for compliance enforcement no doubt strained policymaking and examination resources in the Division of Banking Supervision and Regulation in the late 1970s. Many of the compliance statutes enacted in the 1970s directed the Federal Reserve Board to write the formal rules. Of course, regulators in each of the agencies were and still are required to interpret the rules and set guidelines for supervisors in the field, but the Fed's resources were stretched especially thin. This increased burden could have meant deteriorating quality of the corps of commercial examiners, as well as less attention to compliance. By creating a separate division responsible for writing the rules, the agency avoided this possibility.

Although a compliance program closely integrated with the commercial program can allow an agency to assign priorities with more confidence, a more autonomous program, with not only an independent corps of examiners but separate operations and policy development, is more likely to develop seasoned examiners knowledgable about the compliance systems of the banks they oversee. Consequently, as has been true of commercial examinations, the time required to conduct examinations can be reduced, an obvious benefit both to the agency and the banks, and cooperation improved. Because CRA ratings are public information, if a bank receives a negative evaluation, it will certainly contact the compliance examiner's district office to criticize his or her work. For this reason, inexperienced examiners, especially, will want to document their evaluations and go by the book. Yet because they are inexperienced, going by the book will be more time consuming. It might also mean overlooking bankers' creative efforts to meet community needs or missing ideas from consumer and community groups. Without the skills to gather information that is difficult to obtain and harder yet to interpret, the inexperienced examiner must rely on rigid guidelines that are a poor substitute for familiarity and expertise.

A more independent program is more likely to facilitate this expertise. Examiners who are given the opportunity to specialize in compliance through course work that is part of their core curriculum are likely to develop the experience necessary to exercise good judgment more readily than those trained in a supplementary fashion. Perhaps more important, the separate management hierarchy for monitoring and policy development of compliance supervision will provide examiners with more focused oversight as well as incentives to become compliance examiners in the first place.

There is, however, an organizational check on the Division of Consumer and Community Affairs: the commitment to reasonableness. Just as the commercial policy team is expected to exercise restraint and to seek consensus with the Fed's sister agencies, the compliance management team must practice policy development in moderation. Much of the pressure for moderation comes from the Federal Reserve Board members. "Consumer laws and compliance is not a traditional central bank responsibility," noted a senior manager, "so the board relies heavily on staff. . . . From my point of view, it is important to have the credibility of the board." Part of ensuring that credibility is to approach policy development in a reasonable, balanced manner. This is no easy task. First, managers must develop policy amid the divisive and quirky political dynamics that define compliance policy. Following the debate over the burdens of compliance in early 1990, one manager recalled, the arguments in favor of additional compliance policy erupted: "Then we have LA in flames, and everyone begins saying what are we doing for these people. What initiatives do you have?"

Second, the expertise of the compliance staff at the Fed is routinely used by members of Congress for developing compliance legislation. In the case of Truth in Savings, it was awkward, one senior manager said. "We were involved because we have considerable expertise. Congress calls on us in these areas . . . for technical advice. . . . The board was not in favor, yet we knew here how best to draft the legislation. We knew the best way to do X, but we were not in favor of it." Despite the conflicts, as another manager noted, "one of the things we have always striven for is to do what we think is right, with all that stuff going on."

Compliance and Character

In all three agencies, commercial examiners and their superiors at the district, regional, and national levels were less than sanguine about the mandated responsibilities of compliance oversight. Fulfilling the mandates was outside their traditional areas of expertise and created competition for organizational resources. The ways managers charged with compliance incorporated the responsibilities into each agency's routine has depended mostly on the character of the agency. The new compliance mandates, at odds in their origins and tumultuous in their politics of implementation, posed the greatest challenge to the OCC, the least autonomous of the three agencies. Its greater exposure to the political arena made it particularly vulnerable to added responsibilities and conflicting efforts to define its mandate. Nevertheless, its commitment to promote the national banking industry and the professionalism of its examiners encouraged the resolution of the new external expectations with internal operations and priorities.

Similarly, the more autonomous FDIC drew upon its commitment to protect the fund, first to marginalize its compliance program, and then to hire the necessary expertise to limit the strain placed on commercial examination resources.

Finally, for the Fed, access to the resources of a central bank and commitment to expertise made the development of a specialized division a fitting choice. Its commitment to reasonableness tempered the fear expressed by commercial managers in all three agencies of compliance zealots who would supervise without regard to questions of commercial viability.

By understanding organizational character one can explain the translation of mandates into consumer and community protection programs. And character can explain the variation in compliance programs between the three agencies—each with the same political overseers in Congress, each responsible for implementing the same legislation, but varied in their levels of autonomy and thus in the effort required to integrate the new duties with existing supervisory priorities.

7

Is There One Best Way to Manage Bank Supervision?

Given the different ways bank supervisory agencies are organized and overseen, and the implications of these ways for how they do their job, is there a best way to structure banking agencies, make banking supervision more efficient, and hold supervisors and examiners more accountable?[1] The answers depend on two factors.

First, is there one best way to supervise banks? For more than fifty years critics have avoided answering the question by focusing instead on the rationality of the individual supervisor and the uniqueness of the United States in relying on three agencies for supervision.[2] Consolidation, they have contended, would improve accountability to elected officials, reduce administrative overlap, and sharpen the effectiveness of supervision. It would also encourage a supervisory structure more comparable to the ones in the rest of the world. But this begs the question: What is it we want a consolidated supervisory agency to do? Do we want to promote banking innovation, competitiveness and growth, or stability

1. The term *one best way* is used in reference to the work of Frederick W. Taylor, who argued that the scientific analysis of any given task would reveal the one best way to perform the task. See *The Principles of Scientific Management* (Harper and Brothers, 1911).

2. For an overview of the many proposals see Robert S. Pasley, "Consolidation of the Federal Financial Regulatory Agencies," graduate thesis, Stonier Graduate School of Banking, University of Delaware, 1989. The General Accounting Office has conducted overviews of several foreign supervisory systems as requested by members of Congress interested in consolidation. See, for example, *Bank Regulatory Structure: France*, GAO/GGD-95-152 (August 1995); *Bank Regulatory Structure: The Federal Republic of Germany*, GAO/GGD-94-134BR (May 9, 1994); and *Bank Regulatory Structure: The United Kingdom*, GAO/GGD-95-38 (December 29, 1994). The GAO itself has recommended consolidation on a limited scale. See Statement of Charles A. Bowsher, comptroller general of the United States, in *Bank Regulation: Consolidation of the Regulatory Agencies*, Hearings before the Senate Committee on Banking, Housing and Urban Affairs, 103 Cong. 2 sess. (Government Printing Office, March 4, 1994).

and care in taking risks? If we favor the management practices of the Federal Reserve, for example, we forgo the more innovative supervision of the Office of the Comptroller of the Currency that has kept pace with changes in the banking industry. If we favor the management practices of the OCC, we forgo the emphasis on protecting the bank insurance fund (and ultimately the taxpaying public) and the stable supervisory practices of the Federal Deposit Insurance Corporation. Other countries might have the more rational structure of a single supervisory agency, but these organizations do not necessarily keep pace with changes in the banking industry and simultaneously provide checks to promote safe banking. When Daiwa Bank of Japan failed to report $1.1 billion in trading losses in New York in November 1995, it was expelled from doing business in the United States. Japan's single supervisor, the Ministry of Finance, announced shortly thereafter that its approach to supervision had not kept pace with new banking practices and the internationalization of the industry, which required more rigorous supervision that put more "distance between the government and the financial institutions."[3]

Second, whether there is one best way to structure the supervision of banks also depends on the political circumstances surrounding the creation of a single supervisory agency. If the goals of supervision are still in dispute, the problem will be reflected in the more contentious way a consolidated agency would be held accountable. If political overseers disagree about the structure of the new agency, it will likely be organized so as to allow some access for competing political powers and their constituent groups (banks, bank holding companies, and competitors in financial intermediation). And if the banking industry experiences a crisis under the new agency, respect for it will be diminished and its operational autonomy nibbled away. How a new agency would be structured and held accountable, and therefore how it would perform, is very much contingent on the politics that would create it and what the agency would do with any autonomy it might have. Structure and accountability cannot depend on nothing more than a clean sheet of paper and a rational calculus of how best to maximize efficiency, effectiveness, and accountability.[4]

---

3. Sandra Sugawara, "Japan Plans to Tighten Its Banking Regulations: Move Meant to Calm World's Daiwa Jitters," *Washington Post*, November 11, 1995, p. D1.

4. See Terry M. Moe, "The Politics of Bureaucratic Structure," in John E. Chubb and Paul E. Peterson, eds., *Can the Government Govern?* (Brookings, 1989), pp. 267–329, for a similar argument.

Nevertheless, the effort to rationalize supervision boasts a long history of scholarly investigation. Starting from the premise that the administration of government programs could be separated from the politics that created them, Frank Goodnow, Leonard White, and Luther Gulick, among others, contended that administration was a science whose principles of organization and management—aimed at maximizing efficiency—could be derived from careful research and practice. Their work contributed to a model that emphasized hierarchy, clear and narrow spans of control, expertise, written rules and procedures, and, of course, functional specialization as fundamental to more efficient, effective, and accountable organizations.[5]

Critics of this "scientific" approach to administration have focused on the unrealistic premise of a separation of politics and administration as well as the often dysfuntional consequences of administrative efficiency. Politics, they said, mattered a great deal, not only for the way bureaucracies were designed and overseen, but also for how bureaucrats exercised discretion in decisionmaking.[6] More critically, despite an organization's reliance on narrow spans of control, expertise, functional specialization, and written rules and procedures, politics at all levels interfered with the efficient execution of public policy.[7]

Yet despite this trenchant criticism, the model remains very much a part of government reform efforts. Rarely is administrative reform considered within a context that might pose distinctive political or historical challenges to effective implementation. Instead, academics and policymakers alike tend to view administration in the abstract and set out to find the formula that guarantees better performance and better accountability across the board. Perhaps, as political scientist Craig

5. See Frank J. Goodnow, *Politics and Administration: A Study in Government* (Macmillan, 1900); Luther H. Gulick and L. Urwick, eds., *Papers on the Science of Administration* (New York: Institute of Public Administration, Columbia University, 1937); and Leonard D. White, *Introduction to the Study of Public Administration*, 3d ed. (Macmillan, 1948). For an overview of organizational principles and the arguments favoring their application, see Jack H. Knott and Gary J. Miller, *Reforming Bureaucracy: The Politics of Institutional Choice* (Prentice Hall, 1987).

6. Dwight Waldo, *The Administrative State: A Study of the Political Theory of American Public Administration* (Ronald Press, 1948); Herbert A. Simon, "The Proverbs of Administration," *Public Administration Review*, vol. 6 (Winter 1946), pp. 53–67; and Paul H. Appleby, *Policy and Administration* (University of Alabama Press, 1949). For a more recent study of the dysfunctional aspects of spans of control in particular, see Paul C. Light, *Thickening Government: Federal Hierarchy and the Diffusion of Accountability* (Brookings, 1995).

7. Graham T. Allison Jr., *Essence of Decision: Explaining the Cuban Missile Crisis* (Little, Brown, 1971); and Donald P. Warwick, *A Theory of Public Bureaucracy: Politics, Personality, and Organization in the State Department* (Harvard University Press, 1975).

Thomas commented, this is why the evidence for reorganizations of public institutions prescribed by administrative scholars, in particular, is "relatively scant [and] often contradicts theoretical claims."[8]

Administration of banking supervision cannot be detached from its historical and political foundations. The system's relationship with federalism and the struggle for control over financial intermediation, the long-standing political debate as to whether "safe and sound" means "competitive" or "cautious" and therefore what the role of the bank supervisor ought to be, and the political interest in limiting examiner discretion that varies with the condition of the industry and the strain on the bank insurance fund have each helped shape the relationships of the OCC, Fed, and FDIC with their political overseers. Rationalization, or consolidation, demands the irrational assumption that these influences can be ignored. Rationalization also ignores the benefits, in this case, of distinctive structures that result in distinctive management systems.

The Argument for Consolidation

A single, consolidated supervisory authority, its advocates argue, would eliminate unnecessary layers of bureaucracy and promote greater efficiency in two ways.[9] One large agency would cost less to operate than three smaller ones: there would be one personnel system, one training system, one rule-making process, and one network of regional and field offices. The Office of Management and Budget, for example, performed a savings estimate for the Clinton administration's proposal to consolidate the three banking agencies and the Office of Thrift Supervision that focused on the costs of direct supervision and of indirect and direct overhead and support. The OMB estimated a savings to the federal government of $151 million to $208 million to be realized through new examination technologies and the elimination of the "current, duplicative exam process," both of which would require fewer full-time em-

8. Craig W. Thomas, "Reorganizing Public Organizations: Alternatives, Objectives, and Evidence," *Journal of Public Administration Research and Theory*, vol. 3 (October 1993), p. 457. Paul Light offers an excellent analysis of this phenomenon. In *Thickening Government* he examines the consequences of structuring government according to the theoretical principle of narrow spans of control. Rather than promote tighter control by those at the top of the hierarchy, government merely thickens, placing the chief executive at a greater distance from the administration of policy.

9. Wolfgang H. Reinicke, "Consolidation of Federal Bank Regulation?" *Challenge* (May-June 1994), p. 26. See also *Consolidating the Federal Bank Regulatory Agencies*, proposal requested by the Senate Committee on Banking, Housing and Urban Affairs, November 23, 1993, p. 3.

ployees. The estimate, however, excludes the cost of examiners who would be maintained by the Fed and FDIC to gather information necessary for making monetary policy and examiners maintained by the FDIC to fulfill the agency's responsibilities as backup supervisor.[10]

A consolidated system, critics contend, would also eliminate discrepancies in supervisory regulations and the territorial battles that occur in determining which agency is responsible for the supervision of a particular bank or bank holding company. As the insurer, the FDIC has backup authority over banks supervised by the Fed or OCC. Although FDIC supervisors hesitate to exert this authority (granted in the Federal Deposit Insurance Corporation Improvement Act of 1991), the potential for conflict is there should the agency decide to second-guess one of the others' assessments of a bank. Similarly, most of the nation's largest banks have national charters and are frequently the lead banks in bank holding companies. Consequently, several OCC district offices have expressed an interest in examining the bank holding companies of national banks, a clear challenge to the territory of the Federal Reserve. Resolving such disputes can be arduous, as managers in the three agencies readily acknowledge. When asked about the most significant challenges he faced in managing supervisory policymaking, an OCC manager stated,

> Getting consensus from my counterparts in . . . other agencies. . . .
> There are no right yes or no answers. When we deal with policies that
> will affect every examiner, there are disagreements with the legal
> people; even [with] my own staff it's difficult to reach consensus, and
> it's hard to work things out with other agencies. They have their own
> concerns. . . . We have the same definitions, but we don't apply them
> the same way. . . . Reaching a consensus, it's a bureaucratic maze.

In addition to improving efficiency, consolidation would, its advocates argue, improve the effectiveness of supervision. First, it would reduce the regulatory burden of the banking industry, especially of multibank holding companies. Under the current system, a holding company that controls (through stock ownership) state and nationally chartered banks as well as savings and loans cannot consolidate all its operations. Each part of the company could have a different supervisor. The holding company itself would also have a primary supervisor, the

---

10. Office of Management and Budget, *Bank Regulatory Consolidation Savings Estimate: Technical Assumptions* (February 1994).

Fed, for its operations. Operations would be made more complex for the holding company if the OCC, for example, decided it must know certain things about the holding company in order to supervise a member bank with a national charter. (The regulatory burden for an individual banking unit, whether or not it belonged to a bank holding company, would not be reduced by consolidation.) Individual banks and thrifts in a holding company have one primary supervisor, as do the thousands of banks that are not members of a larger holding company. The burden that individual banks face is not overlapping supervisors, per se, but volumes of mandated regulations that govern their business activities. Consolidating supervision in one agency will not reduce the number of regulations. If the president and members of Congress want to streamline the supervisory process, the solution is not a consolidated supervisory authority but the elimination of some regulations.

Effectiveness, critics contend, would also be improved by eliminating the agencies' alleged "competition in laxity." Banks have their pick among the three agencies for a primary regulator. They can be chartered under state or national laws and can choose to become members of the Federal Reserve system. To keep a viable group of banks under their jurisdiction, these agencies are said to supervise in a manner that keeps their existing constituency happy and attracts other banks. As described by a bank regulatory task force appointed during the Ford administration, the competition for constituent banks can manifest itself in "the interpretation of explicit statutes governing bank behavior" or in "those decisions that are subjective in nature."[11] In other words, an agency might offer a more liberal interpretation of statutory provisions governing the behavior of banks, forcing the other agencies to follow suit to maintain their competitiveness, or competition might involve granting or denying mergers, new branches, or entry into the industry. Consolidation would supposedly eliminate this competition.

Finally, advocates of a consolidated system argue that specialization would improve accountability. To those who counter that consolidation is the equivalent of monopoly, they respond that one agency (the Fed) is responsible for monetary policy, one (the FDIC) for insurance, one (the Securities and Exchange Commission) for regulating the securities markets, and so on.[12] Why not apply the same principle to banking supervi-

11. *Perspectives on Bank Regulation*, report of the Bank Regulatory Task Force, folder "Bank Regulation," Box 115, L. William Seidman files, Gerald R. Ford Library, pp. 21–22.

12. L. William Seidman, "A New Way to Govern Banks," *Wall Street Journal*, February 3, 1994, p. A14.

sion? Representatives of the executive branch and of the banking committees in Congress would then need to oversee only one agency. The point was brought home by a less-than-enthusiastic supporter of consolidation who oversaw supervisory activities in one of the agencies: "Congress would like to have one agency, independent and appropriated [funded through Congress], so that they would be the master of its fate. The administration, though, is anxious to keep control." The point is that a single agency is more likely susceptible to influence by Congress or the president or to be caught in the struggle between the two branches.

The supposed rationality of consolidation, however, does not necessarily make it a sensible policy. The arguments for both consolidation and limiting agency autonomy are taking place without consideration of the agencies' responsibilities, the politics of banking supervision, or organizational and managerial realities. Indeed, with scant exception, the discussion of administrative and regulatory efficiencies has ignored the costs—from character clashes to fundamental differences in training, decisionmaking, personnel needs, and basic forms of communication—associated with consolidation.[13] Also missing from the debate is an investigation of what work the agencies—individually and together—currently do particularly well. Although there might be (and I am not convinced of this) administrative savings associated with a merger, it would be wise to remember that downsizing government activities through consolidation does not guarantee better performance.[14] Policymakers must ask if the good performance of the current system would be sacrificed for the promise of greater accountability, efficiency, and effectiveness.

In Defense of Supervisory Overlap

National bank failures accounted for 73 percent of the losses incurred by the bank insurance fund between 1986 and 1991, and the OCC took the brunt of congressional wrath over the crisis. But there is some vindication of the agency, evidence that also supports the argument that several supervising entities, each with its own style, provide an impor-

13. The OMB assessment, *Bank Regulatory Consolidation Savings Estimate*, is one of the few empirical efforts to estimate savings that might result from consolidation.

14. Donald F. Kettl, *Reinventing Government? Appraising the National Performance Review* (Brookings, 1994), esp. pp. 58–59.

tant tension for the overall health of the banking industry that would be lost under consolidation.

One More Look at Disbursements

The OCC supervises some of the nation's largest banks. If disbursements from the insurance fund are considered as a percentage of total banking assets under the supervision of each agency, nationally chartered banks performed at least as well as Fed-supervised banks throughout the 1980s and better than those supervised by the FDIC (figure 7-1). FDIC-supervised banks drew the largest number of disbursements as a percentage of assets in the first seven years of the 1980s. This higher percentage represents, in part, the agency's conservative approach: it prefers to close an ailing bank more rapidly than the other agencies rather than risk greater losses through forbearance—a practice that can lead to higher future disbursements if the institution does not recover. The FDIC's approach is also reflected in the decrease of disbursements going to its banks in the late 1980s as the ailing banks were closed quickly, leaving healthier state nonmember banks. It also no doubt reflects the greater difficulties of small banks during the crisis and the fact that the FDIC supervises more than 50 percent of the banks in the dual banking system with assets of $100 million or less.

From 1967 to 1989 banks under the jurisdiction of each of the three agencies claimed the highest percentage of disbursements at one time or another. Banks under the jurisdiction of all three agencies experienced an increase in disbursements as a percentage of total assets during the 1980s, but the rate of increase experienced by Fed- and OCC-supervised banks was less steep through 1986 than that of the FDIC. When Fed- and OCC-supervised bank disbursements increased in 1988, disbursements for FDIC-supervised banks began to drop. There has been, in other words, an overall balance in the performance of banks under the jurisdiction of the three agencies.

A Competition in Laxity?

As noted earlier, a prominent argument for consolidation is the supposed competition in laxity among the agencies in their quest for constituent banks. If this is the case, one might expect the OCC, as the innovator among them, to lead in the competition because it could more readily alter its examination and supervisory techniques to appease more banks. A test of the argument, however, not only vindicates the

FIGURE 7-1. *Bank Insurance Fund Disbursements as Percentage of Total Bank Assets, by Bank Supervising Agency, 1965–90*

Percent

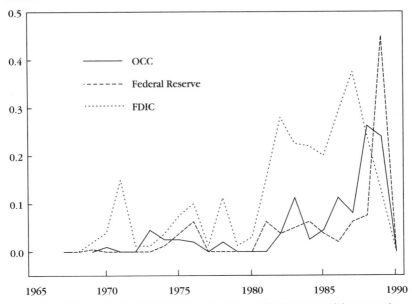

SOURCE: The *FDIC Annual Report* (1967–89), table 123, lists insured banks requiring disbursements by the FDIC for any given year. Banks are listed as either national banks, nonmember state banks, or state member banks. Disbursements for each class of bank were gathered for each year and totaled, providing total disbursements to banks supervised by the OCC, FDIC, and Fed, respectively, each year. Assets were gathered from the *FDIC Statistics on Banking*, table 104, which lists total assets of FDIC-insured institutions, grouped by charter class, for each year. Disbursements were then calculated as a percentage of assets for each year.

OCC, it shows little evidence of any effort among the agencies to get banks to switch supervisors.

Figures 7-2 and 7-3 show the charter losses (the losses of constituent banks) and additions of the three agencies from 1978 to 1991. For example, a national bank might switch its charter to a state bank with membership in the Federal Reserve system, thus leaving the OCC for the Fed. Between 1978 and 1980, when the OCC initiated the multinational examination group and began to introduce top-down examination techniques, fewer than ten banks a year switched from a state to a national charter (additions to the OCC's constituency). At the same time, fifty to seventy banks (approximately 2 percent of all nationally chartered banks) a year left the OCC for supervision by the Fed or the FDIC—not exactly strong evidence that the OCC's innovative policies were aimed at attracting more banks.

FIGURE 7-2. *Additions of Banks to Agency Constituency through Charter Switches, by Bank Supervising Agency, 1978-91*

Number

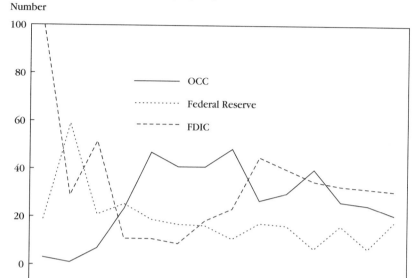

SOURCE: Data are from *FDIC Statistics on Banking*, table 101, for the years examined. Under the category "other changes in classification," losses and gains are provided by charter type (Fed member, nonmember, and national bank).

Between 1981 and 1985 the OCC introduced the hierarchy of risk, portfolio management, and the targeting of examination resources. It also took the lead in charter additions, about forty a year, or 1 percent of all national banks. However, these gains did not keep pace with those of the Fed during the same period. The addition of ten to twenty Fed member banks each year bolstered its constituency by 2 percent. By 1986 the OCC's portfolio management was in full swing, the shift toward training generalist examiners able to consider both a bank's commercial needs and its compliance responsibilities was in place, a specialized policy group was organized, and greater authority was delegated to OCC districts, yet the agency became the largest loser of banks, finishing 1991 in second place.

The FDIC experienced the most dramatic swings in charter losses and gains. It had large gains in 1978, 1979, and 1980, equally large losses in the early 1980s, and a gradual growth of charter additions from 1986 to 1991. But even the agency's high of seventy charter losses in one year

FIGURE 7-3. *Losses of Banks from Agency Constituency through Charter Switches, by Bank Supervising Agency, 1978–91*

Number

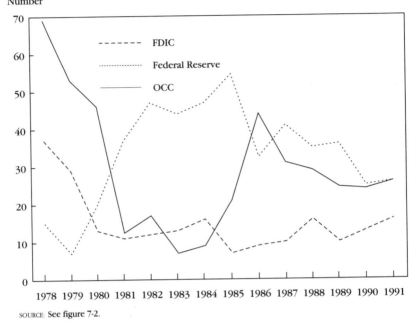

SOURCE: See figure 7-2.

and one-hundred additions amounts to 1 percent or less of all banks that are not Fed members, by far the largest category.

Rather than exhibiting unredeemably inefficient overlap, the system's current structure seems to have added an element of stability. Yes, banks have the option to switch supervisors, but rarely more than 1 percent do so in any given year. The current system provides options for banks, but it does not promote destabilization. Nor is there evidence that banks switch charters to be a client of a more lenient supervisor. Indeed, in the early years of the banking crisis the OCC, targeted by the Senate Banking Committee staff as the most lenient of the three, was the leader in charter losses.

What the current system does provide is a built-in motivation to improve the quality of supervision. Agencies have been able to innovate because each has learned from the successes and occasional failures of the others. The innovations, particularly those of the OCC, have drawn the wrath of political overseers from time to time, but it is these same innovations that serve as catalysts for organizational learning by the agencies. The current system also promotes a form of regulatory coop-eration—through the good examiner ideal—that many observers believe has created greater compliance with federal law and better corporate citizens in the pursuit of consumer and community protections.

Overlap and the Good Examiner Ideal

Political scientist and management scholar Martin Landau has offered a useful way to think about the current system of bank supervision.[15] He contends that a little duplication and overlap can be a smart way to design an administrative system, especially when the best way to ap-proach a task is not clear. Single systems can fail or perform poorly at times. Overlapping systems can back up one another and can also serve as examples of alternative means to do similar jobs. In other words, they provide the opportunity for organizational learning. Rather than encour-aging competition in laxity, overlapping systems can produce a competi-tion for excellence.

Explicit in the histories of the OCC, Fed, and FDIC are management initiatives to preserve the good examiner ideal. As critics of command-and-control regulation have long argued, one rule applied to every regu-lated entity with equal rigor can be a costly and ineffective means to achieve regulatory objectives. For example, in *Going By the Book*, Eugene Bardach and Robert Kagan contend that "programmed application of uni-form protective standards obviously runs a risk of underestimating the diversity of the ways in which things can go wrong."[16] Citing a study of product regulation by Lawrence Bacow, they illustrate the point:

> Millions of products are marketed annually in the United States by thousands of different producers. The risk associated with each prod-uct varies with its design; the quality of materials and the workman-ship; the directions provided to the users; the user's skill, judgment and caution; the age of the product; whether the product is being used for its intended purpose; the way the product has been maintained; and the extent to which the product is used with other products.[17]

15. Martin Landau, "Redundancy, Rationality, and the Problem of Duplication and Overlap," in Francis E. Rourke, ed., *Bureaucratic Power in National Policy Making,* 4th ed. (Little, Brown, 1986), pp. 470-83.

16. Eugene Bardach and Robert A. Kagan, *Going By the Book: The Problem of Regulatory Unreasonableness* (Temple University Press, 1982), p. 58.

17. Lawrence S. Bacow, *Bargaining for Job Safety and Health* (MIT Press, 1980), cited in Bardach and Kagan, *Going By the Book*, pp. 58-59.

The situation is further complicated, they contend, when enforcement takes an overly legalistic approach that treats problems as violations to be punished rather than difficulties to be overcome through education and cooperation. Things are further complicated when theory as to how things ought to work is not linked to the realities of practice and when rules are generated by a centralized entity that attempts to fit round, square, and rectangular pegs into an oval hole. Instead, they argue that unreasonableness could give way to effectiveness if regulators aspired to the ideal of the good inspector. The good inspector would practice reciprocity with regulated entities to gain cooperation, would be responsive to their concerns by sharing information that would facilitate compliance, and would be willing to grant forbearance in return for compliance with regulatory objectives but would not hesitate to use force when compliance was not forthcoming.

It is precisely this concept that defines the regulatory ideal among the managers of supervision in the Fed, FDIC, and OCC. Every bank is considered unique in its combination of risks, so that one supervisory prescription does not fit all. The risks associated with low levels of capital in one bank, for example, might exceed those in another with more seasoned management and higher-quality assets. Similarly, a bank with high earnings might be at greater risk of failure than a bank with low earnings but with more stable, less risky assets. As a result, effective examination and supervision rests upon the independent judgment of the examiner, able to assess the risks of each institution and work to prevent failure rather than seek immediate sanctions that might indeed prompt it. A hefty fine for low levels of capital, for example, might further deplete capital, and the dismissal of a director might prompt shareholders to dump a bank's stock and cause its equity capital to fall.

The question is, why should the three agencies aspire to this ideal? Pursuing it in the midst of the banking crisis got the OCC, especially, into trouble with political overseers. The agency's forbearance, reliance on informal enforcement actions, delegation of authority to examiners and their supervisors in the field, targeting of banks posing systemic risk, and use of portfolio management that tailored individual supervisory strategies for each bank (all elements of the good examiner ideal), were explicitly blamed by congressional overseers as causes of the crisis. Similar enforcement practices, the delegation of authority to examiners, and occasional forbearance brought General Accounting Office criticism of the Fed and FDIC as well. So why continue to hold the ideal as a worthwhile regulatory objective? Academics seeking to reduce the "unreasonableness" of the regulatory process might applaud the effort, but the costs of political scrutiny and the reduction of managerial autonomy can be highly unreasonable for the targeted agency.

The answer lies in part with shared responsibilities. First, preservation of the good examiner ideal is essential for the ability of each agency to compete for the best examiners. Without a strong commitment to examiners' professional judgment, the agencies would be hard put to attract talented people willing to make examination a career. Thus the OCC continues to promote examiner professionalism. As one manager said, "We teach our examiners to be so self-reliant they think they can do anything. . . . Our examiners are thoroughbreds." More so than the Fed and FDIC, the OCC prides itself on the time it takes an examiner to become commissioned and the rigor of the training. The Fed and FDIC also recognize the need to promote professionalism. The Fed is committed to developing examiners' expertise or specialization, and the FDIC has invested significant resources in training and relies on a thorough commitment to protecting the fund as a primary guide of examiner judgment.

Examiners are free to work for any of the supervisory agencies or to move to the private sector and work for a bank. The FDIC hired many Fed examiners trained in compliance by offering them higher salaries. Indeed, turnover among examination personnel can reach as high as 18 percent in any given year (see chapter 2). To remain competitive, each agency must not only pay careful attention to salaries and benefits, but also to maintaining the freedom of examiners to exercise their own judgment. This also means reining in bureaucratic growth that might reduce the amount of interesting work any one examiner gets to perform. In the past three years the banking industry has become healthier and, because of mergers, has fewer banks. In response, the OCC has begun to shrink its examination force, and the FDIC is planning to do so. Given new responsibilities for supervising the U.S. offices of foreign banks, the Fed's examination force has grown.[18]

Second, each agency must be attentive to the good examiner ideal to avoid suffocating banking competitiveness. By the account of many bankers, the good examiner ideal is not realized in practice. Too often regulations require extensive documentation from the meaningful to the menial transaction or administrative action within the bank, and novice

18. Jonathan D. Glater, "Banking Industry Mergers Spur Regulatory Cutbacks: Agencies Trimming Staffs, Moving Personnel," *Washington Post*, August 18, 1995, p. A11.

examiners can cling to their manuals and checklists to conduct an exam rather than exhibit the know-how to assess a bank in the context of the community it serves, the quality of its management, and the risk it might pose to the bank insurance fund. The FDIC Improvement Act made banks anxious about having to endure a one-size-fits-all approach to examination and supervision. In addition to mandated capital levels and enforcement actions that are required when a bank's capital gets too low, the act's efforts to define a comprehensive exam intended to prevent losses from the insurance fund seriously compromised the flexibility epitomized by the good examiner ideal.

Nevertheless, achieving the ideal remains a goal of bank managers. If examiners are poorly trained, banks not only bear the burden of an exam conducted by the book but must also provide the necessary training. If banks are consistently punished for problems that can be corrected informally or if they must spend excessive time in court battling formal enforcement actions, they could clearly be harmed in their efforts to compete with other financial intermediaries.

This is not to say that the agencies should bend too far over backward. Lax supervision could readily lead to failures, a consequence both banks and the agencies are eager to avoid. Pursuit of the good inspector ideal with the examiner willing to be cooperative but not hesitant to invoke formal sanctions when cooperation is not forthcoming helps to maintain a rough parity among the three agencies. This is also not to deny that banks occasionally view some supervisory policies as more appealing than others; shopping around does occur. But the management systems of the three agencies have been historically consistent not only in their approach to the challenges of examiner training, promotion, and direction, but also in the value they place upon the good examiner ideal. Rather than view competition between the agencies as a deplorable consequence of jurisdictional overlap, one can make a strong case that it improves the regulatory process.

Overlap and Organizational Learning

It is conventional wisdom that bureaucracies grow stagnant with age.[19] Yet changes in the past fifteen years in the way banks are supervised and the way the process is managed suggest entrepreneurism on

19. For a formal statement of the phenomenon, see Anthony Downs, *Inside Bureaucracy* (Little, Brown, 1967).

the part of the agencies in their efforts to reallocate resources and adopt new techniques. Shared jurisdictions encourage innovation and learning as each agency observes the successes and occasional failures of the others.

In 1986 the OCC introduced targeted examinations. Senior examiners were given responsibility for determining the examination needs of a portfolio of national banks in order to target those activities of a bank that posed the greatest risk to itself or a systemic risk to the industry. The nation's largest national banks, banks in trouble, and banks holding the riskiest assets received the most attention. Congress later criticized the OCC for reducing the frequency of on-site supervision of many smaller national banks, but the refocusing of resources could also have prevented more drastic problems in the industry. Although the FDIC and Fed did not adopt targeting, the OCC's innovations in managing supervision over the years have provided important advances for all three agencies. For example, its emphasis in the 1970s on examination procedures focusing on management systems in a bank rather than on the cash in the vault is today a common practice among examiners. But OCC innovation has been balanced by the more conservative examination techniques of the Fed and FDIC, which also have their strengths—not the least of which is the caution the FDIC, in particular, brings to supervision.

During the past ten years the FDIC has focused on examiner training to match a rapidly changing industry with more rigorous training. The L. William Seidman Center in Arlington, Virginia, now serves as an FDIC campus for training new examiners and updating the skills of senior staff. It is also the training site for some Fed examiners and a source of curriculum material shared with the OCC. The FDIC also took bold steps when the bank insurance fund faced insolvency to improve management of resolution activities, contracting with legal firms, and communication with the public and political overseers.

The expertise of individual Federal Reserve banks has facilitated supervision of new banking activities, such as buying and trading derivative products, and improved the collection and management of banking data related to community reinvestment activities and home mortgage lending. And it was the Fed's specialized program for informing banks about their consumer and civil rights responsibilities that informed a similar FDIC program in 1991. As noted in chapter 6, many Fed examiners with consumer and civil rights expertise were hired by the FDIC to jump-start its initiative.

During and immediately following the banking crisis, the three agencies reexamined their efforts to assess problems in a banking operation before they become manifest. They especially focused on the assessment of bank management. A study conducted by the OCC in 1988, for example, examined and dismissed the "common presumption" that most of the bank failures were "caused by adverse economic conditions," a presumption that was "believed to be further borne out by the fact that most failed banks have been located in regions with troubled economies."[20] Instead, the report concluded that "management-driven weaknesses played a significant role in the decline of 90 percent of the failed and problem banks the OCC evaluated." The inadequacy of loan policies and identification systems intended to spot problem loans, as well as the "aggressive behavior" on the part of managers and directors of failed banks, often "resulted in imprudent lending practices and excessive loan growth that forced the banks to rely on volatile liabilities and to maintain inadequate liquid assets." Rather than hide an apparent flaw in its ability to assess a key component of bank safety, the agency has since worked persistently to address its weaknesses (see chapter 2). A task force established by the Federal Reserve Bank of Chicago has also studied ways in which bank management might be better assessed.[21]

In an effort to explain why some organizations are more competent and innovative than others, political scientists J. Steven Ott and Jay Shafritz speculate that "as long as the core [organizational commitments] of an organization are externally oriented—organization members focus their attention and energies . . . on issues and problems that affect outside stakeholders—the probability of an organization being incompetent is less than if they are internally oriented."[22] An external orientation, in other words, can prevent the organization from experiencing dry rot.[23] As the most innovative of the three agencies, the OCC's greater external orientation certainly gives credence to the argument. But the explanation for why internally and externally oriented organizations can

20. Office of the Comptroller of the Currency, *Bank Failure: An Evaluation of the Factors Contributing to the Failure of National Banks* (1988), p. 1.

21. Federal Reserve Bank of Chicago, *Management Assessment, Report by the Taskforce of the Federal Reserve Bank of Chicago* (1993).

22. J. Steven Ott and Jay M. Shafritz, "Toward a Definition of Organizational Incompetence: A Neglected Variable in Organizational Theory," *Public Administration Review*, vol. 54 (July-August 1994), p. 373.

23. The term is Chris Argyris's in *Intervention Theory and Method: A Behavioral Science View* (Reading, Mass.: Addison-Wesley, 1970), cited in Ott and Shafritz, "Toward a Definition of Organizational Incompetence."

equally avoid dry rot (or succumb to it) must also include the significance of other organizations with similar jurisdictions.

Even the most autonomous government agency, such as the Fed, must be attentive to the activities of other agencies. Each bank supervisory agency in a sense competes to demonstrate competence in performing supervisory responsibilities and bolster operational autonomy. The agency that fails in its supervisory efforts or slips significantly will most likely lose some autonomy as political overseers move to prevent recurrence of the problem, most likely by imposing procedural restraints. The incentive helps not only maintain a high level of supervisory effort, but encourages each to pay close attention to the efforts of the others. Whether they are inward or outward oriented, the shared responsibilities of the agencies promote learning.

Overlap, Autonomy, and Accountability

Perhaps the most crucial feature of jurisdictional overlap between the Fed, FDIC, and OCC is an essential tension between the need for accountability and the need for managerial flexibility. Although none can afford to ignore the expectations of political overseers, particularly those in Congress, the three vary considerably in their responsiveness to concerns for performance. The varied degrees of autonomy enable them to create balance between immediate responsiveness to public and political concerns and the need for a stable, consistent approach to supervision that is not as heavily influenced by changing political priorities.

Autonomy and Consistent Performance

The Fed's extensive autonomy is perhaps most evident in the stability of its supervisory practices and of the banks under its jurisdiction. Member state banks have had their share of claims on the bank insurance fund, but with the exception of 1989, disbursements to Fed-supervised banks have remained less than one-tenth of 1 percent of the total assets of those banks (see figure 7-1). And, as the House staff report found, Fed-member state banks contributed more to the bank insurance fund in premiums from 1986 to 1991 than they required in disbursements.

Many academics and public managers would argue that this performance shows that all government agencies would benefit from greater autonomy. They would contend that excessive legislative efforts to make bureaucracies more accountable cause agency dysfunction. The legislative propensity to prescribe and prod program implementation complicates the management of public agencies. Effective public management can give way to implementation by documentation (as required by Congress) and excessive time spent testifying at hearings, responding to letters and requests for information, and facilitating GAO audits and congressional staff investigations. If the scrutiny more often produced guidance for improving management performance, the intervention would be better received. But the administrative aptitude of an agency is rarely a concern for oversight staff looking for mismanagement and fraud, so agencies on the receiving end of close oversight view it as ad hoc and disruptive.[24]

Problems associated with these constraints are compounded by the caution public managers often exercise to preclude close congressional oversight.[25] For the most risk averse, the temptation to use written rules and procedures and tight central direction will probably reduce program flexibility and employee discretion.[26] The agency mission, in other words, can be displaced by the objective of toeing a well-defined procedural line to prevent setting off the congressional fire alarm.[27] Before public managers can be more enterprising, it is argued, before they can give employees more discretion, before they can cut through the red tape that frustrates citizens and regulated entities, Congress must give agencies more room to experiment in the implementation of government programs.

24. Martha Derthick, *Agency under Stress: The Social Security Administration in American Government* (Brookings, 1990); and Harold Seidman and Robert Gilmour, *Politics, Position, and Power: From the Positive to the Regulatory State*, 4th ed. (Oxford University Press, 1986).

25. Donald F. Kettl, "Micromanagement: Congressional Control and Bureaucratic Risk," in Patricia W. Ingraham and Donald F. Kettl, eds., *Agenda for Excellence: Public Service in America* (Chatham, N.J.: Chatham House, 1992), pp. 94–109.

26. Martin Landau and Russell Stout Jr., "To Manage Is Not to Control: Or the Folly of Type II Errors," *Public Administration Review*, vol. 39 (March-April, 1979), pp. 148–56. Landau and Stout discuss the dysfunctional consequences of substituting control for management strategies in a more general context than in conjunction with congressional oversight.

27. Mathew D. McCubbins and Thomas Schwartz, "Congressional Oversight Overlooked: Police Patrols versus Fire Alarms," *American Journal of Political Science*, vol. 28 (Fall 1984), pp. 165–79. As supporters of the congressional dominance hypothesis, McCubbins and Schwartz would argue that this attentiveness by public managers is precisely the objective of Congress. The threat of sanctions in response to a fire alarm is an efficient means to keep agencies attuned to congressional priorities. And to the extent that such attentiveness leads to delay and inflexibility, members will have yet another instance of intransigence to investigate.

Despite its greater autonomy, the Fed has not been as innovative a supervisor as the OCC. As one manager said, "Getting this place to change is a draconian process. We are married to tradition and married to a conservative approach." Part of that conservatism is reflected in the agency's commitment to on-site annual exams of every bank under its jurisdiction. Another aspect is the commitment to reasonableness in supervisory efforts, often translated as *balance*. "What we have always emphasized is balance. . . . We want to ensure the safety and soundness of loans, but we want credit to be available to borrowers for the economy to grow." To achieve that balance, the Fed has long made its supervisory adjustments very cautiously. But its autonomy *has* facilitated pursuit of the good examiner ideal. Fed managers delegate responsibility broadly, both to the Reserve banks and to the personnel conducting examinations. They rely heavily on expertise and individual advancement as a source of consistency in examination and supervision. Both characteristics go a long way toward fostering the good examiner ideal.

Responsiveness and Performance

Autonomy does not, of course, guarantee successful management of regulatory efforts. There is an important role for political scrutiny. Consider the FDIC's actions once the bank insurance fund projected a deficit in 1991. Coming out of the banking crisis, the FDIC shook the label of being a "sleepy little agency." It became a savvy insurer of an industry undergoing enormous economic and technological change. As noted in chapter 5, the agency took forceful actions to improve its management of supervision and its responsibilities to protect the deposit insurance fund. Litigation activities previously contracted were brought under the direction of Legal Division lawyers, while contracting for resolution assistance was stopped and resolution made a permanent function with its own division. The agency's communication with Congress, the public, and insured banks was enhanced through additional staff and greater central direction.

It is unlikely that the FDIC's management changes would have been as prompt or as far-reaching without the intensive oversight exercised by Congress (in large part through the GAO) to expose the problems of the fund and consider ways to avoid their recurrence. It is also unlikely that the agency's relationship with Congress will ever be as uncomplicated and distant as in the past. Although the improved communication with Congress will help the FDIC keep abreast of activities on Capitol Hill, it will also let Congress know what is happening (or not happening) in the agency. There is a fine line between scrutiny that prompts improved management and scrutiny that paralyzes an agency, but the congressional interest in FDIC management clearly was a prod for change—even if only to keep congressional interest in the agency's activities to a minimum in the future by improving management of the fund.

Perhaps more so than with the FDIC, the OCC was energized by the congressional scrutiny heaped on it in the late 1980s to upgrade its training program, particularly the training of examiners pursuing compliance as a specialty. When the Clinton administration took a strong interest in fair lending and in increasing the investment of banks in their communities and in poorly developed urban areas, the OCC announced a program for sending testers into the field to identify discriminatory lending practices.[28] Managers involved in training now emphasize not only the necessity for soundness but also that banking must be fair and equitable, a concern not likely to have been expressed before intense congressional and presidential attention.

The three agencies clearly vary in their autonomy and their need to be responsive to expectations for effective performance. None can afford to ignore political overseers, particularly those in Congress, but the greater autonomy of the Fed is evident. Managers in the Fed all acknowledged the increased burden placed on it during the banking crisis, particularly leading up to and following the passage of the Federal Deposit Insurance Corporation Improvement Act. More staff time was required for writing the new mandated regulations as well as responding to congressional and GAO inquiries for data and assistance. But the common perception was that the FDICIA was a vindication of the Fed's management of supervision. As one manager said, "We cling to the traditional approach. Congress would appear to have endorsed the traditional approach by requiring full-scale exams. . . . That approach is seen as the most reliable for identifying problem banks . . . to take problem banks to sound bank status, and to mitigate losses to the insurance fund."

It is in the aggregate that the supervisory process presents a balance between the need for responsiveness to political overseers and the consistency provided by autonomy. Both are valuable objectives. The system benefits from responsiveness that requires a rethinking of organizational structure and procedure from time to time as well as an emphasis on consistency uninhibited by variations in the political winds.

28. Office of the Comptroller of the Currency, *Examining Issuance*, 93-3 (1993); and Office of the Comptroller of the Currency, news release, 93-38, April 5, 1993.

Politics and Administration

Americans are comfortable in demanding that their government regulate certain markets, distribute entitlements, enforce the law, and so forth. At the same time, they are quick to denounce government when it tries to do too much or does not do well what it is supposed to do. The obvious target for disillusioned citizens and their elected officials is the bureaucracy. It is the manifestation of both well-developed and poorly developed legislation, the arbitrator for competing disgruntled interests, the distributor of funds under cumbersome guidelines, the authority that shuts down a failed bank and sells off the assets, and the entity that provides benefits to special interests while the public interest (everyone else) may be poorly served or not served at all. In the debate over what is wrong with government, what needs fixing, and how, hundreds of agencies are lumped into one category—the bureaucracy—allowing for a simplification of problems to enable quick solutions. Unfortunately, the solutions are often devised without reference to the politics and histories of the agencies policymakers seek to reform.

In *The Administrative State*, Dwight Waldo cites A. B Hall as a critic of the traditional principles of administration that promote a single best approach to resolving problems:

[We] are becoming increasingly aware that problems of public administration can be adequately understood only in the light of the policies to be administered. Administration cannot be studied in a vacuum. The nature and scope of administrative techniques are conditioned largely by the content of the policies involved. The theory that all the different and diverse functions of government could be fitted into a uniform, symmetrical administrative set-up has become obsolete. A more pragmatic, experimental point of view now prevails.[29]

The one-size-fits-all formula for reform remains popular, especially among those seeking to reform banking supervision. It should not be argued that we must give up trying to improve the management of public programs, but it should be recognized that the nature of the task does matter, and that political and historical differences equip agencies for a task in different ways. Not all agencies are created equal, and not all

29. A. B. Hall in Dwight Waldo, *The Administrative State: A Study of the Political Theory of American Public Administration* (Ronald Press, 1948), p. 165.

policies are equally clear, popular, or come with a sure measure of performance. We cannot understand how bank supervision is currently administered without understanding the political and historical foundations of each agency, nor can we design a more effective system without first grappling with the political questions that define supervision in the current system. Even if we could agree on having a single supervising agency, there is no guarantee that the politics surrounding its creation would produce the structure and, ultimately, the level of autonomy necessary to conduct the task as anticipated.

Index